Psychological Insights on the Role and Impact of the Media during the Pandemic

This volume places the spotlight on the role different media and communications systems played in informing the public about the pandemic, shaping their views about what was happening and contributing to behavioural compliances with pandemic-related restrictions.

Throughout the pandemic, media coverage has played an important role in drawing attention to specific messages, influencing public risk perceptions and fear responses. Mainstream media and other electronic communication systems such as Facebook and WhatsApp have been pivotal in getting pandemic information out to the public, thereby influencing their beliefs, attitudes and behaviour and engaging them generally in the pandemic as stakeholders. In this timely volume, author Barrie Gunter considers how people reacted to this coverage and its contribution to their understanding of what was going on, including the influence of fake news and misinformation on public beliefs about the pandemic, from anti-lockdown protests to the "anti-vaxx" movement. In addition, looking at how government messaging was not always consistent or clear and how different authorities were found not always to be in harmony or compliance with the messages they put out, Gunter examines the harm done by presenting different publics with ambiguous or conflicting narratives.

Drawing out important communications strategy lessons to be learned for the future, this is essential reading for students and researchers in psychology, public health and medical sciences and for policymakers who assess government strategies, responses and performance.

Barrie Gunter is an Emeritus Professor in Media at the University of Leicester, United Kingdom. A psychologist by training, he has published more than 80 books on a range of media, marketing, business, leisure and psychology topics.

Psychological Insights on the Role and Impact of the Media during the Pandemic

Lessons from COVID-19

Barrie Gunter

LONDON AND NEW YORK

Cover image: Getty

First published 2022
by Routledge
4 Park Square, Milton Park, Abingdon, Oxon OX14 4RN

and by Routledge
605 Third Avenue, New York, NY 10158

Routledge is an imprint of the Taylor & Francis Group, an informa business

British Library Cataloguing-in-Publication Data
A catalogue record for this book is available from the British Library

Library of Congress Cataloging-in-Publication Data
Names: Gunter, Barrie, author.
Title: Psychological insights on the role and impact of the media during the
pandemic : lessons from COVID-19 / Barrie Gunter.
Description: Abingdon, Oxon ; New York, NY : Routledge, 2022. | Includes
bibliographical references and index. | Summary: "This volume places the
spotlight on the role played by different media and communications systems
on informing the public about the pandemic, shaping their views about what
was happening, and contributing to behavioural compliances with pandemic-
related restrictions"-- Provided by publisher.
Identifiers: LCCN 2022013157 (print) | LCCN 2022013158 (ebook) |
ISBN 9781032228792 (v. 3 ; hardback) | ISBN 9781032228754 (v. 3 ;
paperback) | ISBN 9781003274629 (v. 3 ; ebook)
Subjects: LCSH: Behavior modification. | COVID-19 Pandemic, 2020- , in
mass media. | COVID-19 Pandemic, 2020--Psychological aspects.
Classification: LCC BF637.B4 G855 2022 (print) | LCC BF637.B4 (ebook) |
DDC 158.1--dc23/eng/20220504
LC record available at https://lccn.loc.gov/2022013157
LC ebook record available at https://lccn.loc.gov/2022013158

ISBN: 978-1-032-22879-2 (hbk)
ISBN: 978-1-032-22875-4 (pbk)
ISBN: 978-1-003-27462-9 (ebk)

DOI: 10.4324/9781003274629

Typeset in Sabon
by MPS Limited, Dehradun

Contents

1 Pandemic, Media and the Public   1

2 News Media and Quality of COVID News   17

3 Online Chatter about COVID-19   36

4 Public Confidence in News and Journalism   49

5 News Media and Impact on Public Understanding   68

6 The Internet and Public Perceptions of the Pandemic   86

7 Misleading Pandemic Information and the Public   100

8 Media, Risk Perceptions and Fear   121

9 Media and Behavioural Compliance   135

10 Social Media, Behavioural Compliance and Other
   Outcomes   151

11 Pandemic, Media and Ageism   163

12 The Pandemic, the Media and Mental Health   177

13 Importance of the Media during a Pandemic   194

   Index   211

Chapter 1

Pandemic, Media and the Public

This book will examine the roles played by the media in communicating information to communities around the world about the 2020-2021 COVID-19 pandemic, the nature of these communications and how they shaped the people's psychological responses to the crisis. In this context, the term "media" refers to the traditional "mainstream" media including television and radio broadcasting and print media. It also refers to the vast stream of communications found via the Internet on the World Wide Web. These information sources comprised of websites operated by the major mass news media and also newer online-only sources. They also included the massive sites operated by the biggest micro-blogging and social networking companies. The best-known names here are Facebook, Instagram, Twitter, WhatsApp, and YouTube, each with a global reach of hundreds of millions or even billions of people, and sites originating from, based in or operating out of China (with most of these serving Chinese users only), such as QZone, Ren Ren, Sina Weibo, TikTok, We Chat and You Ku.

The major news media were known to play potentially important roles in keeping populations informed about major outbreaks of new and established diseases long before the 2020 COVID-19 pandemic (Anwar et al., 2020). News reporting can let people know about the latest developments in epidemics and more importantly teach them about the symptoms caused by a new disease and how they can minimise their chances of catching it. Scare stories can quickly circulate about new diseases especially if they have caused deaths and those deaths have occurred in or close to the communities in which people live. The media can contribute to these reactions if they give significant attention to the worst-case scenarios and most damaging outcomes. The tendency of the "news" to gravitate towards the unusual can often mean that epidemic stories fail to focus sufficiently on the normal or normative. If it is the case that a new disease is relatively harmless to the great majority, but can be life-threatening to the few, the major news media will often focus on the latter (Yan et al., 2016).

The lessons learned from pre-pandemic research need to be revisited again to see whether they can be or have been re-learned. As the pandemic

DOI: 10.4324/9781003274629-1

spread dramatically around the world during early 2020 with an initial peak in the spring of that year, followed by a second wave in many countries later the same year and in some places for a third time in 2021, national governments maintained tight restrictions over people's behaviour and introduced repeated lockdowns in which they closed down most of their economies and societies. These responses were deemed necessary to bring this highly infectious new coronavirus under control, but they were also, in many ways, as damaging to societies and individuals as the disease itself.

The traditional mass media and the newer online media became vital points of contact for most people with information sources about COVID-19. For extended periods, some national and regional government leaders and their scientific advisers broadcast daily briefings on television. Most broadcast news airtime and newspaper page space were devoted to news about the pandemic and its impact. Early coverage provided regular reminders to people of rapidly rising hospitalisation and death rates linked to COVID-19. Stories told tales of people not being allowed to visit elderly loved ones in residential care homes or family members in hospitals even if they were dying. Other reports reminded everyone that government lockdowns had forced companies out of business by compulsorily closing their premises while many employees lost their jobs and were left unable to pay their bills. Given the significance of this media coverage to national publics, what impact, if any, did it have?

The Onset of a Global Pandemic

Before considering the role and impact of media coverage during the pandemic, a major theme in this book, it is probably helpful to pause to review how it all started. At the end of December 2019, scientists in Wuhan, China identified a new disease manifesting in patients showing pneumonia-like symptoms and discovered its cause was a new coronavirus. It caused severe respiratory illness. In this respect it was similar to an earlier outbreak in 2003, that had been labelled SARS-CoV – severe acute respiratory syndrome coronavirus. The new virus was labelled SARS-CoV-2 or COVID-19 (after the year – 2019 – when it had emerged). It was less deadly than the first SARS virus, but highly infectious and over time produced many new variants of itself.

SARS-CoV-2 was originally thought to be another zoonotic virus that had originated in an animal species which then migrated into humans as result of close physical contact between people and infected animals. Case numbers escalated in and around Wuhan within weeks and started to be detected in other parts of China signalling the start of a new epidemic. SARS-CoV-2 cases quickly outstripped those of SARS-CoV.

At the outset, the Chinese medical authorities were unable to pinpoint the origin of this new viral pneumonia. By 7th January 2020, however, the cause was identified as a new coronavirus and its genomic sequence was published and shared with other countries. By 11th January, China reported its first known death from this new virus. This happened just before the big Chinese New Year's celebrations expected to involve millions of people, many of whom would travel across the country to visit relatives and friends. Further cases were reported outside China in Japan, South Korea and Thailand. Reports emerged of cases in other parts of the world, including Europe and North America across February 2020 (Taylor, 2021, 17th March).

In spite of initial claims by the Chinese authorities that they had this new disease under control, later modelling calculated that anything between 2,300 and 4,000 of its citizens may have been infected by the virus by the time China first publicly owned up to this outbreak on 31st December 2019 (McMullen, 2021, 26th January).

It was the World Health Organization that, on 11th February 2020, labelled the virus as SARS-CoV-2 and the disease it caused as COVID-19. It soon became clear, as early cases mounted, that this new virus had a range of surface symptoms but that it primarily affected the respiratory system and could give rise to serious illness. Other organs in the body could also be damaged by the virus if it penetrated that far. Fortunately, it emerged that while it could be life-threatening to some, COVID-19's mortality rate was quite low and that most people infected by it would either be asymptomatic or experience only mild symptoms. Despite this reassuring discovery, its highly infectious nature meant that it could spread extensively and that in absolute numerical terms, those needing hospital treatment were numerous enough to put most health systems under considerable strain.

By the 30th January 2020, the World Health Organization had classed COVID-19 as a "public health emergency of international concern" (World Health Organization, 2020, 30th January) Scientists around the world had been triggered into examining the nature of the virus and its symptoms and also started work on developing vaccines against it. Public health systems instigated preparations for a major disease outbreak and governments and their support administrations were placed on a higher state of alert in line with protocols for dealing with epidemics (Perlman, 2020).

Once the initial China-based epidemic evolved into a pandemic, where it infiltrated populations worldwide, it was clear that international cooperation would be needed to deal with this new disease (Kokudo & Sugiyama, 2020). This meant that experts from around the world would need to pool resources and share intelligence openly and early to expedite understanding and devise effective interventions to bring this new virus under control (Lee et al., 2020). Governments would also need to be open about the facts with the populations. The discovery that while the virus could survive on surfaces, it was principally transmitted through the air, meant that coping strategies had to evolve to deal with the problems this new disease created (Morawska & Cao, 2020).

The UK government, for example, initially advised people in media announcements to increase their personal hygiene vigilance. This included avoidance, wherever possible, of touching surfaces when out of home, regular hand washing or sanitising and advising people not to touch their face without having first thoroughly washed their hands. There was some further advice to avoid crowded spaces indoors and to try to keep a physical distance from others, unless you lived with them. As the narratives about the new disease rapidly evolved, the mass media were increasingly brought into play as the principal sources for keeping the public aware of what was going on. While media reports were useful for getting out the latest news about the pandemic, they could also generate public disquiet if they cast doubt on the ability of their government and health services to cope (Maciel-Lima et al., 2015; Wang et al., 2015).

During the 2020 coronavirus pandemic, both the traditional mass media and newer online media had roles to play in getting information out to the public. It was imperative that people were aware of this new disease and how to spots its symptoms, and then knew what to do if they felt unwell and believed from their symptoms that they had COVID-19. It was also important that people received and understood official health guidance in relation to this new disease. Inevitably, as regular updates about infection rates and then death rates from COVID-19 started became more prominent on the mainstream news, there were questions about how this coverage might influence people's personal risk perceptions and also trigger associated anxiety and fear responses. With frightening death rates projections being published in March 2020, the eventual locking down of societies and economies meant that many people were dramatically suspended from their usual work routines either through orders to work from home or because they lost their job. This created a climate of uncertainty and worry that over time could potentially trigger damaging health consequences.

The tone of much media coverage in the early days – and sometimes later on as well – was dire. No finite time frame could be placed on the duration of the pandemic and this only served to generate further uncertainty and anxiety. Hence, the media coverage of the pandemic, though in so many ways essential, could also relay information that caused considerable psychological distress for many people (Garfin et al., 2020).

It was already known that persistent and acute stress could be very damaging to people's long-term health. An extremely stressful event such as the attacks on the United States of 11th September 2001 could shape the risk perceptions, anxiety levels and subsequent loss of confidence and hope across populations with long-lasting and damaging consequences to the national psyche. These profound and potentially damaging psychological responses could have long-term implications for public health (Garfin et al., 2018).

Pandemics and the Media

The virus underpinning the COVID-19 pandemic was first publicly noticed in December 2019 and then during the first three months of 2020 spread rapidly around the world and across the world's news agendas. It emerged initially as a matter of potential international concern, and then as a clear and present danger to virtually every nation. Many societies, distant from where the virus was first noticed in central China looked on, via news media reports, initially with some degree of complacency, dismissing this new viral outbreak as yet another "Asian" disease (like SARS and MERS before it) that probably would not reach their shores (Cheung, 2020, 21st March). This initial reaction turned into nervousness as it reached Europe and North America and then Australia and into full-blown panic once it began to infect indigenous populations and news about rapidly rising hospitalisation rates surfaced and then the first reports of deaths.

The major news media around the world filled their news schedules with COVID-19 stories. News coverage underlined the multi-faceted issues triggered by the COVID-19 pandemic. There was the disease itself and concerns about how many people could become seriously ill or die once infected. In some countries, such as the United Kingdom, there was additional concern about how much this new disease would stretch the resources of the health services.

There was evidence that news organisations initially held back from reporting on death rates even as they rose. A study of Italian media interpreted this finding as indicative of a degree of "death denial" in the nation's news. This might have been motivated by a wish not to alarm people unduly. At the same time, there were still many unknowns about this new virus and reporters lacked the confidence to attribute some deaths conclusively to COVID-19. One downside to this reporting was that in playing down the worst-case scenario risks to people, this could have false assurance and less public vigilance in taking precautions to minimise infection (Solomon et al., 2021).

The patterns of early news coverage were observed to mirror historical evidence about the way the media had treated epidemics in the past (Wahl-Jorgensen, 2020). The increased strains on people confined to their own homes, and also confused about what was happening and who to trust, also led to growing news reports about people displaying inwardly directed aggression and taking their own lives and others displaying increased outwardly directed aggression in the form of domestic abuse of those they were living with. In sum, an impression was cultivated that there was no escape from the consequences of the pandemic (Feder et al., 2020; John et al., 2020).

The mass media could, of course, support the authorities by promoting safety-first behaviours such as hand washing, wearing face coverings and keeping your distance from others. It could encourage people to leave home only when it was absolutely necessary and then to desist from travelling too far. Underpinning these urging, however, were the subtle threats that non-compliance could prove disastrous for self and others (Anwar et al., 2020).

In the modern 21st century era of communications, many people could turn to online media systems, made available via the Internet, to find vast quantities of COVID-related information. Some of this derived from the big news brands, but much did not. Tuning into the major news suppliers meant that large numbers of people received essentially the same messages about COVID-19. Going online more often meant that people received their information from a wider array of sources, not all of which were reliable. Despite its availability not everyone used the information the Internet could provide especially if their technology literacy and Internet skills were limited (Van Deursen, 2020).

As we will see, the World Wide Web can be highly informative and beneficial for the public when hungry for information about a national crisis but it can also be a source of widespread misinformation and false messages about what is happening. Differentiating what to believe from what to reject is the major challenge for those relying on the online world for their information.

Importance of the Media during Pandemics

Research over time has indicated that the public frequently turn to the mainstream media for information and advice at times of crisis. When there are threats to normal, everyday life, people on a community-wide scale need to know what to do (Ball-Rokeach & DeFleur, 1976). They will expect governments and authorities to give them certainty and one of the quickest ways to reach people on a mass scale is via the major mass media, and especially through the broadcast media. The major news broadcasters tend to be trusted – at least in open liberal democracies (Lachlan et al., 2016). Although, as we saw earlier, at the start of the SAR-CoV-2 pandemic, journalists were among the least-trusted information sources. Hence, public trusts can fluctuate and could be linked to the occasion.

The importance of the media can reside in its enhancement of awareness of a crisis situation and in enabling people related risks to themselves and their families. Clear, verified information presented via the mass media can play an important part in enabling people to make risk judgements (Fischhoff et al., 2018). This approach to helping the public cope with uncertainty and risk has been shown to work in the context of a major, local crime and a national health crisis (Jones et al., 2017; Taha et al., 2014).

When a major new disease breaks out, people need to know the status of the outbreak and about any changes to the threat level. Under such circumstances, the public are most likely to be reassured by credible sources with authority and relevant expertise. If the threat is posed by a new phenomenon, such as a new virus, about which little is known even by experts, the threat level in the public's mind become elevated and along with it their anxiety level (Hong & Collins, 2006).

When official information is lacking detail or fails to be presented in a a timely way, another risk emerges and that is that people begin to search for their own explanations of what is going on in order to gain some insights into what is happening and what they can do to help themselves. Under these circumstances, misinformation and conspiracy theories can flourish. These alternatives "truths" about, for example, a new virus, can undermine official frames once these have become properly established. In a world populated by social media, to which more and more people now turn first for their information, the official or authority frames can get suppressed or overlain by alternatives that result in behaviour among some groups or communities that are disadvantageous for them and for wider society (Lachlan et al., 2016).

Hence, in examining the role played by media in times of major crisis such as global pandemics, the right balance has to be struck between providing sufficient coverage that is informative and creates the right kinds of motivation to act without also generating debilitating fear. Research conducted in the United States during the 2014 Ebola outbreak in Africa which was known to pose a minimal risk to America, those exposed to greater amounts of news coverage about it also developed greater risk perceptions and exaggerated fear of the threat level to themselves (Thompson et al., 2017).

Prior to that greater media exposure to coverage during the days after the 9/11 events was associated with greater post-traumatic stress symptoms, which in some cases persisted for two to three years (Silver et al., 2013; Holman et al., 2008). Such fears related not just to the distress caused by the events themselves but also arose from enhanced perceptions of risk from future acts of terrorism. Similar findings occurred among people exposed media to coverage of the Boston Marathon bombings (Holman et al., 2014). For some people, repeated exposure to media coverage of emotionally distressing events can build cumulatively to seed more chronic and persistent stress and anxiety symptoms (Garfin et al., 2015; Thompson et al., 2019). There was further evidence that the more graphic the media content to which people were exposed, the more severe were their psychological reactions (Holman et al., 2020).

A degree of public fear could be useful in motivating behavioural compliance with the restrictions on their movements during pandemic lockdowns. Too much anxiety and perceived threat however can result in far less constructive behaviour such as panic buying or over-use of specific facilities. Research into previous pandemics produced evidence that a lot of exposure to media reports about infectious disease outbreaks that generates an exaggerated sense of personal risk can result in surges in visits to healthcare services even among communities that do not face significant immediate risk themselves (McDonnell et al., 2012). Despite the message of the UK lockdown to stay home and protect the NHS, if risk and fear drove people to visit GPs or hospitals unnecessarily when significant health care capacity was and needed to be directed towards managing the pandemic and its effects, this would be a less than desirable outcome.

The media therefore can have a vitally important role to play in a pandemic, but there are side-effects that are less helpful that need to be borne in mind. Media stories need to be compelling to command audience attention in crowded media environments, but they need also to be factually accurate, offer the appropriate reference frame which cultivates appropriate beliefs and behavioural orientations, and ensure that people are encouraged to comply with restrictions that cause them to put their normal lives on hold. There will be times when critical information needs to be communicated to the public as a whole very quickly. The media are very well placed to support this process.

The Negative Potential of Media News

The news that a new coronavirus had emerged in China following stories about a number of cases of serious pneumonia of initially unknown origin had surfaced led to a number of early accusations. As the virus spread beyond China and other countries began to perceive a threat to their own populations, xenophobic reactions occurred, including from the President of the United States, Donald Trump, who referred to it as the "China virus", despite the WHO announcing that it would be referred to as SARS-CoV-2 and the disease it caused as COVID-19 (Fifield, 2020, 22nd March; Rogers et al., 2020, 18th March).

Incidents of racial slurs were reported in different countries that were targeted at Chinese and sometimes other Far Eastern nationals associated with accusations about the new virus (BBC News, 2020, 3rd March; Ng, 2021, 4th January). China was criticised for allowing so-called "wet markets" to operate under poor standards of hygiene. The Chinese government did act quickly to close down these markets, but once the word got out in the world's news that this new virus could have originated in one of these markets, the intervention was too late to stave off reputational damage.

In response, another story surfaced that the novel coronavirus had been developed as a biological weapon (Kortepeter, 2020, 19th June). Yet, some sources accused China and others suggested that the virus had been brought into China by visiting overseas troops during a militarygames (Pickrell, 2020, 12th March). Meanwhile, other observers claimed that the military sports event which took place in Wuhan may have served as an early spreader of the disease (Sengupta, 2020, 15th June).

It is understandable that many questionably substantiated stories will fly around at a time of international crisis when general understanding of a new disease is sketchy. At the same time, there is a propensity of media news operations, when chasing exclusives and seeking to be the first to break them, as well as in their constant competition with each other and the commercial implications of being the most used, to dramatize events. In their haste, stories are published that turn out later to be untrue or at least incomplete.

The news business must be entertaining as well as informative to command audiences' attention in the highly competitive media environment of the 21st century. This means that it will naturally look for stories that are interesting and this usually means that they concern events that are unusual. By focusing on the unusual, which is what tends to grab more news attention than the usual or "normal", news frames are developed that can distort public understanding perceptions and beliefs.

This professional aesthetic arbiter of standards within news publishing also leads news gatherers almost inevitably towards negative rather than positive news. "Bad" news tends more than "good" news to be about relatively rare events or events that have highly distinctive qualities. They also tend to trigger stronger emotional reactions in the audience which tends to serve as a principal benchmark of news entertainment value (Pinker, 2018, 17th February). Attention to deaths from COVID-19 might be expected, hypothetically, to raise public perceptions of personal risk. Accompanying fear is also promoted. Yet, in statistical terms, the probability of dying for most people was small.

The suggestion that the closure of many businesses might undermine important supply chains can lead people to engage in panic buying. During the early days of the pandemic, this behaviour was all too apparent as supermarket shelves were rapidly emptied of toilet rolls, first-aid kits, bottled water and pre-packed food items as well as fresh food, and soap and hand-sanitizer. This excessive behaviour became a self-fulfilling prophesy as it did temporarily cause shortages – even though quit unnecessarily as people bought to stockpile more than they immediately needed.

Online Media and the Pandemic

There were reasons to believe that the newer online media, including social media sites, could play a constructive role in supporting the population and the authorities in dealing with the pandemic. First, billions of people access the Internet and many are signed up with micro-blogging and social networking sites that represent massive online communities some of which are almost as expansive as the entire Internet. Sites such as Facebook, Instagram, Reddit, Snapchat, Tik Tok, Twitter, WhatsApp and YouTube and many others provide sources of news information from the big news brands as well as from family, friends and multiple others. With the restrictions of lockdown, many people have turned in even larger numbers and more often to these "social media" sites. As face-to-face meetings were banned, people turned instead to digital technologies and video calls (De et al., 2020).

The closures of schools, universities and many workplaces meant that significant proportions of students and employees were required to work from home. The closure of many cultural and entertainment venues meant that remote substitutes, such as virtual excursions and tours, and online performances, were presented instead. Some video-conferencing services, such as Zoom, saw a tenfold increase in use (Branscombe, 2020).

There are important caveats to be borne in mind with social media. They circumvent the gatekeeping protocols of mainstream media that embody editorial checks on the accuracy and authenticity of information content. On social media, everybody potentially can become a mass broadcaster if they have the information technology skills and know how to use specific sites. This means that these sites can hold and distribute content that is inaccurate or misleading and even potentially harmful if people act upon it. When confronted with uncertainty such as that created by the outbreak of a new and highly infectious virus that makes some people very ill, it is understandable that widespread fear with circulate. At an optimal level this fear can motivate people to follow official advice about how to behave. At a suboptimal level, such advice might generate less widespread compliance. At an above optimal level excessive fear could give rise to other unpleasant and potentially damaging side-effects and result in some being afraid to surface again into normal life one the danger has passed.

Research into social media behaviour as the pandemic and lockdowns against it were implemented showed that social media use increased as infection rates increased. Users of these sites sought out pandemic-related information. They were likely to use both reliable and unreliable information sources, and the extent to which social media users turned increasingly to each of these sources did not differ all that much as infection rates took off. In a sense, social media sites witnessed a parallel "epidemic" in information search behaviour linked to the novel coronavirus, otherwise known as an "infodemic" (Cinelli et al., 2020). These findings have important implications for public behaviour given that unreliable sources can cultivate false beliefs about crises and their causes and consequences, which can lead to less willingness to comply with behavioural advice from authorities (Hameleers et al., 2020). In the case of a major pandemic, such as COVID-19, for which no medically-established protections were available in the beginning, only behavioural restrictions could bring contagion under control, rendering behavioural compliance with officially sanctioned restrictions critical.

The public appetite for information to alleviate uncertainty during the pandemic, especially at the start of it, inevitably meant that available media systems played vital parts in enhancing understanding and giving reassurance to ignorant and increasingly anxious populations but could also act potentially to undermine these objectives. As part of a broader review of the pandemic experience and the way it was managed by authorities around the world, it will be important to consider the roles and responsibilities of media systems and their impact on those who used them. In this book, evidence gathered through research will be considered, critiqued and interpreted to provide insights into how the media performed and with what effects.

This Book

The SARS-CoV-2 or COVID-19 pandemic of 2020-2021 was a once in a lifetime experience for virtually all affected by it. Even though regional pandemics and local epidemics had occurred in specific pats of the world that resulted in deaths from viruses that were either unknown or familiar but rare, and dangerous, this was the first time a public health crisis of this magnitude had occurred for 100 years. Despite the existence of public health protocols in most countries, in few places had these been tested for real on the scale witnessed in 2020.

During the course of the pandemic, the absence of medical or pharmaceutical treatments or preventatives meant that national governments had to place their reliance on a raft of non-pharmaceutical interventions that comprised personal hygiene measures and behavioural restrictions. Among the major challenges here was procuring and maintaining public compliance with the restrictions that defined extensive societal-level lockdown. Among the major concerns was the collateral damage wrought by these measures, especially on the health and well-being of the population. The success of these measures depended upon the cooperation of the people and not being overwhelmed by the damage caused by their implementation. The pandemic spawned huge volumes of scientific research in the medical sciences and behavioural sciences.

The evidence covered in this book is restricted to behavioural science research. It examines research on the role played by the mainstream news media and Internet-based communications in representing public thoughts and feelings and contributing towards knowledge and awareness, and shaping behaviour. It begins by examining how information about COVID-19 and government interventions was represented in the major news media (Chapter 2) and on the Internet (Chapter 3). It then turns to evidence concerning the confidence that people had in news services as sources of pandemic-related information (Chapter 4). Next, research concerning the impact of the news media on public understanding of the pandemic and lockdown measures (Chapter 5) and of Internet communications on perceptions of the pandemic (Chapter 6). It turns attention then to ways in which the public might be misled by false information in circulation and mostly to be found on sites accessed over the Internet (Chapter 7). It was important that the public had trust in authorities and experts from which they were receiving advice. The impact of communications and information received through news media and the Internet on public perceptions of risk from COVID-19 and their fear responses to the pandemic were explored (in Chapter 8).

On a behavioural level, the success of governments' interventions was dependent on public compliance with behavioural restrictions and adoption of hygiene and related protective measures. How were these behaviours linked to exposure to news and other online information sources? This was examined in Chapter 9 and Chapter 10. The collateral effects of pandemic interventions on mental health represented a significant issue in determining whether to persist with these restrictions.

It was established early in the pandemic that COVID-19 was potentially a much more serious disease and posed more immediate health risks for older people than for younger people. There were concerns about the way the risks and vulnerabilities of older people were represented by the media and how this might have in turn affected public responses to the pandemic. This subject was examined in Chapter 11. The media and Internet were important sources of information about the pandemic, not least in providing reassurance to people that normality would eventually return. The impact of media exposure to the severity of these psychological side-effects was the focus of attention in Chapter 12. Finally, Chapter 13 wraps up the analysis of media and the pandemic by considering the importance of the media at times of public health crisis and what has been learned about the positives and negatives of people's reliance on different mediated information sources during the SARS-CoV-2 pandemic.

References

Anwar, A., Malik, M., Raees, V., & Anwar, A. (2020) Role of mass media and public health communications in the COVID-19 pandemic. *Cureus*, 12(9): e10453. doi:10.7759/cureus.10453

Ball-Rokeach, S. J., & DeFleur, M. L. (1976) A dependency model of mass-media effects. *Communication Research*, 3(1): 3–21. doi:10.1177/009365027600300101

BBC News. (2020, 3rd March) Student from Singapore hurt in oxford Street attack. Retrieved from: https://www.bbc.co.uk/news/uk-england-london-51722686

Beatty, T. K., Shimshack, J. P., & Volpe, R. J. (2019) Disaster preparedness and disaster response: Evidence from sales of emergency supplies before and after hurricanes. *Journal of the Association of Environmental and Resource Economists*, 6: 633–668. doi:10.2139/ssrn.3208765

Branscombe, M. (2020, 14th April) The network impact of the global COVID-19 pandemic. *The New Stack*. Retrieved from: https://thenewstack.io/the-network-impact-of-the-global-covid-19-pandemic/

Cheung, H. (2020, 21st march) Coronavirus: What could the West learn from Asia. *BBC News*. Retrieved from: https://www.bbc.co.uk/news/world-asia-51970379

Cinelli, M., Quattrociocchi, W., Galeazzi, A., Valensise, C. M., Brugnoli, E., Schmidt, A. L., Zola, P., Zollo, F., & Scala, A. (2020) The COVID-19 social media infodemic. *Scientific Reports*, 10: Article No. 16598. Retrieved from: https://www.nature.com/articles/s41598-020-73510-5

De, R., Pandev, N., & Pal, A. (2020) Impact of digital surge during COVID-19 pandemic: A viewpoint on research and practice. *International Journal of Information Management*, 55: 102171. doi:10.1016/j.ijinfomgt.2020.102171

Feder, G., Flavia, A., Rishal, P., & Johnson, M. (2020) Domestic violence during the pandemic. *The BMJ*, 372. doi:10.1136/bmj.n722

Fifield, A. (2020, 22nd March) Wolf Warrior' strives to make China first with coronavirus vaccine. *The Washington Post*. Retrieved from: https://www.washingtonpost.com/world/asia_pacific/chinas-wolf-warrior-strives-to-be-first-with-coronavirus-vaccine/2020/03/19/d6705cba-699c-11ea-b199-3a9799c54512_story.html

Fischhoff, B., Wong-Parodi, G., Garfin, D. R., Holman, E. A., & Silver, R. C. (2018) Public understanding of Ebola risks: Mastering an unfamiliar threat. *Risk Analysis: An International Journal*, 38: 71–83 (published ahead of print June 8, 2017). doi:10.1111/risa.12794

Garfin, D. R., Holman, E. A., & Silver, R. C. (2015) Cumulative exposure to prior collective trauma and acute stress responses to the Boston Marathon bombings. *Psychological Science*, 26: 675–683. doi:10.1177/0956797614561043

Garfin, D. R., Silver, R. C., & Holman, E. A. (2020) The novel coronavirus (COVID-2019) outbreak: Amplification of public health consequences by media exposure. *Health Psychology*, 39(5): 355–357.

Garfin, D. R., Thompson, R., & Holman, E. A. (2018) Mental and physical health effects of acute stress following traumatic events: A systematic review. *Journal of Psychosomatic Research*, 112: 107–113. doi:10.1016/j.jpsychores.2018.05.017

Hameleers, M., Van der Meer, T. G. L. A., & Brosius, A. (2020) Feeling "disinformed" lowers compliance with COVID-19 guidelines: Evidence from the US, UK, Netherlands, and Germany. *Mis/Information Review*. Retrieved from: https://misinforeview.hks.harvard.edu/article/feeling-disinformed-lowers-compliance-with-covid-19-guidelines-evidence-from-the-us-uk-netherlands-and-germany/

Holman, E. A., Garfin, D. R., Lubens, P., & Silver R. C. (2020) Media exposure to collective trauma, mental health, and functioning: Does it matter what you see? *Clinical Psychological Science*, 8: 111–124 (published ahead of print October 8, 2019). doi:10.1177/2167702619858300

Holman, E. A., Garfin, D. R., & Silver, R. C. (2014) Media's role in broadcasting acute stress following the Boston Marathon bombings. *Proceedings of the National Academy of Sciences of the USA*, 111: 93–98 (published ahead of print December 9, 2013). doi:/10.1073/pnas.1316265110

Holman, E. A., Silver, R. C., Poulin, M., Andersen, J., Gil-Rivas, V., & McIntosh, D. N. (2008) Terrorism, acute stress, and cardiovascular health: A 3-year national study following the September 11th attacks. *Archives of General Psychiatry (JAMA Psychiatry)*, 65: 73–80.

Hong, S., & Collins, A. (2006) Societal responses to familiar versus unfamiliar risk: Comparisons of influenza and SARS in Korea. *Risk Analysis*, 26(5): 1247–1257. doi:10.1111/j.1539-6924.2006.00812.x

John, A., Pirkis, J., Gunnell, D., Appleby, L., & Morrissey, J. (2020) Trends in suicide during COVID-19 pandemic. *The BMJ*, 371. doi:10.1136/bmj.m4352

Jones, N. M., Garfin, D. R., Holman, E. A., & Silver, R. C. (2016) Media use and exposure to graphic content in the week following the Boston Marathon bombings. *American Journal of Community Psychology*, 58: 47–59. doi:10.1002/ajcp.12073

Jones, N. M., Thompson, R. R., Dunkel Schetter, C., & Silver, R. C. (2017) Distress and rumour exposure on social media during a campus lockdown. *Proceedings of the National Academy of Sciences of the USA*, 114: 11663–11668 (published ahead of print October 17, 2017). doi:10.1073/pnas.1708518114

Kleemans, M., Schlindwein, L. F., & Dohmen, R. (2017) Preadolescents' emotional and prosocial responses to negative TV news: Investigating the beneficial effects of constructive reporting and peer discussion. *Journal of Youth and Adolescence*, 46(9): 2060–2072.

Kokudo, N., & Sugiyama, H. (2020) Call for international cooperation and collaboration to effectively tackle the COVID-19 pandemic. *Global Health and Medicine*, 2(2): 60–62. doi:10.35772/ghm.2020.01019

Kortepeter, M. (2020, 19th June) Did COVID-19 come from a lab? Was it deliberate bioterrorism? A biodefense expert explores the clues. *Forbes*. Retrieved from: https://www.forbes.com/sites/coronavirusfrontlines/2020/06/19/did-covid-19-come-from-a-lab-was-it-deliberate-bioterrorism-a-biodefense-expert-explores-the-clues/?sh=5a2ecfe4356d

Lachlan, K. A., Spence, P. R., Lin, X., Najarian, K., & Del Greco, M. (2016) Social media and crisis management: CERC, search strategies, and Twitter content. *Computers in Human Behaviour*, 54: 647–652. doi:10.1016/j.chb.2015.05.027

Lee, D., Heo, Y., & Kim, K. (2020) A strategy for international cooperation in the COVID-19 pandemic era: Focusing on national scientific funding data. *Healthcare (Basel)*, 8(3): 204. doi:10.3390/healthcare8030204

Maciel-Lima, S. M., Rasia, J. M., Bagatelli, R. C., Gontarski, G., & Colares, M. J. (2015) The impact that the influenza A (H1N1) pandemic had on news reporting in the state of Paraná, Brazil. *História, Ciências, Saúde-Manguinhos*, 22: 273–291.

McDonnell, W. M., Nelson, D. S., & Schunk, J. E. (2012) Should we fear "flu fear" itself? Effects of H1N1 influenza fear on ED use. *The American Journal of Emergency Medicine*, 30: 275–282. 10.1016/j.ajem.2010.11.027

McMullen, J. (2021, 26th January) COVID-19: Five days that shaped the outbreak. *BBC News*. Retrieved from: https://www.bbc.co.uk/news/world-55756452

Morawska, L., & Cao, J. (2020) Airborne transmission of SARS-CoV-2: The world should face the reality. *Environment International*, 139: 105730. doi:10.1016/j.envint.2020.105730

Ng, K. (2021, 4th January) Attack on London law student over coronavirus was "racially motivated". *The Independent*. Retrieved from: https://www.bbc.co.uk/news/uk-england-london-51722686

Ng, Y. J., Yang, Z. J., & Vishwanath, A. (2018) To fear or not to fear? Applying the social amplification of risk framework on two environmental health risks in Singapore. *Journal of Risk Research*, 21: 1487–1501. 10.1080/13669877.2017. 1313762

Perlman, S. (2020) Another decade, another coronavirus. *New England Journal of Medicine*. doi:10.1056/NEJMe2001126

Pickrell, R. (2020, 12th March) Chinese officials say US army may have "brought the epidemic to Wuhan". *Military.com*. Retrieved from: https://www.military. com/daily-news/2020/03/12/chinese-official-says-us-army-may-have-brought-epidemic-wuhan.html

Pinker, S. (2018, 17th February) The media exaggerates negative news. This distortion has consequences. *The Guardian*. Retrieved from: https://www. theguardian.com/commentisfree/2018/feb/17/steven-pinker-media-negative-news

Rogers, K., Jakes, L., & Swanson, A. (2020, 18th March) *Trump defends using "Chinese Virus" label, ignoring growing criticism*. New York Times. Retrieved from: https://www.nytimes.com/2020/03/18/us/politics/china-virus.html

Sengupta, K. (2020, 15th June) Security agencies investigating possibility coronavirus spread in Wuhan as early as October. *The Independent*. Retrieved from: https://www.independent.co.uk/independentpremium/world/coronavirus-china-wuhan-military-games-investigation-who-a9567206.html

Silver, R. C., Holman, E. A., Andersen, J. P., Poulin, M., McIntosh, D. N., & Gil-Rivas, V. (2013) Mental- and physical-health effects of acute exposure to media images of the September 11, 2001, attacks and the Iraq War. *Psychological Science*, 24, 1623–1634. doi:10.1177/0956797612460406

Solomon, S., Rostellato, D., Testoni, I., Calabrese, F., & Biasco, G. (2021) Journalistic denial of death during the very first traumatic period of the Italian COVID-19 pandemic. *Behaviour Science (Basel)*, 11(3): 41. doi:10.3390/bs11030041

Taha, S. A., Matheson, K., & Anisman, H. (2014) H1N1 was not all that scary: Uncertainty and stressor appraisals predict anxiety related to a coming viral threat. *Stress and Health*, 30: 149–157. 10.1002/smi.2505

Taylor, D. B. (2021, 17th March) A timeline of the coronavirus pandemic. *The New York Times*. Retrieved from: https://www.nytimes.com/article/coronavirus-timeline.html

Thompson, R. R., Garfin, D. R., Holman, E. A., & Silver, R. C. (2017) Distress, worry, and functioning following a global health crisis: A national study of Americans' responses to Ebola. *Clinical Psychological Science*, 5: 513–521 (published ahead of print April 26, 2017). doi:10.1177/2167702617692030

Thompson, R. R., Jones, N. M., Holman, E. A., & Silver, R. C. (2019) Media exposure to mass violence events can fuel a cycle of distress. *Science Advances*, 5, eaav3502. doi:10.1126/sciadv.aav3502

van Deursen, A. J. (2020) Digital inequality during a pandemic: Quantitative study of differences in COVID-19-related internet uses and outcomes among the general population. *Journal of Medical Internet Research*, 22(8): e20073. doi:10. 2196/20073

Wahl-Jorgensen, K. (2020, 14th February) Coronavirus: How media coverage of epidemics often stokes fear and panic. *The Conversation*. Retrieved from: https://

theconversation.com/coronavirus-how-media-coverage-of-epidemics-often-stokes-fear-and-panic-131844

Wang, Q., Zhao, L., Huang, R., Yang, Y., & Wu, J. (2015) Interaction of media and disease dynamics and its impact on emerging infection management. *Hist Cienc Saude Manguinhos*, 20: 215.

Wang, Y., McKee, M., Torbica, A., & Stuckler D. (2019) Systematic literature review on the spread of health-related misinformation on social media. *Social Science & Medicine*, 112552. doi: 10.1016/j.socscimed.2019.112552

World Health Organization. (2020, 30th January) Statement on the second meeting of the International Health Regulations (2005) Emergency Committee regarding the outbreak of novel coronavirus (2019-nCoV). Retrieved from: https://www.who.int/news-room/detail/30-01-2020-statement-on-the-second-meeting-of-the-international-health-regulations-(2005)-emergency-committee-regarding-the-outbreak-of-novel-coronavirus-(2019-ncov)

Yan, Q., Tang, S., Gabriele, S., & Wu, J. (2016). Media coverage and hospital notifications: Correlation analysis and optimal media impact duration to manage a pandemic. *Journal of Theoretical Biology*, 390: 1–13. 10.1016/j.jtbi.2015.11.002

Chapter 2

News Media and Quality of COVID News

As the uncertainty about the future grew during early phases of the pandemic with increasingly interventionist action on the part of governments resulting in suspension of normal life, so people's thirst for information about COVID-19 became more acute. In keeping up with frequent changes in restrictions and infection rates, people turned to different sources for information. These sources included family and friends, work colleagues and health professionals and significantly to the mass media and online communications networks. Traditionally, in times of crisis, people have turned principally to the mainstream news media. In the 21st century, this has continued for some sections of society, but it has changed radically for others. Older generations remained loyal to long-established broadcast and print media. At the same time, younger generations have emerged that display less loyalty to the big broadcast and newspaper brands, and turn instead to newly emergent online information sources, with the generically labelled "social media" platforms being at the forefront of news suppliers. This book will examine research about the role of both these sources during the pandemic.

Whichever news sources people turn to, it is important that they can trust the information they receive if it is to have any impact on them. During the COVID-19 pandemic, national governments relied upon the major media suppliers such as national news broadcasters and daily newspapers as platforms to reach their populations with advice, requests and commands that many aspects of normal everyday life be put on hold. Although the big news brands have traditionally been the most trusted, they can still be used to cultivate specific agendas. Despite claims of objectivity, news coverage can still be subtly nuanced to place emphasis on specific facts over others (Gunter, 1997, 2015).

The power of the mainstream news media to influence public agendas, shape people's attention to events and understanding of issues means that they can be utilised as devices of public control. Subtle nuances in the reporting of events, through their visualisation on film or video and the narratives that are constructed around them can result in variances in the impressions people form

DOI: 10.4324/9781003274629-2

about these things (Scheufele & Tewksbury, 2006). It is critical that this power is used responsibly especially during times of national crisis and emergency.

The mass media can play a vital role in informing the public about pandemics. The broadcast media, in particular, have a significant part to play in this process because they can update their news bulletins continuously throughout the day. The printed press can provide greater detail about new disease outbreaks, what steps their government and health authorities are taking to tackle the problem and about the levels of risk to people and the steps they can take themselves to mitigate against personal risk. Research studies were conducted as the pandemic took hold and spread around the world to assess the nature of media coverage and the impact it had on different communities.

Volume of News Coverage

From early in the pandemic, the coronavirus outbreak attracted a considerable volume of media coverage around the world. *Time Magazine* identified 41,358 English-language articles about the new coronavirus in China during January 2020 and nearly half of these stories (18,800) were headliners. The much more deadly Ebola outbreak in 2018, in contrast, generated 1,778 articles and 682 headliners in the month of August that year (Ducharme, 2020, 7th February). Yet, while Ebola killed 2,246 out of 3,500 cases (64% death rate among those infected, of the known 31,500 novel coronavirus cases in January 2020, only 2% had died.

An analysis of 3,000 high-traffic news sites online revealed that one per cent of all articles posted in early 2020 were about the new coronavirus. These stories, however, generated 13 per cent of all article views during January-February 2020. This was further evidence that this new virus had quickly grabbed the world's attention (Molla, 2020, 17th March).

An early study of over 7,000 relevant news reports about the novel coronavirus outbreak in newspapers in China, in January and February 2020, found that pandemic-related reports focused most often on prevention and control procedures for dealing with the new virus (33%), on medical treatment of it and research connected to such treatment (16%) and on the social and economic impacts at community-level, national-level and international-level of actions designed to control virus transmission rates (12%) (Liu et al., 2020). These monitoring exercises did not measure any effects of the news coverage on public knowledge and understanding about the virus, or on beliefs and attitudes towards intervention policies or public behaviour, but they did provide a model for assessing the nature of news coverage.

Even when being factual, the coverage of some stories could have profound effects on the public. One example of this was the death of an Arizona resident after drinking chloroquine (which is used in aquariums) following exposure to news reports that some sources had claimed it could be used to treat COVID-19 (Waldrup et al., 2020). Some media sources were identified by journalism academics as being guilty of misreporting of the virus and treatments for it (Brennan et al., 2020). Fox News was singled out for criticism in this context. Yet, many Fox viewers claimed to trust its news and did not perceive a problem with the way it reported the pandemic (Jurkowitz & Mitchell, 2020). Although in mid-March 2020, as the pandemic was taking hold, nearly half of Americans (47%) said they had come across a lot of COVID-19 news they did not trust (Jurkowitz & Mitchell, 2020).

Analysis of media coverage of COVID-19 in more than 100 high-circulation newspapers produced in 50 countries found that there were dramatic increases in mention of COVID or the novel coronavirus in February and March 2020. Is evidence confirmed how quickly the pandemic emerged as the dominant news story around the world (Pearman et al., 2021). This media tracking exercise was conducted in 11 languages (English, Spanish, French, Italian, Japanese, Norwegian, Swedish, Danish, Russian, German and Portuguese) covering news sources in Africa, Asia, Europe, Latin America, Middle East, North America and Oceania. There was evidence that the media coverage of the pandemic had stabilised after a couple of months and even started to decline a little by the end of March, even though regular updates showed infection rates and death rates continuing to climb. Moreover, the cases registered in the 50 countries where this news outputs analysis took place contributed most (85%) of total registered global COVID-19 cases.

One explanation for divergence between COVID-19 cases and media coverage of the pandemic in some markets was "COVID fatigue". Pre-pandemic evidence has also shown that when pandemics persist for some time, news media become hungry for new news agendas and will cease giving these important events significant coverage after a while especially if new issues arise to feed the need for a diverse news menu. Pandemics might therefore remain active and a genuine public risk but even so disappear or are at least relegated in significance in news agendas (Klemm et al., 2016; Reintjes et al., 2016).

After a time, with the news reporting little else, audiences grew tired of hearing about COVID-19. Furthermore, in some parts of the world, other issues began to surface as warranting news coverage. Although there was still plenty of news emerging about COVID-19 even as the pandemic wore on, over time there was less genuinely "new" news to report or else it was simply a continuation of standard, long-running reports of the progress of the disease with little in the way of dramatic new developments (Lytimäki et al., 2020).

By spring 2021, evidence emerged that even though the COVID-19 pandemic was prevalent in many different parts of the world, the public's appetite for relentless media coverage of it was starting to wane. This shift did not amount to a complete public attentional switch-off from pandemic news. Yet, because in many countries there had been partial and temporary suspension of COVID-19 restrictions, as transmission rates fell, other "news" on non-pandemic issues gained traction as well. Perhaps, for many news consumers, this shift came as a relief. Some stories that commanded prominence in news agendas concerned issues of equal importance to the pandemic, for example, climate change. Moreover, in some stories, the pandemic and climate change were inter-linked (Forster et al., 2020).

Pandemic news in the mainstream news media retained some level of public interest, however, while the pandemic remained a dynamic and constantly evolving public health problem. Even after vaccines against COVID-19 had been developed and passed as safe for public use by medical regulators, people continued to get ill and die from this coronavirus. The news media therefore continued to have an important social role in informing and reassuring people about the disease and in advising them to remain vigilant and cautious in their own behaviour (Bolsen et al., 2020; Hart et al., 2020).

An analysis of over 100 high-circulation newspapers in 50 different countries found that coverage of the pandemic increased dramatically across the early months of 2020 and, as evidence of its displacement of other important topics, the volume of coverage devoted, for instance, to climate change fell away (Boykoff et al., 2020; Pearman et al., 2021). After that, newspapers' coverage of the pandemic progressively fell away in those parts of the world where it had once been at a high level of infectivity or where it had remained consistently at a low level and where public attention to it had been modest anyway (Pearman et al., 2021).

The Emotionality of News

The primary objective of the news in the mainstream mass media such as television, radio and newspapers, is to present the public they serve with up-to-date, comprehensible, balanced and truthful coverage of events. Its primary intended psychological impact therefore is cognitive in nature. Yet, as studies of news outputs have shown over many years, the news is about more than simply information. It also has to be entertaining to command the attention of its audiences and readers. This also means it must appeal to people at an emotional level (Gunter, 2015). Moreover, evidence has emerged that the news has become more "emotional" over the years. Although this might render it more interesting and attention-grabbing, it could undermine information quality and uptake by the public (Uribe & Gunter, 2007).

On 24th January 2020, a number of British newspapers carried reports about a video that had spread dramatically across social media sites apparently showing people collapsing in Wuhan, China from a mysterious new disease (Dodsworth, 2021). News of this outbreak had already reached the West from China but had caused little more than ripples of interest beyond the medical science community. At the time of the video, only a few hundred cases and a handful of deaths had been reported in China and the first reported UK case of the respiratory disease that came to be known worldwide as COVID-19 did not appear until 31st January. Yet, the video presented a seemingly apocalyptic scene that was designed to instil fear in its audience, or at least according to some critical observers.

In writing about the pandemic, and in making reference to this case, the journalist Laura Dodsworth's principal premise was that government's use fear to control their populations' behaviours during the pandemic (Dodsworth, 2021). Taking her proposition further she argued that many mainstream news media were complicit in peddling this fear through reporting that lacked the balance and objectivity normally expected of responsible and professional journalism.

One early source of fear was to present accounts that countered attempts by the Chinese government to downplay what was happening. Reporting in the West questioned the integrity of the Chinese leaders and suggested they were covering up a situation that was far worse than they had claimed. References were made to similar events in recent history where the Chinese government had been shown to conceal the truth in its accounts of other pandemics that had originated in China. It had been exposed for being less than honest about the first pandemic caused by a coronavirus (SARS) in 2003. Further stories surfaced that the Chinese government hired large numbers of its citizens to post fake messages online that appear to be independent endorsements of government policies and to promulgate favourable propaganda in the West (Dodsworth, 2021). By questioning raising the honesty of the Chinese, other messages that purportedly showed a burgeoning health crisis in China set the scene for stronger audience reactions to media coverage of the same crisis as it weas exported around the world.

There is no doubt that when the novel coronavirus (SARS-CoV-2) reached Europe and then the United Kingdom, governments in the region was caught out by the speed with which the virus spread and then by the numbers of cases it generated that needed hospital attention. Journalists also found themselves chasing a story that moved do fast it got away from them. In keeping up with the latest developments while also trying to understand what was going on so that they could explain it to their readers, listeners and viewers, they often lack the time to get to grips with the detail.

As they struggled to get to grips with factual complexities that were evolving all the time, they relied on emotion to draw attention to their reports or perhaps fund themselves unwittingly writing emotive accounts of rapidly changing events as they unfolded. One central characteristic of initial media coverage of the novel coronavirus, that became prominent again as the pandemic ebbed and flowed, was its mortality rate. The statistical reality was that only a tiny minority of the population would die as a result of infection with this virus, but this risk grew with age. Older people, especially those aged 60+, had a higher risk of hospitalisation and death than did younger people. For children, that is, people under 18, COVID-19 generally caused only mild symptoms or none at all.

The attention given to death rates by the mainstream media, however, gave the impression to everyone that they were more commonplace than the statistical reality. Psychologists have studied a construct known as the "availability heuristic" that represents a tendency for people to over-estimate event frequencies, especially of relatively rare events, when these events have received a lot of publicity and people are conditioned into thinking about the specific outcomes that received most attention as being relatively likely to occur (Tversky & Kahneman, 1973, 1979).

The emotionality of the news had been recorded as on the increase long before the 2020 pandemic. This feature is not invariably bad because used effectively it can draw in an audience's attention to important information (Lang et al., 1995, 2003). However, news that takes on a "sensationalist" hue has been found frequently to focus on bad rather than good outcomes (Shoemaker & Reese, 1996; Grabe & Kamahawi, 2006). When this happens during epidemic crises, people who become infected and their families can find themselves stigmatised by other people because of the nature of the news reporting about the disease (Wang et al., 2015).

What this means is that it has adopted presentational attributes known to trigger emotional reactions in the audience. This sensationalising of the news can have positive benefits by drawing viewers' attention to stories that might not otherwise interest them (Cooper & Roter, 2000; Cooper et al., 2000). When the emotions triggered are negative (e.g., reports of events with bad outcomes for those involved), however, viewers can subsequently experience a downswing in their own mood state (Johnston & Davey, 1997). Specifically, in the case of televised news (but no print news), sensationalising health-related stories could trigger exaggerated risk percep-tions in the audience (Driedger, 2007).

The key point in the context of the pandemic is that routine news re-porting of death rates from COVID-19 with little further qualification potentially had the effect of triggering public anxiety. One reason for doing this, on the part of governments and their public health authorities, was to use it as a motivator of compliance with unprecedented restrictions on public behaviour.

Television news and newspapers might cover the same stories but not always in the same way. News stories of public health issues can not only inform people about such problems, but also influences their perceptions of risk where they encroach on the lives of people. One Canadian analysis found that televised news tended to give more emotional coverage of this story and newspapers offered more in-depth and rational coverage. The latter probably offered the kind of coverage that would enable readers to develop a more evidence-based and realistic perception of risk, while televised coverage could have exaggerated the risk (Driedger, 2007).

In another large study of 141,208 news headlines about COVID-19 from online English-language news sources, researchers used sentiment analysis to measure the emotionality of COVID-19 news coverage. This analysis covered a period from 15th January to 3rd June 2020 when the pandemic spread around the world and caused most countries to close down their economies and societies and some to close their borders (Aslam et al., 2020). The analysis techniques primarily divided stories into those displaying positive, neutral or negative sentiments. Overall, more than one in two (52%) of the headlines were classified of net negative in their emotional sentiments. Three in ten (30%) were classed as positive in emotionality. The remainder (18%) were neutral. Among the most prevalent emotions identified by the analysis were anger, fear and sadness and anticipation and trust.

There was significant coverage that had the potential to spark fear in the public. Although this study did not investigate causal relationships between news stories that were formally judged as conveying fear in the language being used and the emotional reactions of people exposed to these stories. Nor was there evidence that the degree to which public fear about COVID-19 might have been directly influenced by this content, but opinion polls internationally did detect considerable levels of fear about the pandemic and about its wider repercussions flowing from government interventions. The fear could have a constructive influenced if it motivated people to comply with government advice and restrictions in settings where it there had to be a degree of trust in the civic responsibility of the public.

In sentiment analysis, linguistic techniques are deployed for classifying the nature of words being used in texts and to identify meanings and feelings that were being conveyed. This form of analysis is not restricted to cataloguing words according to semantic type, but can also examine how words are combined into sentences and paragraphs to convey representations of events, issues and topics and impressions about how these entities might then impact upon readers, listeners or viewers. Sentiment analysis cannot guarantee that people will experience the same emotions that were formally identified in specific texts, or even how different people might individually experience specific feelings upon reading the text. It can however, be used to infer the intentions of authors in terms of the potential (or hoped for) emotional impact of what they write.

The Information Value of COVID-19 News Coverage

During times of crisis, publics around the world rely on reputable news media to present the facts, to enhance their understanding, to dispel misinformation and fake news and to catalyse internalised psychological coping mechanisms that would enable individuals to gain a sense of personal control over an uncertain situation (Renn et al., 1992; Southwell et al., 2018; Scheufele & Krause, 2019). Facts are expected to be checked, but in rapidly changing scenarios such as the COVID-19 pandemic where there were so many unknowns among even the expert community, facts can change and misinterpretations can occur (Krause et al., 2020).

As the pandemic spread around the world, it dominated the news agenda and commanded huge amounts of public attention. Most other issues were swamped by COVID-19 coverage. At the same time, media coverage of the pandemic, despite being led by senior politicians for much of the time, also gave extended airtime to medical and science experts. This raised the profile of science disciplines and the work of scientists like at no other time. This could be particularly important not only in terms of educating people about the pandemic and how their behaviour could help to control it, but also profiled science more generally. This profiling of science can be so important if the public is to develop a wider awareness of major issues confronting the world such as climate change (Boykoff, 2011).

People continued to turn to the mass media and despite the emergence of online microblogging and social networking sites, the big news media brands still command considerable public attention and, as importantly, their trust. Having science made digestible on popular media is therefore a crucial aspect of enhancing public understanding and triggering necessary action. Evidence was swift to emerge during the 2020 pandemic that news stories about COVID-19 and governments' interventionist policies could shape public awareness of what was going on and about the impact this new virus was having (Bolsen et al., 2020; Boykoff et al., 2020).

Television news broadcasting is good at getting information out to people quickly, but the visual imperatives of news story-telling in this medium means that pictures can dominate the words, even though most of the important information is conveyed by the words (Schwitzer, 2004; Schwitzer et al., 2005). The need for brevity can also mean much simplification of complex issues with the risk being run that explanations are incomplete. In a public health crisis, this lack of attention to detail and need to fit news reports into the limited timeframes available, might result in people making poor judgments or making the wrong decisions with serious consequences for their own health and that of others in their care (Voss, 2002).

An analysis of news coverage of the novel coronavirus in China across January and most of February 2020, examined the nature of health information being distributed through the news during the initial stage of the epidemic (Liu et al., 2020). Coverage was located through online search protocols. A sample of 7,791 articles was classified into 20 initial topics and nine primary themes. The three themes mentioned most often were prevention and control of the virus (33%), medical research and treatment (16%) and local social and economic effects (12%).

To assess the value of United States and international broadcast news, one research group used Google Videos to access video recordings of broadcast news transmitted in January and February 2020 that covered the coronavirus. They compiled a sample of 837 videos and then with further pruning reduced the sample down to 401 for analysis. These videos were content analysed by trained coders who catalogue their information content (Basch et al., 2020).

The study found that a substantial proportion (44%) of the items reported on death rates but relatively few covered information about preventing the spread of the virus, for instance by disinfecting regularly touched objects or surfaces (8%), wearing a face mask when caring for the ill (6%) or coughing into a tissue and then throwing the tissue away carefully (3%). Hence, in general there was a lot of focus on bad news and much less on coping behaviours.

A study of newspapers, both offline and online, in Canada, the United States and the United Kingdom provided insights into their contribution towards narratives in circulation about the pandemic over the first six months of the pandemic in these countries (March too August 2020). During the period covered by this study, Canada had the lowest per capita death rate, the United States had a much higher rate throughout the period, and the Unted Kingdom had more than Canada overall, but largely contained in an early spike. The analysis of newspapers examined what the researchers referred to as the "scientific quality" and the "sensationalism" of reporting. As the researchers put it in their own words: "scientific quality refers to the alignment between reporting and the state of scientific evidence and its uncertainties, and sensationalism is a discursive strategy rendering news as more extraordinary, interesting, or relevant than it really is" (Mach et al., 2021).

Across a sample of over 1,300 articles extracted from 12 newspapers in the three countries, scientific quality was judged to be generally moderate and sensationalism was mostly low-level. This finding suggested an attempt by these publications to treat the pandemic seriously and to attain good standards of accuracy. There were some variances on these measures, however, between newspapers of different political persuasion. Populist right-leaning newspapers were judged to have poorer quality reporting in a factual sense although this did not mean that they turned to sensationalism instead.

In the United States, newspapers on the left side of the political spectrum were more likely than those to the right to report on disease risks, policy failures and misinformation about COVID-19. When pandemic-related coverage was low in quality it often failed to warn people sufficiently about the health implications of the disease and did not tackle critically the veracity of stories based on misinformation.

The importance of good quality news information during times of national crisis had already been illustrated by experiences of earlier health emergencies. During times of widespread uncertainty when people might feel personally at risk, the major news media are crucial sources of information to which people turn for reassurance. It can also influence public perceptions of event that in turn will shape the way the public respond to policy decisions (Klemm et al., 2016; Laing, 2011; Pieri, 2019).

When policy-makers need to persuade people to change their behaviour, therefore, as was the case during the COVID-19 pandemic, news media coverage must get key policy messages across loud and clear and at the same time strongly challenge misinformation narratives that seek to undermine public confidence in authorities. The news media can impart important advice and knowledge to people to help them to help themselves. They can reach large numbers of people very quickly. They must ensure that they provide accurate information, however, even when this means playing down how much science already knows when knowledge of a new disease outbreak is, in fact, still limited (Hoffman & Justicz, 2016; Klemm et al., 2016).

One of the challenges for the news media is to choose how to construct narratives around a health crisis when "the science" cannot yet offer firm assurances about how an epidemic or pandemic might play out. Advice to the public must try to be helpful but should try to avoid overstating or understating the seriousness of a situation. This can be a difficult balance to strike when information and understanding about an issue remain patchy.

The Politicisation of COVID-19 News

What also became apparent from inspection of media news coverage of the pandemic was that it was not just based upon scientific data and analysis, but was also politicised, and sometimes significantly so. It is important to recognise this point and to the extent that it was an accurate description of news coverage, to consider its implications for the psychological impact it had on audiences. As noted earlier, the politicisation of COVID-19 news coverage was more apparent in newspapers than in broadcast news.

Hart et al. (2020) investigated the amount of politicization and polarization of COVID-19 coverage in American newspapers and television network news. Their analysis covered a period from March to May during the early phase of the pandemic. The findings showed that politicians were more visible than scientists. On network television news, scientists and politicians had parity in their coverage. This was believed to account in part for the political divide in opinions about COVID-19 in the United States.

Given the significant health risk of COVID-19, it is crucial that the public understand this risk and the reasons for imposing restrictions on their behaviour. If political polarisation, cultivated both by politicians and the news media, in partnership, undermines public safety by creating conditions under which large swathes of the population reject the pandemic controls and advice from public health authorities, this could have dire consequences for all concerned (Milligan, 2020; Roberts, 2020). This was especially true when public distrust of their governments and other authorities weakened their motivations to comply with pandemic-related restrictions on their behaviour.

Willingness to comply with these restrictions, however, depended upon the sense of civic responsibility that pervaded specific societies and also upon whether politicians were trusted. There was further evidence that compliance was also driven by fear (Dodsworth, 2021). Compliance with behavioural restrictions was weakened when people distrusted what they were being told because the message source was believed to be untrustworthy. Political divisions and prejudices could also play into this scenario and in politically divided countries, such as the United States, created polarised populations where some people accepted the nature of the crisis and the rest did not. Which camp people finished up in was closely associated, among Americans, with whether their politics leaned towards the Democrats or Republicans (Mordecai & Connaughton, 2020, 28th October).

When the pandemic struck the United States, Donald Trump was President. Initially, he dismissed the seriousness of the new virus from China. He claimed that it would not affect the United States and then when it did, he downplayed its seriousness and spoke up the ease with which it would be controlled by his government and the medical authorities. These pronouncements turned out to be empty words as the virus tore across the country infected millions and eventually killing hundreds of thousands. Many Americans believed he had not done a good job in handling this crisis, but his core Republican supporters were not among them. Most Republicans (83%) rated the job done by Trump's in dealing with COVID-19 as good or excellent (Van Green & Tyson, 2020).

Recognition was given to the role played by scientists in response to the pandemic but once again public opinion was divided along partisan lines. Democrat supporters had greater faith in scientists than did Republican supporters. Over the first months of the pandemic in the United States, Democrats' belief in scientists grew, but among Republicans it flatlined (Funk et al., 2020). Public belief in behavioural constraints also split along party political lines. Most Democrat supporters believed that social distancing was helping a lot to contain the virus, where only a minority of Republicans were convinced of this (Funk et al., 2020).

These different beliefs often translated into different behaviour patterns. Public behaviour was tracked via smartphones using GPS data and indicated that Republicans exhibited less social distancing than did Democrats (Allcott et al., 2020; Goldstein & Wiedemann, 2020; Painter & Qiu, 2020). The more Republican supporters had confidence in President Trump, who had been seen on television playing down the pandemic and refusing to wear a face mask, the less they complied with pandemic-related behaviour restrictions (Graham et al., 2020).

Political partisanship was also found to be related to public perceptions of the media coverage of COVID-19. Democrat supporters were much more likely than Republican supporters to agree that this coverage was accurate (66% vs 31%), was working to benefit people (63% vs 27%), was helping the country (63% vs 27%) and was getting people information they needed (73% vs 44%) (Gottfried et al., 2020). There may be numerous factors at play for these differences in opinion. The actions and pronouncements of President Trump, who had questioned whether the virus was a serious matter more than once both on mainstream media and social media (Franck, 2020). People who watched the outputs of media organisations that were sympathetic to the Republican Party and to Trump were more likely to support conspiracy theories or exhibited a poor understanding of the pandemic (Motta et al., 2020).

The media played their part in all of this. People rely on the mainstream news media for authoritative information in times of national crisis. It becomes all the more important for news providers to adhere to the highest standards of journalistic objectivity and to feature experts who are best equipped to provide evidence-backed reassurance to the public. When coverage is highly politicised, this imperative can be lost.

News reports become more personalised and feature politicians, often with disparate, politically-motivated viewpoints, sowing dispute and confusion. This can create dramatic and entertaining coverage, but it is not necessarily informative (Bennett et al., 2007; Feldman et al., 2015). Such coverage can nevertheless influence public beliefs and through these can set in place motives for behaviour that may or may not be compliant with what is everyone's best interests. The dramatic qualities politicians bring to the news can command public attention more than the more measured remarks of scientists (Bolsen et al., 2014; Chinn et al., 2020). When this happens and politicians receive more attentional focus than scientists by news audiences, public opinion can be shaped more by what politicians say. As politicians are likely to tow a "party line", both the news coverage and public opinion end up being more politicised and perhaps polarised (Druckman et al., 2013).

In an analysis of news coverage in the United States during the early stages of the pandemic, Sacerdote et al. (2020) found that an overwhelming proportion of those originated by American news outlets (91%) were negative in tone compared with articles found in non-Amercan English-language news sources (54%) and scientific journals (65%). The general negativity of mainstream U.S. news coverage persisted even when there were major scientific breakthroughs linked to COVID-19 such as vaccine trials to report or stories about relaxation of behavioural resrictions, such as re-openings of schools. Stories that reported increased COVID-19 cases significantly outnumber (by fivefold) stories about falling numbers of cases. Yet when "positive" but misinformed stories emerged, such as President Donald Trump's claims about swallowing bleach or the use of hydroxy-chloroquine, coverage was extensive.

Hart et al. (2020) conducted another analysis of news coverage of COVID-19 in the United States on the three leading television networks (ABC, CBS, NBC) and six national and regional newspapers from January to May 2020. Their news sample comprised over 36,000 news stories. They used a linguistic analysis methodology to identify the use of words that signalled political partisanship. The methods had been developed, tried and tested in other political narrative analysis settings. News references involving the Democrats and Republicans could be both qualified and quantified across the news sample.

Newspaper coverage was found to be highly politicised from early in the pandemic. Politicians featured more heavily than did scientists. In comparing the findings of this analysis with an earlier one by the same authors on news coverage of global warming, COVID-19 coverage emerged as more politicised (Chinn et al., 2020). Television network news coverage exhibited different qualities. Political polarisation was still high, although not as prominent as in newspapers, but scientific experts had greater visibility on televised news (Hart et al., 2020).

Lessons Learned

The novel coronavirus (SARS-CoV-2) pandemic commanded significant news attention. Coverage expanded rapidly as virus transmission rates accelerated across the globe. In many countries, news agendas were not just dominated by the pandemic but, for a time, were given over almost entirely and exclusively to COVID news. There was evidence that most news media tried to provide good quality coverage that followed emerging scientific evidence, but news operators known for more "populist" approaches performed less well on tis metric.

In some news markets, some "fatigue" set in after a few months and news coverage stabilised before falling away a little along with audiences. Some news suppliers benefited from the audience interest in the pandemic and saw their audiences climb higher than usual, following pre-pandemic declines. Other news media, especially print media, witnessed the opposite trend.

Despite the obvious significance of the pandemic-related news to people across many news markets, this dependency did not always lead to enhanced and universal trust among publics in what they were being told. Some countries, perhaps most notably the United States, witnessed a profound divided in pubic trust that was underpinned by political allegiances. The news media had already been rejected by some categories of the electorate as collectively untrustworthy. This mindset did not change during the pandemic.

There was also evidence that the news became quite "emotional" at times. This was not surprising given the emphasis placed by governments in their regular media briefings on hospitalisation and death rates from COVID-19. The use of emotional language and images was nothing new. This had been common currency among television broadcasters for many years (Gunter, 1987, 2015). It became pronounced during the pandemic. It may have served an initial purpose of cultivating public concern and fear that, in turn, motivated compliance with behavioural restrictions. Yet, over-use of emotion in the news can impede information uptake and enhanced cognitive understanding of the facts. Emotion pulls people into stories which is important. Overplayed, however, it can restrict what they take away from the experience. Triggering fear responses in audiences over time also runs the risk of cultivating a chronic pubic anxiety that becomes difficult to shift once the pandemic is over and life must return to normal.

The use of story-telling techniques that overemphasize risks and promote anxiety and fear might serve useful short-term political and public health objectives, but can cause longer-term problems once countries decide to relax pandemic restrictions and invite their publics to return to normality before the disease has been completely eradicated. Residual risk perceptions and accompanying anxieties might discourage some from returning to less restrictive behaviour and greater levels of interaction with others for continuing fears of personal infection. This reluctance to return to normal could itself be damaging to recovering public services, businesses and economies.

References

Allcott, H., Boxell, L., Conway, J. C., Gentzkow, M., Thaler, M., Yang, D. Y. (2020) *Polarization and public health: Partisan differences in social distancing during the coronavirus pandemic (Working Paper No. 26946)*. National Bureau of Economic Research. doi:10.3386/w26946

Aslam, F., Awan, T. M., Syed, J. H., Kashif, A., & Parveen, M. (2020) Sentiments and emotions evoked by news headlines of coronavirus disease (COVID-19) outbreak. *Humanities and Social Sciences Communications*, 7(1): 1–9. doi:10.1057/s41599-020-0523-3

Basch, C. H., Hillyer, G. C., Meleo-Erwin, Z., Mohlman, J., & Cosgrove, A. (2020) News coverage of the COVID-19 pandemic: Missed opportunities to promote health sustaining behaviours. *Infection, Disease & Health*, 25(3): P205–P209.

Bennett, W. L., Lawrence, R. G., & Livingston, S. (2007) *When the press fails*. University of Chicago Press. https://press.uchicago.edu/ucp/books/book/chicago/W/bo5186389.html

Bermingham A., & Smeaton A. F. (2010) Crowdsourced real-world sensing: Sentiment analysis and the real-time web. AICS 2010 – Sentiment Analysis

Workshop at Artificial Intelligence and Cognitive Science, Galway, Ireland, pp. 1–8.

Bolsen, T., Druckman, J. N., & Cook, F. L. (2014) How frames can undermine support for scientific adaptations: Politicization and the status-quo bias. *Public Opinion Quarterly*, 78(1): 1–26. doi:10.1093/poq/nft044

Bolsen, T., Palm, R., & Kingsland, J. T. (2020) Framing the origins of COVID-19. *Science Communication*, 42: 562–585.

Boykoff, M. T. (2011) *Who speaks for the climate? Making sense of media reporting on climate change*. Cambridge, UK: Cambridge University Press, Cambridge.

Boykoff, M., Aoyagi, M., Ballantyne, A. G. et al. (2020) World newspaper coverage of climate change or global warming, 2004–2020. Retrieved from: https://scholar.colorado.edu/concern/datasets/ng451j54h

Brennan, J. S., Simon, F., Howard, P. N., & Nielsen, R. K. (2020, 7th April) *Types, sources and claims of COVID-19 misinformation*. Oxford, UK: Reuters Institute, University of Oxford.

Chinn, S., Hart, P. S., & Soroka, S. (2020) Politicization and polarization in climate change news content, 1985-2017. *Science Communication*, 42(1): 112–129. doi:10.1177/1075547019900290

Cooper, C. P., & Roter, D. L. (2000) "If it bleeds it leads"? Attributes of TV health news stories that drive viewer attention. *Public Health Reports*, 115(4): 331–338.

Cooper, C. P., Roter, D. L., & Langlieb, A. M. (2000) Using entertainment television to build a context for prevention news stories. *Preventive Medicine*, 31(3): 225–231.

Dodsworth, L. (2021) *A state of fear*. London, UK: Pinter & Martin Ltd.

Driedger, S. M. (2007) Risk and the media: A comparison of print and televised news stories of a Canadian drinking water risk event. *Risk Analysis*, 27(3): 775–786.

Druckman, J. N., Peterson, E., & Slothuus, R. (2013) How elite partisan polarization affects public opinion formation. *American Political Science Review*, 107(1): 57–79. doi:10.1017/S0003055412000500

Ducharme, J. (2020, 7th February) How news coverage of coronavirus in 2020 compares to Ebola in 2018. Retrieved from: https://time.com/5779872/coronavirus-ebola-news-coverage/

Feldman, L., Hart, P. S., & Milosevic, T. (2015) Polarizing news? Representations of threat and efficacy in leading US newspapers' coverage of climate change. *Public Understanding of Science*, 26(4): 481–497. doi:10.1177/0963662515595348

Fletcher, R., Kalogeropoulos, A., Simon, F. M., & Nielsen, R. K. (2020c) *Information inequality in the UK coronavirus communications crisis*. Oxford: Reuters Institute for the Study of Journalism.

Forster, P. M., Forster, H. I., Evans, M. J., et al. (2020) Erratum: Publisher correction: Current and future global climate impacts resulting from COVID-19. *Nature Climate Change*, 10: 1–7.

Franck, T. (2020, February 29) Trump says the coronavirus is the Democrats' "new hoax". *CNBC*. https://www.cnbc.com/2020/02/28/trump-says-the-coronavirus-is-the-democrats-new-hoax.html

Funk, C., Kennedy, B., Johnson, C. (2020, May 21) Trust in medical scientists has grown in U.S., but mainly among Democrats. *Pew Research Center Science & Society*. https://www.pewresearch.org/science/2020/05/21/trust-in-medical-scientists-has-grown-in-u-s-but-mainly-among-democrats/

Goldstein, D. A. N., & Wiedemann, J. (2020) Who do you trust? The consequences of political and social trust for public responsiveness to COVID-19 orders (SSRN Scholarly Paper ID 3580547). *Social Science Research Network*. doi:10.2139/ssrn.3580547

Gottfried, J., Walker, M., & Mitchell, A. (2020, May 8) Republicans and democrats sharply divided in views of news media's coronavirus coverage. *Pew Research Center's Journalism Project*. https://www.journalism.org/2020/05/08/americans-are-more-likely-than-not-to-think-the-news-media-are-fulfilling-key-roles-during-the-coronavirus-outbreak-but-partisans-are-starkly-divided/

Grabe, M. E., & Kamahawi, R. (2006) Hard wired for negative news? Gender differences in processing broadcast news. *Communication Research*, 33(5): 346–369.

Graham, A., Cullen, F., Pickett, J., Jonson, C., Haner, M., & Sloan, M. (2020) Faith in Trump, moral foundations, and social distancing defiance during the coronavirus pandemic (SSRN Scholarly Paper ID 3586626). *Social Science Research Network*. doi:10.2139/ssrn.3586626

Gunter, B. (1987) *Poor reception: Misunderstanding and forgetting broadcast news*. Hillsdale, NJ: Lawrence Erlbaum Associates.

Gunter, B. (1997) *Measuring bias on television*. Luton, UK: University of Luton Press.

Gunter, B. (2015) *The cognitive impact of television news: Production attributes and information reception*. Basingstoke, UK: Palgrave Macmillan.

Hart, P. S., Chinn, S., & Soroka, S. (2020) Politicization and polarization in COVID-19 news coverage. *Science Communication*, 42: 679–697.

Hoffman, S. J., & Justicz, V. (2016) Automatically quantifying the scientific quality and sensationalism of news records mentioning pandemics: Validating a maximum entropy machine-learning model. *Journal of Clinical Epidemiology*, 75: 47–55. doi:10.1016/j.jclinepi.2015.12.010

Johnston, W. M., & Davey, G. C. L. (1997) The psychological impact of negative TV news bulletins: The catastrophizing of personal worries. *British Journal of Psychology*, 88 (pt 1): 85–91.

Jurkowitz, M., & Mitchell, A. (2020, 1st April) *Cable TB and COVID-19: How Americans perceive the outbreak and view media coverage differ by main news source*. Washington, DC: Pew Research Center.

Klemm, C., Das, E., & Hartmann, T. (2016) Swine flu and hype: A systematic review of media dramatization of the H1N1 influenza pandemic. *Journal of Risk Research*, 19: 1–20. doi:10.1080/13669877.2014.923029

Krause, N. M., Freiling, I., Beets, B., & Broussard, D. (2020) Fact checking as risk communication: The multi-layered risk of misinformation in times of COVID-19. *Journal of Risk Research*, 23(7–8): 1052–1059.

Kyriakidou, M., Morani, M., Soo, N., & Cushion, S. (2020) Government and media misinformation about COVID-19 is confusing the public. LSE blog.

Lang, A., Potter, D., & Grabe, M. E. (2003) Making news memorable: Applying theory to the production of local television news. *Journal of Broadcasting and Electronic Media*, 47: 113–124.

Lang, A., Sias, P., Chantril, P., & Burek, J. A. (1995) Tell me a story: Narrative structure and memory for television messages. *Communication Reports*, 8(2): 1–9.

Laing, A. (2011) The H1N1 crisis: Roles played by government communicators, the public and the media. *Journal of Professional Communication*, 1: 123–149. doi:1 0.15173/jpc.v1i1.88

Liu B. (2012) Sentiment analysis and opinion mining. *Synthesis Lectures on Human Language Technologies*, 5(1): 1–167.

Liu, Q., Zheng, Z., Zheng, J., Chen, Q., Liu, G., Chen, S., Chu, B., Zhu, H., Akinwunmi, B., Huang, J., Zhang, C. J. P., & Ming, W.-K. (2020) Health communication through news media during the early stage of the COVID-19 outbreak in China: Digital topic modelling approach. *Journal of Medical Internet Research*, 22(4): e19118. doi:10.2196/19118

Lytimäki, J., Kangas, H.-L., Mervaala, E., & Vikström, S. (2020) Muted by a crisis? COVID-19 and the long-term evolution of climate change newspaper coverage. *Sustainability*, 12: 8575.

Mach, K. J., Salas Reyes, R., Pentz, B., Taylor, J., Cook, C. A., Cruz, S. G., Thomas, K. E., Arnott, J. C., Donald, R., Jagannathan, K., Kirchhoff, C. J., Rosella, L. C., & Klenk, N. (2021) News media coverage of COVID-19 public health and policy information. *Humanities and Social Sciences Communications*, 8: 220. doi:10.1 057/s41599-021-00900-z

Milligan, S. (2020) The political divide over the coronavirus. US News & World Report. https://www.usnews.com/news/politics/articles/2020-03-18/the-political-divide-over-the-coronavirus

Mohammad, S. M., & Turney, P. D. (2013) Crowdsourcing a word-emotion association lexicon. *Computer Intelligence*, 29(3): 436–465.

Molla, R. (2020, 17th March) It's not just you. Everybody is reading the news more because of coronavirus. *Recode*. Retrieved from: https://www.vox.com/recode/2020/3/17/21182770/news-consumption-coronavirus-traffic-views

Mordecai, M., & Connaughton, A. (2020, 28th October) Public opinion about coronavirus is more politically divided in U. S. than in other advance economies. *Pew Research Centre*. Retrieved from: https://www.pewresearch.org/fact-tank/2020/10/28/public-opinion-about-coronavirus-is-more-politically-divided-in-u-s-than-in-other-advanced-economies/

Motta, M., Stecula, D., & Farhart, C. (2020) How right-leaning media coverage of COVID-19 facilitated the spread of misinformation in the early stages of the Pandemic in the U.S. *Canadian Journal of Political Science*, 1–8. doi:10.1017/S0008423920000396

Painter, M., & Qiu, T. (2020) Political beliefs affect compliance with COVID-19 social distancing orders (SSRN Scholarly Paper ID 3569098). *Social Science Research Network*. doi:10.2139/ssrn.3569098

Pang, B., & Lee, L. (2008) Opinion mining and sentiment analysis. *Foundations and Trends® in Information Retrieval*, 2(1–2): 1–135.

Pang, B., Lee, L., & Vaithyanathan, S. (2002) Thumbs up? Sentiment classification using machine learning techniques. *Proceedings of the ACL-02 Conference on Empirical Methods in Natural Language Processing*, 10: 79–86.

Pearman, O., Boykoff, M., Osborne-Gowey, J., Aoyagi, M., Ballantyne, A. G., Chandler, P., Daly, M., Doi, K., Fernández-Reyes, R., Jiménez-Gómez, I., Nacu-Schmidt, A., McAllister, L., McNatt, M., Mocatta, G., Petersen, L. K., Simonsen, A. H., & Ytterstad, A. (2021) COVID-19 media coverage decreasing despite deepening crisis. *Lancet Planet Health*, 5(1): e6–e7. doi:10.1016/S2542-5196(20)30303-X

Pieri, E. (2019) Media framing and the threat of global pandemics: The Ebola crisis in UK media and policy response. *Sociology Research Online*, 24: 73–92.

Reintjes, R., Das, E., Klemm, C., Richardus, J. H., Keßler, V., & Ahmad, A. (2016) "Pandemic public health paradox": Time Series analysis of the 2009/10 Influenza A/H1N1 epidemiology, media attention, risk perception and public reactions in 5 European countries. *PloS one*, 11(3): e0151258. doi:10.1371/journal.pone.0151258

Renn, O., Burns, W. J., Kasperson, J. X., Kasperson, R. E., & Slovic, P. (1992) The social amplification of risk: Theoretical foundations and empirical applications. *Journal of Social Issues*, 48(4): 137–160. doi:10.1111/j.1540-4560.1992.tb01949.x

Roberts, D. (2020, March 31) Partisanship is the strongest predictor of coronavirus response. Vox. https://www.vox.com/science-and-health/2020/3/31/21199271/coronavirus-in-us-trump-republicans-democrats-survey-epistemic-crisis

Roser, M., Ritchie, H., Ortiz-Ospina, E., & Hasell, J. (2020) Coronavirus disease (COVID-19). *Our World in Data*. Retrieved from: https://ourworldindata.org/coronavirus

Sacerdote, B., Shegal, R., & Cook, M. (2020, November) Why is all COVID-19 news bad news? Bureau of Economic Research, Working Paper No. 28110. doi:10.3386/w28110. Retrieved from: https://ideas.repec.org/p/nbr/nberwo/28110.html

Scheufele, D. A., & Krause, N. M. (2019) Science audiences, misinformation and fake news. *Proceedings of the National Academy of Sciences of the United States of America*, 116(16): 7662–7669.

Scheufele, D. A., & Tewksbury, P. (2006) Framing, agenda setting and priming: The evolution of three media effects models. *Journal of Communication*, 57: 9–20.

Schwitzer, G. (2004) Ten troublesome trends in TV health news. *British Medical Journal*, 329: 1362. doi:10.1136/bmj.329.7478.1352

Schwitzer, G., Mudur, G., Henry, D., Wilson, A., Goozner, M., Sweet, M., & Baverstock, K. A. (2005) What are the roles and responsibilities of the media in disseminating health information? *Plos One*, 2(7): e215. doi:10.1371/journal.pmed.0020215

Shoemaker, P. J., & Reese, S. D. (1996) *Mediating the message* (2nd Ed.). White Plains, New York: Longman.

Sokolova M., & Bobicev V. (2013) What sentiments can be found in medical forums?. Proceedings of the *International Conference Recent Advances in Natural Language Processing RANLP 2013*. INCOMA Ltd. Shoumen, BULGARIA, Hissar, Bulgaria, pp. 633–639.

Southwell, B. G., Thorson, E. A., & Sheble, L. (2018) *Misinformation and mass audiences*. Austin, TX: University of Texas Press.

Strapparava C., & Mihalcea R. (2008) Learning to identify emotions in text. Proceedings of the *2008 ACM symposium on Applied computing. Association for Computing Machinery New York*, NY, United States, pp. 1556–1560.

Taboada M., Brooke J., Tofiloski M., Voll K., & Stede M. (2011) Lexicon-based methods for sentiment analysis. *Comput Linguist*, 37(2): 267–307.

Turney P. D., & Littman M. L. (2003) Measuring praise and criticism: Inference of semantic orientation from association. *ACM Transactions on Information Systems (TOIS)*, 21(4): 315–346.

Tversky, A., & Kahneman, D. (1973) Availability: A heuristic for judging frequency and probability. *Cognitive Psychology*, 5(2): 207–232.

Tversky, A., & Kahneman, D. (1979) Prospect theory: An analysis of decision under risk. *Econometrica*, 47(2): 263–291.

Uribe, R., & Gunter, B. (2007) Are sensational news stories more likely to trigger viewers' emotions than non-sensational news stories? A content analysis of British TV news. *European Journal of Communication*, 22(2): 207–228.

Van Green, T., & Tyson, A. (2020, April 2) 5 facts about partisan reactions to COVID-19 in the U.S. Pew Research Center. https://www.pewresearch.org/fact-tank/2020/04/02/5-facts-about-partisan-reactions-to-covid-19-in-the-u-s/

Voss, M. (2002) Checking the pulse: Midwestern reporters' opinions on their ability to report health care news. *American Journal of Public Health*, 92: 1158–1160.

Waldrup, T., Alsup, D., & McLaughlin, E. C. (2020, 25th March) Fearing coronavirus, Arizona man dies after taking a form of chloroquine used to treat aquariums, CNN. https://www.cnn.com/2020/07/23/health.arizona-coronavirus-choloroquine-death/index/html

Wang, Q., Zhao, L., Huang, R., Yang, Y., & Wu, T. (2015) Interaction of media and disease dynamics and its impact on emerging infection management. *Discrete Continuous Dynamical Systems Series B*, 20(1): 215–230.

Wilson T., Hoffmann P., Somasundaran S., Kessler J., Wiebe J., Choi Y., Cardie C., Riloff E., & Patwardhan, S. (2005) OpinionFinder: A system for subjectivity analysis. *Proceedings of HLT/EMNLP 2005 Interactive Demonstrations. Association for Computational Linguistics*, Vancouver, British Columbia, Canada, pp. 34–35.

Zeng-Treitler Q., Goryachev S., Tse T., Keselman A., & Boxwala A. (2008) Estimating consumer familiarity with health terminology: A context-based approach. *Journal of the American Medical Informatics Association*, 15(3): 349–356.

Chapter 3

Online Chatter about COVID-19

The dissemination of accurate and relevant information was essential during the 2020 pandemic both to get people to play their part in a responsible way and also to ensure they followed offical health guidance and advice accurately. During the 21st century, online media have become important adjuncts to the mainstream news media for more and more people. The use of the Internet to access news, at first enthusiasticlly adopted by the young, has spread across the generations, although for many of these later adopters remains strongly tied to major news brands. Among the younger generations, however, news consumers have often turned away from the big news names in favour of newer news providers, including aggregator services that seek out and construct personalised news menus for their patrons. While exposure to a more diversified news supply might seem, potentially, to be a good thing because it might broaden perspectives on major news issues, there are inherent risks associated with it.

The Internet transmitted huge quantities of information about COVID-19 and the pandemic. Hence, the pandemic was accompanied by what became known as an "infodemic" comprising a viral-like spreading of news and information about the pandemic from a multitude of sources. This phenomenon triggered a range of questions about how helpful or harmful this activity might be. If the information being spread was accurate and constructive, then it might be helpful in all kinds of ways. Equally, if the messages being disseminated about COVID-19 were spreading falsehoods, scare stories and conspiracies, then the outcomes might be much less positive, encouraging people to ignore official advice, reject behavioural restrictions and fail to protect themselves and others by taking appropriate safeguards and not engaging in risky behaviour (Schillinger et al., 2020).

Pandemics Drive Internet Search Volumes

During the 21st century, the Internet has emerged as a major source of public health information (Gunter, 2005). People search online for generic health content, often to shed further light on diagnoses received from health

DOI: 10.4324/9781003274629-3

professionals. Many searches are also motivated by the need to find specific information about an individual's particular health circumstances (Reis & Brownstein, 2010). Past pandemics have also been found to drive online health information search behaviour. This behaviour might also be used as a warning system for pandemics or certainly an indication of growing public interest in specific symptoms even before official figures about infection rates had been released (Ginsberg et al., 2009; Lampos et al., 2021).

During the H7N9 influenza outbreak in China in 2013, significant increases in traffic volumes to microblog websites were observed which spread across the country as the virus spread. Online behaviour increased substantially within days of infection outbreaks being announced in specific regions as people sought information about the virus and the progress being made by the epidemic and exchanged opinions with others about what was happening (Zhou et al., 2020).

Korean research found that from the early phase of the pandemic in February 2020, sites such as Twitter were mobilised by people to find news about the new coronavirus and to share what they knew with others. Twitter users drew upon major news channels for information here, but also exchanged much information with each other. Medical and non-medical topics were searched and discussed. Under non-medical discussion, conversations often turned to deviant behaviour on the part of the public and also the role being played by celebrities in the early publicity about this new disease. Twitter was used as a useful supplementary platform to the main news media to get health information out of people but also provided its users with alternative information sources to spokespersons from government and health authorities who dominated mainstream media coverage (Park et al., 2020).

Further Korean research noted that sites such as Twitter can serve as early warnings of what is to come. Researchers developed a Twitter traffic monitoring methodology and identified shifts in volumes of chatter on the site in the United States concerning specific early developments in the pandemic. There was a buildup of interest in the new coronavirus already underway up to the point at which the World Health Organization (WHO) declared a Public Health Emergency of International Concern at the end of January 2020. Interest fell away again, although exhibited small undulations when the WHO named COVID-19, and then when the first cases were announced in Italy. A much larger peak occurred around the time of the first case in the United States in early March and then equally dramatically fell away again over subsequent weeks (Chen et al., 2020).

Primary among the risks is the uncertainty about the identity of some news sources, their agendas and the accuracy and unbiased nature of the news they provide. In times of global crisis, misinformation can circulate as widely as authoritative knowledge and if people on the receiving end are inclined to believe false news, this could lead to the development of false beliefs which might in turn feed into the emergence of internal motivations to behave in ways that only exacerbate the crisis. Misinformation could then undermine efforts on the part of the authorities to get people to change their behaviour patterns in ways that would enhance the safety of all (Pimenta et al., 2020).

Sentiments Expressed

Online platforms enabled ordinary members of the public to engage in debates about the pandemic on a mass scale. Microblogging and social media platforms provided opportunities for people to express their feelings about the pandemic and the restrictions being imposed on their everyday behaviour. While some people found being placed under lockdown and told not to go to work to represent a change of scene that was not altogether unwelcome initially, for others it created an extremely damaging state of affairs, especially if they lost their business, their jobs and their income.

Abd-Alrazaq et al. (2020) investigated the topics ientified from posts made by Twitter users that were linked to the COVID-19 pandemic. Search terms, such as "corona", "COVID-19" and "2019-nCov" were used at the start. Responses to tweets including "likes" and "rewteets" were also catelogied for analysis. The analysis covered a period from 2nd February to 15th March 2020. An initial sample was identified comprising 2.8 million tweets of which around 167,000 produced by around 160,000 users met inclusion criteria. From these, 12 topics were identified that covered four main themes: (1) origin of the virus; (2) its sources; (3) impact on people, countroes and the ecoonmy; and (4) ways of mitigating infection risks from the virus. Ten of the topics were broadly classed as positive in sentiment and two as negative (i.e., deaths caused by COVID-19 and increased racism). Tweets about economic losses atracted the highest average number of "likes" (15.4) and travel bans and warnings attracted the lowest (3.9).

Another investigation of Twitter activity and the topics covered and sentiments expressed in posts examined how tweets had changed from before the pandemic to during it (Chandrasekaran et al., 2020). This analysis spanned a period from 1st January to 9th May 2020. The researchers compiled a sample of 13.9 million English-language tweets that had bene posted by individual Twitter users. They identified 26 topics that they grouped into 10 broader themes. Over one in five of the tweets (21%) concerned the economic impact of COVID-19. In terms of prevalence this was followed by tweets about the spread of the virus (15%), treatment and recovery (13%), impact on the health care sector (11%) and their government's response (11%).

On topics such as spread of the virus, symptoms, racism, origins of outbreak and political impact, sentiments tended generally to be more negative than positive. When considering matters such as prevention, treatment and recovery, impact of the economy, government response and impact on health care, sentiments tended to be more positive.

An analysis of Twitter activity in the United States between 20th March and 19th April 2020 examined once again topics discussed and sentiments expressed. Hung et al. (2020) compiled a sample of over 900,000 tweets, which also generated over 14 million "likes" and over three million retweets. Nearly half the tweets (48%) were classed as expressing positive sentiment, one in five (21%) as neutral and three in ten (31%) as negative. Five dominant themes emerged: health care environment, emotional support, business and economy, social change and psychological stress. It emerged that there were regional differences in emotions being expressed in Twitter across the United States. The most negative sentiments were found to occur in tweets from site users in Alaska, Florida, New Mexico, Pennsylvania and Wyoming. The most positive sentiment emerged in Colorado, North Carolina, North Dakota, Tennessee, Utah and Vermont.

Xui et al. (2020) collected four million Twitter messages related to COVID-19 uploaded between 7th March and 21st April 2020 and discovered 13 discussion topics that covered five themes. As in other studies, similar themes emerged including the nature of public health measures designed to slow the spread of the virus, COVID-19 in the United States (where the study was based), COVID-19 across the world, news about the virus and deaths caused by it and, also, somewhat more distinctively to this study, discussion of the social stigma associated with COVID-19. Sentiment analysis revealed widespread expressions of anger and fear linked to different topis but also some degree of public trust. Discussion of deaths evoked significant negative emotional responses, especially fear.

These analyses of Twitter discussions about the pandemic provide interesting insights into the status of public feeling and understanding, and also where people felt the priorities lay in relation to this public health crisis. The fluid nature of Twitter and other online platforms on which users can regularly update their thoughts and feelings provides insights into the dynamics of constantly evolving public reactions to a constantly changing scenario, which are not so easily identified, monitored and updated via conventional survey methods.

A Brazilian study of Twitter also included analysis of news media outputs about the pandemic. The recognition of themes covered by the online discussions and the feelings or sentiments expressed by Twitter users was linked to the wider reporting about COVID-19. De Melo and Figueiredo (2020) compiled a sample of over 18,000 reports from news media and nearly 1.6 million tweets posted by nearly 1.3 million Brazilian users of the site. Similarities were detected between the topic coverage in the news and in tweets, but the attention given to specific themes varied between these two domains. There were political themes that drew negative sentiments in both news coverage and Twitter commentary.

Another Brazilian study analysed over 3.3 million tweets in English and over 3.1 million in Portuguese from Brazil and the United States across a later pandemic period than the studies already reviewed here. Between April and August 2020, news coverage and Twitter chatter was characterised by 10 major topics. News coverage dealt with the politics of the pandemic and also its impact on economies. In the United States, public health messages were presented and encouraged people to comply with restrictions and communities not to open back up prematurely. Other coverage examined treatments and vaccine development. As the pandemic evolved and the initial wave subsided news appeared from different parts of the world about the re-opening of their economies and societies. There was also discussion of continuing precautionary measures such as social distancing and wearing face masks.

Evidence emerged that the topic coverage of Twitter chatter matched that in major news coverage. This mirroring between Twitter coverage and mainstream news coverage in each country was reflected not just in topic profiles but also in the dominant sentiments being expressed. Different stories evoked different sentiments, some positive and other negative. For the authors of this study, this finding invited further research into the influence of news coverage on public sentiments abut COVID-19 (Garcia & Berton, 2021).

A Chinese study examined China's equivalent to Twitter, Sina Weibo and its use by ordinary people to raise concerns about COVID-19. Analysis of this micro-blogging site from 1st December 2019 to 31st July 2020 identified the topics most frequently discussed by the site's users. Seventeen topics were identified across over 203,000 posts and these were then grouped into eight themes. People on this site discussed pandemic statistics, the epidemic in China, the spread of the virus overseas, treatments for COVID-19, medical resources, economic impact, quarantine restrictions, patients needing help, making material donations, resumption of work and productivity, the psychological impact, prevention and help, the situation in neighbouring countries, vaccine development congratulating those on the forefront of tackling the pandemic, detection of the virus and (for children and young adults) resumption of their studies. With 11 topics, the sentiments expressed tended to be positive and for six of them, they tended to be more negative. Concerns about the epidemic within China triggered the most "retweets" of messages. Discussion of quarantining accumulate the mot "likes" (Wang et al. (2020).

This research provided further evidence of the potential significance of social networking sites during the COVID-19 pandemic. Sina Weibo, in particular, represented a widely used platform for people to express their concerns, the find out information and to get reassurance at an uncertain time. It also provides are area in which governments and health authorities can monitor how well their populations are coping and track outbreaks of illness in different locations.

Li et al. (2020) combined quantitative and qualitative analyses of use of the Weibo microblogging platform in China, with the focus placed on posts originating in Wuhan City where the coronavirus was initially detected. Their analysis began on 23rd December 2019 and went through to 31st January 2020. There was special interest in whether Weibo COVID-19 posts predicted the number of cases reported. The researchers collected over 115,000 Weibo posts and found that the numbers of posts found each day (ranging from zero to 13,587) was related to the number of cases formally detected in Wuhan. For every 10 additional COVID-19 cases there were 40 additional Weibo posts. This relationship was stronger that had been found in the rest of China and suggests a particularly strong sensitivity to the novel coronavirus in a locality where the severity of its outbreak and spread was greater than anywhere else at that time.

Qualitative analysis revealed that the topics commanding the most attention on Weibo concerned how the disease was caused, the rate at which the virus was spreading, how people were reacting to the new disease and what responses were being taken to it. There was a sense of considerable public uncertainty at this time with many people possessing little information or knowledge about the virus and being unsure how to feel it.

What became clear from early on in the pandemic was that the new coronavirus was highly infectious and could spread very quickly challenging even the best equipped and most skilled health systems. Not only that, but in monitoring how the public was reacting to the unfolding crisis, traditional research methods were too cumbersome to keep pace. Government responses to the pandemic had to rely initially on a range of non-pharmaceutical measures and this meant implementing the closure of many routine activities such as going to work, sending the children to school, being able to visit the hairdresser and so on.

Yet in the ubiquitous online world, people disclosed details of their lives daily. These messages represented potentially hugely valuable resources to track public opinion and behaviour. By analysing the themes people talked about on microblogging and social networking sites, the authorities could learn tremendous amounts about how their nation was coping. It could also provide early warning signals about fresh outbreaks of the disease and the willingness of people to comply with behavioural restrictions.

In the United States, researchers investigated the kinds of discussions people had online about COVID-19, whether this behaviour increased after the onset of the pandemic and what kinds of feelings or sentiments were being expressed. Over 86 million tweets were analysed on Twitter and attention focused on 354,738 individuals located in 20 US cities. Initially there was chatter about the arrival of the disease, but as time wore on and the authorities began imposing restrictions, more chatter turned to lifestyle changes caused by interventions. Sentiment analysis indicated the negative emotional impact of the pandemic (Valdez et al., 2020).

Information Quality

The World Wide Web has become an increasingly important and widely used information source for those seeking to understand health conditions better. It can provide ready access to a wide range of information sources. The downside is that not all of these sources can be trusted in terms of the quality of information provided. The web is also used for the wilful distribution of misinformation designed to mislead people. This has led to calls for filtering systems to identify reliable and problematic websites. Automated quality control systems have been developed to check the content of websites against specific criteria designed to test content accuracy and credibility (Dunn et al., 2021). It has been found that many people will have exposure to low credibility websites, but that in general, the high credibility sites perform better in terms of volume of usage (Shah et al., 2015).

Misinformation can damage public understanding during a pandemic. When public health authorities need to persuade the public to join with them in taking staeps to combat a new disease, it is essential that everyone acts consistently and in harmony with extant knowledge and understanding about the disease. Fact-checking systems can play an important part in this process, as already noted, but they may not be enough. Sources of misinformation can run counter to the advice given out by the authorities.

Some online communities demonstrate observable distrust their authorities and governments. They construct distorted or false interpretations of the reasons why specific preventative steps are being taken. In one example of this phenomenon, a study conducted in the United States during February and March 2019 and then again in September and October 2019, found that misinformation about measles had struck home with some people. In particular, a movement opposed to giving children vaccination against measles (and mumps and rubella) had advised that this vaccine was linked to the onset of autism (Stecula et al., 2020).

Some of these communities have value systems that discorages them from compliance with any government requests. For instance, communities that abstain for alcohol or certain kinds foods might be understandably reluctant to be innoculated if they believe that a vaccine contains alcohol or essences of specific prohibited food products. Hence, new story-telling narratives must be developed that are persuasive and therefore communicated not just by the mainstream media, but also by sources that doubters can trust (Chou et al., 2021).

A number of pre-pandemic narratives about vaccination had made unsubstantiated claims that vaccines contained toxins, that they could be delayed with risk so there was no need to be rushed into getting them, that the population would gain natural immunity over time without the need for vaccination and that vaccination can cause autism (Smith, 2017). In the 2019 study, noted above, nearly one in five respondents (18%) signed up to the opinion that vaccines could cause autism and one in six (15%) believed vaccines were full of toxins. One in five (20%) also believed that it made no difference if parents delayed getting their children vaccinated because it would be better for their children to develop natural immunity (Stecula et al., 2020). Clearly most people did not subscribe to these theories. Yet, as indicated by earlier research, even the minorities that did accept unsound theories were large enough, if acted upon, to enable the virus to remain in circulation in society to a potentially dangerous level (Oxford Vaccine Group, 2016).

Previous research had shown that changing people's misconceptions about vaccines is not easy to achieve (Chan et al, 2017; Walter & Murphy, 2018). By the time of the pandemic, new research found that, despite the extensive mainstream media coverage that tried to promote vaccination, there remained in circulation a lot of anti-vaxxer messaging which was widely available online. Over the five-month period of their observations, one in five participants (19%) exhibited a significant margin of change in their level of vaccination misinformation. The most worring finding was that among these people, two-thirds (64%) appeared to be more strongly signed up to vaccination misinformation compared to one-third (34%) who became less so (Stecula et al., 2020).

Although the researchers were unable to map belief changes precisely onto the interim media diets of the people they studied, they knew there had been widespread coverage of the importance of vaccination on the major media, much of which featured endorsements from medical experts. Yet, if their participants had been exposed to this coverage, it appeared to have very little impact on the overall status of their vaccination beliefs. There was evidence, however, that where vaccination beliefs did shift, if they changed in the direction of being more strobgly against it, this was most associated with people who relied a lot on social media for their information.

News Frames on Twitter

As the novel coronavirus spread, there was increased chatter on the world's most used micro-blogging site, Twitter. This platform was extensively used by news organisations and individual journalists as an extension of their normal professional outputs and also invited news consumers and multiple other interested parties to contribute to ongoing commentaries and debates about the pandemic and the way it was being handled by national governments and their health authorities.

Studies were launched around the world of the use being made of this site and of the type and quality of information circulating on it. These sites attracted much public criticism for those occasions on which false information was presented by its users and sometimes gained traction with others. Yet, Twitter conveyed much useful and truthful information about the coronavirus and the pandemic it had caused. The ascertain the nature of COVID-related content being posted on Twitter, systematic analysis is needed in which a transparent methodology has been fully described and explained.

Twitter can convey information very quickly and content can be published very soon after the events it described have taken place. The content can also be ephemeral and can disappear as quickly as it appeared. Researchers must therefore take snapshots of this very fluid information environment to study the messages it conveys. Analyses tended to examine whether content originates from a few or many sources and whether and how often these sources link up and exchange information with each other. One such study in South Korea illustrates this approach (Park et al., 2020).

In this study, the researchers collated a sample of Twitter content on 29th February 2020. It had involved over 43,000 Twitter users between whom over 78,000 inter-connections were traced. Four "networks" were identified that were defined in terms of the issues they were each preoccupied with. They also identified major news services that were involved in these networks. Finally, they examined the way news topics were framed, that is, approached and explained.

One initial finding was that Twitter networks worked fast, but some of their internal use networks mover faster than others. Twitter users who often used the word 'coronavirus' tended to be among the quickest at communicating with each other, compared to activity in three other networks. They were generally more active than other Twitter networks and they spread information quicker. They highlighted news stories about the new virus and were instrumental in directing other network members' attention to these reports. Hence, Twitter users catalysed the spread of news information about the pandemic. Among the topics highlighted in this specific network were discussion of the ethics of deviating from behavioural restrictions linked to the pandemic and also the involvement of celebrities in debates about the pandemic. While some tweets clearly spun off from mainstream news stories, others presented more specific discussions of medical issues linked to the virus and at the time of this research, the medically framed posts were the more popular with other users. This indicated the priority for many Twitter users of getting as informed as they could with the most relevant of advice and know-how about this new disease.

Lessons Learned

As we have seen in this chapter, the Internet conveyed massive amounts of information about the pandemic. This information could vary greatly in its quality. Analyses of micro-blogging and social media sites provided insights into public discussions that took place about the novel coronavirus at different points in the pandemic. The understanding that people had about the virus and the feelings they harboured about the pandemic and the interventions of their governments were dynamic and changing constantly. Expressions of belief and concern on these online platforms therefore provided one of the best sources of insight into how the pandemic was received and reacted to by ordinary people.

Just as the pandemic dominated mainstream media news agendas, it also garnered a great deal of attention online. There were large volumes of Internet searches for information about the pandemic and much chatter about it on microblogging and social media sites. Some of this chatter mirrored mainstream news coverage. In addition, there was much distinctive content generated by the information exchanges between users of these sites. There were important questions of information accuracy, credibility and trustworthiness that applied to these sources just as much as to the major news providers.

Studies that monitored the topic themes of online discussions about the pandemic found that people's concerns were similar in different locations and often reflected the issues being reported in the major news media. Online, however, there was always an issue of information quality and of whether sources, whose authority and credibility often could not be easily verified represented vested interests that were inclined to distort the facts to serve their own objectives. Certainly, in the future any repeat of the COVID-19 crisis, should trigger deployment of fact-checking systems by platform providers, as well as news organisations, to sort out reputable from disreputable information sources. An inaccurate story can quickly gain traction on microblogging and social media sites and once repeated and re-posted by multiple users of these sites can take on an air of authenticity they do not deserve.

Some research did show, however, that online platforms could have very positive effects in quickly reaching out to large numbers of people with critical information even before mainstream news media can. In the context of emergencies in which events evolve rapidly, online behaviour can give early indications of public response on the ground and enable authorities to distribute actionable messages to large populations to trigger prompt defensive and safeguarding behaviours. Examples of these positive effects emerged from early pandemic-related research conducted in China, where the novel coronavirus was first detected.

The virus was first identified in China and shortly afterwards it started to gain traction online. Users of Sina Weibo, a twitter-like platform used exclusively in China, were monitored for their ongoing reactions. Shen et al. (2020) established a pool of 250 million Weibo users, which comprised half the total user base. They used a list of 167 key words to search the site for COVID-related posts from 1st November 2019 to 31st March 2020. Their analysis, as these dates indicate, started some time before the new virus was formally recognised by the Chinese government. They analysed around 15 million Sina Weibo posts. Among other things, the researchers identified what they called "sick posts", that is, messages that reported users' own or other people's symptoms and diagnoses relating to COVID-19. They monitored this behaviour on a daily basis. They also differentiated between posts uploaded from users in Hubei province where the virus was first identified and for those in the rest of the China mainland.

One interesting finding was that the data specifically for reports of symptoms and diagnoses predicted daily case counts 14 days ahead of official statistics. Other COVID-related posts did not have the same predictive power. The predictive power of symptoms and diagnoses posts was found both among users in Hubei and for those across the rest of China. This finding was consistent for different parts of China regardless of the timings of first cases and the status of local health services. The researchers advised that online chatter about disease could provide useful early warnings sources about impending epidemics. Such data can also be used to track how and where a pandemic is evolving over time.

A further analysis of over 9,800 Sina Weibo posts about COVID-19 between 3rd and 20th February 2020 focused on people who had presented with clinical symptoms of laboratory confirmed cases. The average of these individuals was 63 (range: 55-71 years). Over eight in ten (84%) reported a fever and three-quarters (75%) were found subsequently to have a chest infection. Eight days lapsed on average between first reporting symptoms online and being tested. It was proposed that Sina Weibo could serve as an early notification system for people experiencing COVID symptoms. The patients identified here were most classed as "elderly" and were the ones most at risk from this disease. Early identification and treatment were especially important for this age group (Huang et al., 2020).

What these early Chinese studies indicated was that online chatter can provide a source of advance warnings about pandemics and how the public might be responding to them. Chatter about specific symptoms could indicate when a new disease is starting to spread even before hospital case loads confirm that there might be a problem. Further online chatter can be indicative of how people are reacting to government restrictions on their behaviour or health authorities' advice about the personal protective steps people can take to reduce their chances of infection far in advance of any tracking surveys. Although online searches and chatter that spread false narratives and conspiracy theories can be unhelpful in the cultivation of civic responsibility, some of it can also provide valuable and early insights into emerging health crises.

References

Abd-Alrazaq, A., Alhuwaid, D., Househ, M., Hamdi, M., & Shah, Z. (2020) Top concerns of Tweeters during the COVID-19 pandemic: An infoveillance study. *Journal of Medicine and Internet Research*, 22(4): e19016. doi:10.2196/19016

Chan, M. S., Jones, C. R., Hall Jamieson, K., & Albarracín, D. (2017) Debunking: A meta-analysis of the psychological efficacy of messages countering misinformation. *Psychological Science*, 28(11): 1531–1546. doi: 10.1177/0956797617714579

Chandrasekaran, R., Mehta, V., Valkuna, T., & Moustakas, E. (2020) Topics, trends, and sentiments of tweets about the COVID-19 pandemic: Temporal infoveillance study. *Journal of Medicine and Internet Research*, 22(10): e22624. doi: 10.2196/22624

Chen, E., Lerman, K., & Ferrara, E. (2020) Tracking social media discourse about the COVID-19 pandemic: Development of a public coronavirus Twitter data set. *JMIR Public Health and Surveillance*, 6(2): e19273. doi: 10.2196/19273

Chou, W. S., Gaysynsky, A., Trivedi, N., & Vanderpool, R. C. (2021) Using social media for health: National data from HINTS 2019. *Journal of Health Communication*, 26(3): 184–193. doi: 10.1080/10810730.2021.1903627

De Melo, T., & Figueiredo, C. M. S. (2020) Comparing news articles and tweets about COVID-19 in Brazil: Sentiment analysis and topic modelling approach. *JMIR Public Health Surveillance*, 7(2): e24585. doi: 10.2196/24585

Dunn, A. G., Steffens, M., Dyda, A., & Mandl, K. D. (2021) Knowing when to act: A call for an open misinformation library to guide actionable surveillance. *Big Data & Society*, 8(1).

Garcia, K., & Berton, L. (2021) Topic detection and sentiment analysis in Twitter content related to COVID-19 from Brazil and the USA. *Applied Software Computing*, 101: 107057. doi: 10.1016/j.asoc.2020.107057

Ginsberg, J., Mohebbi, M., Patel, R., Brammer, L., Smolinski, M. S., & Brilliant, L. (2009) Detecting influenza epidemics using search engine query data. *Nature*, 457: 1012–1014. doi: 10.1038/nature07634

Gu, H., Chen, B., Zhu, H., Jiang, T., Wang, X., Chu, L., Jiang, Z., Zheng, D., & Jiang, J. (2014) Importance of internet surveillance in public health emergency control and prevention: Evidence from a digital epidemiologic study during avian influenza A H7N9 outbreaks. *Journal of Medical Internet Research*, 16(1): e20. doi: 10.2196/jmir.2911

Gunter, B. (2005) *Digital health: Meeting patient and professional needs online*. Mahwah, NJ: Lawrence Erlbaum Associates.

Huang, C., Xu, X., Cai, Y., Ge, Q., Zeng, G., Li, X., Zhang, W., Ji, C., & Yang, L. (2020) Mining characteristics of COVID-19 patients in China: Analysis of social media posts. *Journal of Medicine and Internet Research*, 22(5): e19087. doi: 10.2196/19087

Hung, M., Lauren, E., Hon, E. S., Birmingham, W. C., Xu, T., Su, S., Hon, S. D., Park, J., Dang, P., & Lipsky, M. S. (2020) Social network analysis of COVID-19 sentiments: Application of artificial intelligence. *Journal of Medicine and Internet Research*, 22(8): e22590. doi: 10.2196/22590

Lampos, V., Majumder, M. S., Yom-Tov, E., Edelstein, M., Moura, S., Hamada, Y., Rangaka, M. X., McKendry, R. A., & Cox, I. J. (2021) Tracking COVID-19 using online search. *npj Digital Medicine*, 4: 17. doi: 10.1038/s41746-021-00384-w

Li, J., Xu, Q., Cuomo, R., Purushothaman, V., & Mackey, T. (2020) Data mining and content analysis of Chinese social media platform Weibo during the early COVID-19 outbreak: Retrospective observational infoveillance study. *JMIR Public Health Surveillance*, 6(2): e18700. doi: 10.2196/18700

Oxford Vacicine Group (2016) *Herd immunity: Hows does it work?* Oxford, UK: Department of Paediatrics, University of Oxford. Retrieved from:https://www.ovg.ox.ac.uk/news/herd-immunity-how-does-it-work

Park, H. W., Park, S., & Chong, M. (2020) Conversations and medical news frames on Twitter: Infodemiological study on COVID-19 in South Korea. *Journal of Medical Internet Research*, 22(5): e198897. doi:10.2196/18897

Pimenta, I., de Sousa Mata, Á. N., Braga, L. P., de Medeiros, G., de Azevedo, K., Bezerra, I., de Oliveira Segundo, V. H., de França Nunes, A. C., Santos, G. M., Grosseman, S., Nicolás, I. M., & Piuvezam, G. (2020) Media and scientific communication about the COVID-19 pandemic and the repercussions on the population's mental health. *Medicine*, 99(50): e23298. doi:10.1097/md.0000000000023298

Reis, B. Y., & Brownstein, J. S. (2010) Measuring the impact of health policies using Internet search patterns: The case of abortion. *BMC Public Health*, 514. doi: 10.1186/1471-2458-10-514

Schillinger, D., Chittamuru, D., & Ramirez, A. S. (2020) From "infodemics" to health promotion: A novel framework for the role of social media in public health. *American Journal of Public Health*, 110(90): 1393–1396.

Shen, C., Chen, A., Luo, C., Zhang, J., Feng, B., & Liao, W. (2020) Using reports of symptoms and diagnoses on social media to predict COVID-19 case counts in mainland China: Observational infoveillance study. *Journal of Medicine and Internet Research*, 22(5): e19421. doi:10.2196/19421

Shah, A. A., Ravana, S. D., Hamid, S., & Ismail, M. A. (2015) Web credibility assessment: Affecting factors and assessment techniques. *Information Research*, 20(1).

Smith, T. C. (2017) Vaccine rejection and hesitancy: A review and call to action. *Open Forum Infectious Diseases*, 4(3): ofx146. doi:10.1093/ofid/ofx146

Stecula, D. A., Kuru, O., Albarracin, D., & Jamieson, K. H. (2020) Policy views and negative beliefs about vaccines in the United States, 2019. *American Journal of Public Health*, 110(10): 1561–1563. doi:10.2105/AJPH.2020.305828

Valdez, D., Thij, M. T., Bathina, M., Rutter, L. A., & Bollen, J. (2020) Social media insights into US mental health during the COVID-219 Pandemic: Longitudinal analysis of Twitter data. *Journal of Medicine and Internet Research*, 22(12): e21418. doi:10.2196/21418

Walter, N., & Murphy, S. T. (2018) How to unring the bell: A meta-analytic approach to correction of misinformation. *Communication Monographs*. doi:10.1080/03637751.2018.1467564

Wang, J., Zhu, Y., Zhang, W., Evans, R., & Zhu, C. (2020) Concerns expressed by Chinese social media users during the COVID-19 pandemic: Content analysis of Sina Weibo microblogging data. *Journal of Medicine and Internet Research*, 22(11): e22152. doi:10.2196/22152

Xui, J., Chen, J., Hu, R., Chen, C., Zheng, C., Su, Y., & Zhu, T. (2020) Twitter discussions and emotions about the COVID-19 pandemic: Machine learning approach. *Journal of Medicine and Internet Research*, 22(11): e20550. doi:10.2196/20550

Zhou, G., Chen, S., & Chen, Z. (2020) Back to the spring of 2020: facts and hope of COVID-19 outbreak. *Frontiers of Medicine*, 14(2): 113–116. doi:10.1007/s11684-020-0758-9

Chapter 4

Public Confidence in News and Journalism

As the pandemic spread around the world, it occupied more and more of the daily news agendas across all mainstream news media. More airtime in broadcast bulletins and space in newspapers and magazines were devoted to COVID-19. As we will see, analysis over the duration of the pandemic revealed that many people had increased their news consumption. While news schedules and pages were packed with little other than stories about the pandemic, and despite some evidence noted earlier about audience fatigue in some news markets, most publics developed a keen appetite for information about the status of the disease and the impact of restrictions, as well as scientific progress on the development of vaccines. For news about COVID-19 to have any constructive impact on people, it was critical that they trusted it. As it turned out, any such trust could vary between people and fluctuate over time.

Some general poll soundings in the UK, for example, indicated that even though people had a healthy diet for pandemic news as it spread and restrictions were placed on their everyday behaviours, trust in journalists was poor. In fact, they were trusted less than politicians. In a Sky News/YouGov poll of 1652 people conducted in April 2020, across Britain, journalists came out badly, with just one in four respondents (24%) saying they trusted television journalists (64% not doing so) and fewer than one in five (17%) saying they trusted newspaper journalists (72% not doing so (Coates, 2020). A Press Gazette reader poll in the UK, conducted between 7th and 14th April 2020, found that nearly half (48%) felt that trust in journalists had gone down since the COVID-19 outbreak, while one three (33%) thought that it had increased, and one in five (19%) thought it had not changed (Tobitt, 2020).

In the early days of the pandemic, there was much critical comment in circulation about the quality and balance of news media coverage of the pandemic. In the midst of signs that government was struggling to get control of a rapidly escalating crisis, some critics observed that many television journalists could have been more robust in their questioning of political leaders, as death rates spiralled and frontline health and social care staff could

DOI: 10.4324/9781003274629-4

not obtain enough personal protective equipment. There were concerns that the government and the National Health Service had not been prepared and that hesitancy in critical decision-making had resulted in the new coronavirus spreading far more widely than it needed to (Media Lens, 2020).

News Consumption Habits during the Pandemic

Pandemics that scale up to national crises can fuel public appetite for news. This was true also in the SARS-CoV-2 pandemic that spread around the world in 2020. In the United Kingdom, as in many other developed countries, however, falling levels of consumption had been noted for long-established news providers, especially among printed news media and also for broadcast news. Some commentators had observed that even mainstream broadcast news had been losing audiences up to 2020, especially among young people who turned to other sources for their information (Mair, 2020a). The pandemic provided fresh and powerful impetus across the public to return to major news outlets again as they became driven to find reassurance from the uncertainty of an unprecedented global health crisis.

Audience analysts reported significant year-on-year increases in news viewing on the mainstream television channels, but most of all on the BBC. Commercial television services and print media did not enjoy such as pandemic boost. Of course, the pandemic also boosted the use of online information sources accelerating the trend that had already bene in train for some years before (Mair, 2020a).

Newspapers had been experiencing a decline in their printed sales for many years. The pandemic did little to change this. In fact, there were side-effects of the pandemic, not least the drop off in advertising revenues as advertisers tightened their belts while their businesses temporarily closed or partially suspended some of their activities. Some newspapers were forced to cut their own staff and place them on furlough payments and for some of those, they faced the possibility that they would not be re-hired. It also meant that those left behind to operate the presses were placed under more strain. Some also caught the disease or had been in close contact with others that had and had to stay off work to quarantine. What many might have hoped were temporary interventions during a national emergency could end up being adopted in the longer-term further accelerating the demise of print media (Greenslade, 2020).

In the UK, the broadcast and telecommunications regulator, Ofcom (Office of Communications) monitored the nation's media habits during the pandemic. Fieldwork began during 27th to 29th March 2020, just days after the implementation of the first national lockdown. During that first, virtually the entire population (99%) had accessed news and information about COVID-19 at least once a day. One in four people (24%) were tuning in to news at least 20 times a day! The national broadcaster, the

BBC, was the most used news source. It was endorsed as a news source by four out of five people (82%), while other broadcasters collectively lagged some distance behind (at 56%). Further back were social media (49%) and online or printed newspapers (43%) and then family or friends (42%) (Ofcom, 2020, April).

Further fieldwork by the same organisation conducted between 26th and 28th June, three months after the survey just reported, Ofcom (2020, July – a; 2020, July – b) reported that an overwhelming proportion of people (85%) were accessing COVID-19 news every day. There was an age variation in this behaviour with over-55s (91%) being more likely than 16 to 24 s (77%) to say they access pandemic news at least once a day. Far fewer (4%) were tuning in 20 times or more a day to COVID-19 news, a sixth the proportion of people claiming to do this during week one of the first national lockdown. There was an increase in people saying they were trying to avoid news about the coronavirus (32%) at the end of June compared with those saying this at the end of March 2020 (22%).

In general, among adults who identified as internet users, the most-used news sources continued to be the traditional broadcasters and newspapers (93% in week one, falling to 87% at the end of June). These traditional sources had been nominated at people's most important news source about the pandemic at the start of lockdown (71%) and remained so for two-thirds (67%) still three months later. There was an age difference in the use of traditional media, but even amongst the youngest adults, over eight in ten (81%) still tuned into the traditional news media sources. Social media was nominated as a source of information about the pandemic by nearly one in two (49%) in week one of the first national lockdown, and their popularity had faded somewhat three months later (37%). There was a substantial variation in reliance on social media, with many more 16 to 24 s (56%) than over-65s (19%) using them as pandemic news sources (Ofcom, (2021, February – a; Ofcom, (2021, February – b).

Further fieldwork conducted between 15th and 17th January 2021 by Ofcom found that around nine in ten people (89%) were still tuning in to news about the coronavirus at least once a day. This had been an increase in December 2020 (86%), but was lower than week one of the first national lockdown (99%). Traditional news media were still nominated most often as the most-used news and information sources about the coronavirus in the past week (86%). Of these people, two-thirds (65%) also said that these news media were also their most important news sources (Ofcom, (2021, February – a; Ofcom, (2021, February – b).

Public Satisfaction with News Coverage

While the media played a significant part in keeping mass publics informed of the latest public health developments in bringing the COVID-19 pandemic under control, not everyone was satisfied with this coverage. The media coverage about the pandemic was dominated by government announcements concerning interventions which were largely made up of restrictions on public behaviour. It gave people an opportunity therefore to judge the effectiveness with which their government was handling the crisis.

Research conducted in the United States during the early months of the pandemic showed that politically more conservative respondents were more likely than liberals to complain about the amount of media coverage given to the pandemic, generally feeling that there was too much of it. Further probing revealed that many people reported that the pandemic had caused considerable disruption to their home, work and social lives. Households with children were most likely to report these reactions.

For some social groups, especially women and those on lower incomes, the disruptions to everyday life caused by their government's responses to the pandemic had caused them economic anxieties because of loss of income with many workplaces closing down. Liberals were more likely to report their compliance with social distancing restrictions and they were also more likely to report depressive symptoms. Yet, even though media coverage was important to get the public up to speed with the latest developments in a fast-moving national crisis, appetite for constant spoon-feeding of COVID-19 stories was finite (Christensen et al., 2020).

During the pandemic, information was available from a range of sources including health services, employers and from people who post messages on micro-blogging and social media sites. One UK poll showed that the news media and government were the sources mentioned most widely (by 92-93%), followed by an employer (80%), then the NHS (75%), friends and family (70%) and then the local or county council or regional authority (50%) and for a few by a private healthcare provider (17%). The biggest increase in reported use of any source from mid-March to mid-April 2020 was the local or county council or regional authority (+26%) (Survation, 2020, 30th April).

Relative Confidence in Media News

Major news channels were used by governments and health authorities to convey regular messages to the public about the status of the pandemic. Fear responses in the public emerged as one prominent reaction during the early stages of the pandemic. It was also regarded by some observers as a primary motivational driver of public compliance with governments' interventionist strategies using non-pharmaceutical measures to slow the rate of transmission of this new virus. In a critical appraisal of the role played by the news media in this control process, some degree of complicity with government fear messages and the selective use of facts to reinforce them could apparently be identified (Dodsworth, 2021).

Even the BBC was accused of suspending its usual standards of objectivity to present, largely without penetrating analysis, government pronouncements about the status of the pandemic. One key feature of this news coverage was a focus on worst case outcomes, especially death rates, when these outcomes in a purely statistical sense were in reality unlikely to result for most people who became infected (Dodsworth, 2021).

One reason for the emphasis on growing hospitalisation and mortality rates from COVID-19was to increase the salience of these outcomes and encourage the public to calculate subjectively that they had a much higher likelihood of occurrence than was true in terms of statistical outcome probabilities. Creating a sense of high risk also generated a climate of fear that would motivate public compliance with severe behavioural restrictions even among those less likely to be motivated by a sense of civic duty or responsibility. In one analysis, news headlines were often found to contain negative sentiments about the coronavirus pandemic and most also evoked negative feelings in news consumers (Aslam et al., 2020). Further research showed that people could develop a range of different fear responses to media coverage of the pandemic, as had been observed with other pandemics and major disasters (Coelho et al., 2020). More detailed evidence about the role of public fear responses to COVID-19 will be examined in Chapter 8.

Yet, the public were not always duped by fear-evoking tactics used by governments or news media. One piece of polling evidence emerged, for instance, that a large majority of the public (70%) did not think that journalists had done a good job of holding the government to account in relation to the content if its daily televised briefings (Mayhew, 2020).

Further research produced by the Reuters Institute at the University of Oxford found that, despite their reliance upon it, the public did not always invest the news media with unbridled trust (Fletcher et al., 2020b). There was broader evidence from this investigation that more general public trust in authorities rose and then fell over the first weeks of the first national lockdown in the UK. Soundings taken in mid-April, less than four weeks after the start of lockdown, showed that two-thirds of people (67%) rated the government as relatively trustworthy or better, but this figure fell substantially six weeks later (48%). It is also noteworthy that the British public's trust in news organisations also fell across this period (from 57% to 46%).

There was a further growth in mistrust concerning the veracity of information coming from the mouths of politicians in general and not just those serving in executive government. There was a marked increase in the percentage of people expressing concern about false or misleading information linked to COVID-19 coming from the UK government, with public mention of this rising 11-points to 38% by the end of May 2020). This increased concern about misinformation was not also attributed to news organisations (Fletcher et al., 2020b).

Research undertaken by the Office of Communications, the broadcast and telecommunications regulator in the United Kingdom found than overwhelming majorities of the British public trusted the authorities, including the National Health Service (95%), the World Health Organization (91%), official scientists (90%) and the government (89%) (Ofcom 2020, April). The fieldwork for this research as undertaken just days after the first national lockdown had been implemented by the British Prime Minister.

When it came to the news, the mainstream and longest-established broadcasters were the most likely to be trusted. In Britain, the percentages of people investing a high level of trust were substantial for the BBC (83%) Channel 4 (83%), ITV (82%) and Sky (75%). The least likely sources to command public trust in this way were social media and other closed groups online where between one in five and one in four people said they trusted news and information about Covid-19 supplied by these sources (Ofcom, 2020, April).

Polling in the United States during the pandemic revealed that American public opinion about the news media had become more sophisticated and more polarised over time. Research conducted by the Knight Foundation with Gallup found a growing pessimism about the news media with opinion also deeply divided between supporters of the Democratic Party and those of the Republican Party. This division had characterised American public opinion for some time, but had become more pronounced during the Donald Trump Presidency. The public were keenly attuned to false news narratives, or what were defined by one political tribe or the other, as "fake news" (Knight Foundation, 2020, 9th November).

During the pandemic, and despite the growing cynicism towards many news organisations, an overwhelming majority of Americans (81%) regarded the news media as "critical" or "very important" to democracy. Using the same ratings, even more Americans (88%) thought that the news media must provide accurate and fair news reporting. Yet, many people across the U.S. perceived "a great deal" (46%) or a "fair amount" (37%) of political bias in the news. Where inaccuracies did occur, substantial proportions of Americans felt that reporters misrepresented the facts (52%) or even made them up completely (28%).

As mentioned, there was a clear political divided in the public standing of the news in the United States. Republican supporters (67%) were far more likely to hold an unfavourable view of the news than Democrats (20%) or Independents (48%). Two-thirds of Americans overall (65%) felt that the tendency of the news to report events from a particular point of view was a real problem. Republicans (75%) were much more likely than Democrats (57%) to say this. In general, there are conflicted public attitudes towards in the U.S. Half of Americans (51%) felt there were enough news outlets offering different perspectives that the facts would eventually emerge, but nearly as many (45%) felt that the news was lost in so much intrinsic bias that this was no longer possible. This general dismay with the news media in the U.S. held out little hope that news outlets could command public attention and respect during the pandemic when they might have been expected to take the lead in informing, advising and reassuring the people (Knight Foundation, 2020, 9th November).

Perceived Usefulness of News Sources

Investing news sources with importance and trust is one thing, whether they are perceived to provide useful and beneficial information is another matter. The significance of news coverage about Covid-19 rested, in part, on the reassurance it could give people during uncertain times. It also played a part, as we will see later, in frightening people just enough to encourage them to stay home and to comply with various other restrictions on their everyday behaviour. Critically, however, the full impact of news coverage on people will be mediated by how much of what it tells them, they understand. There are various ways in which the public's comprehension of the news and of issues covered by the news can be objectively measured (Gunter, 1987; 2015).

In addition, there is a concept of "subjective comprehension" which is a judgment made by individuals about whether they feel they understand specific topics, events, issues and so on. In the context of the pandemic, one aspect of the news that was important was in the information it provided about what people should be doing in response to Covid-19. Fewer than one in five (17%) people surveyed in March 2020, just after the start of the first national lockdown in the United Kingdom said they had obtained this kind of clarity from the news. Despite, attaching importance to the news, nearly one in two people (46%) said they had come across false or misleading information about COVID-19 and related matters. A substantial minority (40%) also claimed it was "hard to know what's true and what's false about Covid-19". This confusion was even more prevalent among young adults aged 18 to 24 (52%), but less so among those aged 65 and over (32%) (Ofcom, 2020, April).

In the United Kingdom, people who turn to television for their news often rely on the major established broadcast brands and place much trust in the quality of their journalism. They expect these authoritative news sources to present objective news coverage and not to pander to the prejudices of specific communities (Newman, 2020). At the start of the first national lockdown, there were still a few British people (17%) who felt that "the mainstream media is exaggerating the seriousness of Covid-19". As a further qualifier, there were few (5%) who strongly adhered to this belief (Ofcom, 2020, April). Over time, public opinion about the performance of news provider became more nuanced.

One month into lockdown and Ipsos-MORI found that newspaper journalists were seen as relatively more effective at holding the government to account at the daily coronavirus briefings than the opposition Labour Party (Skinner et al., 2020). More than four in ten (43%) of journalists overall were regarded as doing a "good job" (versus 28% saying they were doing a "bad job"). TV and radio journalists were more often endorsed as doing a good job than were newspaper journalists (40% versus 30%). It is also notable that public opinion was equally split on whether newspaper journalists were doing a good job or a bad job (30% in each case). The Labour leader, Keir Starmer was seen as doing a good job (24%) to a lesser extent than journalists, with one in five people (20%) also saying he was doing a bad job. Given how new he was, however, many people (57%) had not yet made up their minds about him at this point.

The public was found to have confidence in government and in the scientific, and health institutions advising government and supporting the public through this health crisis. This confidence did not extend to the news media, however. YouGov research for Sky News showed that one month into the UK lockdown, of the major groups and institutions that the British public relied upon for information, the medical experts and scientists working as government advisers were trusted the most by the public, while politicians and news media were trusted the least (Coates, 2020).

The Reuters Institute for the Study of Journalism at the University of Oxford teamed up with YouGov to undertake a series of surveys tracking public trust in the British news media (Fletcher et al., 2020c). Confidence in the news media (37%) trailed far behind that in the NHS (92%) and the Government (54%) in terms of "doing a good job in responding to coronavirus. Public opinion about news media, however, varied across different news providers. Most people (60%) thought the BBC was doing a good job, while far fewer held this opinion about the commercial public service broadcasters, ITV (36%) and Channel 4(32%), and the commercial broadcaster, Sky (28%) (Newman et al., 2020b; Roser et al., 2020).

A series of YouGov polls tracked public trust in television and newspaper news sources at 1st to 2nd December 2019, 10th to 11th March, 2020, 3rd to 5th April 2020 and 26th to 27tth April 2020 (Jennings & Curtis, 2020, 29th April). Respondents were given a list of news sources and were asked to rate how much they trusted journalists at each of a number of listed media providers either "a great deal" or "a fair amount". The BBC's journalists were trusted the most across this period (44%, 48%, 50% and 47%) followed by those at ITV News (41%, 43%, 45% and 41%). Among newspaper journalists, those working for upmarket broadsheet newspapers garnered the most widespread trust (35%, 40%, 39% and 38%), followed by the mid-market tabloids (14%, 14%, 16% and 13%) and finally the red-tops (7%, 8%, 11% and 7%).

Relative Importance of Different Information Sources

Research by Survation showed that non-media sources were trusted the most, followed by broadcast news sources and then newspapers. In this survey, a 10-point scale was used to measure trust, with a score of 10 representing complete confidence in a specific information source. The most widely trusted source scoring within the range of seven to 10 out of 10 was the National Health Service (81%), followed the respondent's employer (64%) and then family and friends (51%).

Among broadcast news sources, the most often trusted news supplier at the highest level of confidence was the BBC (52%), followed closely by Channel 4 News (50%), then ITV News (47%), Sky News (44%) and Channel 5 News (34%). Among newspapers, that were generally less widely trusted at the highest levels, the most often trusted were *The Guardian* (39%), the *Financial Times* (38%), *The Times* (33%) and *The Telegraph* (29%). Tabloid newspapers such as the *Daily Mail* (21%), *Daily Express* (19%) *The Mirror* (19%) and *The Sun* (14%) were not widely trusted (Survation, 2020, 30th April).

As time wore on, public opinion was still mixed about how much the major news organizations were seen as trustworthy sources of information. By August 2020, fewer than half the British public (45%) trusted what the major news organizations told them about COVID-19, compared with mover half (57%) in April 2020. There was an even bigger drop in trust invested in the British government over this period (from 67% to 44%). Trust in individual politicians had always been much lower and dropped further still (from 38% to 22%) (Nielsen et al., 2020, 25th August).

In the United States, research by the Pew Research Centre with a nationally representative adult sample of over 8,900 Americans found that nine out of ten (89%) said they were following COVID-19 news very closely. Most people (70%) also felt that the media had covered COVID-19 well. In considering the quality of news coverage further, more people felt that the news media had exaggerated the risks of COVID-19 (62%), than got them about right (30%) or underplayed them (8%). There was evidence that the US public thought that misinformation was in circulation. Nearly half (48%) of those surveyed also said they thought they had witnessed "made-up" news about COVID-19 (Mitchell & Oliphant, 2020, 18th March).

Pew's research provided evidence of partisanship in public reactions to the news. People who were Republicans or leant that way in terms of their politics were more negative about the news media's performance in covering COVID-19 than were Democrat supporters or leaners. Republicans were twice as likely as Democrats to think the virus had been created in a laboratory and were more likely to say that vaccines would be developed within months, which was not confirmed by health experts. Despite the different views about the news held by Democrats and Republicans, most adults generally in the United States (62%) said that they had seen the same set of facts about COVID-19 across different news sources, indicating a sense of consistency in reporting. Far fewer (26%) disagreed with this observation.

In another nationwide survey of American adults, where respondents were asked to identify the major and minor sources for news about the coronavirus outbreak, national news (56%) was most often identified as a major news source, slightly ahead of public health organisations and officials (51%). Local news outlets (46%) were next, with President Trump and his team far behind (31%) (Mitchell et al., 2020, 29th April).

Further questions revealed that even though people came to rely on the news to keep them informed about the latest pandemic developments, this coverage could take its toll on them psychologically. News agendas, during this period, were frequently packed with COVID-19 news almost to the total exclusion of any other news. Many Americans (71%) said they needed to take a break from news about the coronavirus. More than four in ten (43%) said this news coverage could leave them feeling emotionally drained. No doubt the uncertainty that the pandemic had created contributed to adverse psychological reactions. Sometimes, the news coverage itself contributed to this uncertainty. The American public was split in terms of whether they find it difficult (51%) or easy (49%) to determine what was true and what was false in the coverage about COVID-19. A majority (64%) felt that they had seen at least some news about the coronavirus that seemed to have bene made up (Mitchell et al., 2020, 29th April).

In a further survey reported by the Pew Research Centre, American adults were asked for their opinions about the functions fulfilled for them by the news media during the COVID-19 outbreak. Most Americans thought that the news media were providing them with the information they needed with one in four (24%) disagreeing. Around half of American adults (49%) thought that the news media's coverage of COVID-19 had been mostly accurate, with one in four (24%) again disagreeing. Nearly one in two American adults (48%) felt that news coverage was working mainly for the benefit of the country and over one in three (36%) felt that news media were working mainly to benefit themselves. Finally, nearly one in two (46%) felt that news coverage was helping the country and one in three (34%) thought it was hurting the country.

Most Americans said they were paying close attention to news coverage about the outbreak and were doing this with news at the national and local levels. Yet, there were continual tensions between the news media and President Trump and this had contributed to differences of opinion about the coverage among Democrat and Republican supporters. Democrat supporters (66%) were far more likely than Republican supporters (31%) to agree that the COVID-19 coverage had been largely accurate (Gottfried et al., 2020, 8th May).

Over half of American adults (55%) said they had a great deal or a fair amount of confidence in journalists in 2018, and this figure had dropped to under one in two (48%) in 2020. Over four in ten American adults (43%)

believed journalists had ethical standards in 2o20, a marginal drop (-2%) on 2018 (Gottfried et al., 2020, 8th May).

Global Importance of Pandemic News

These national perspectives provide some insights into the trust invested by people in the news media to which they were accustomed and whose significance as information sources magnified during the uncertain times of the pandemic. It is of more general interest however to understand whether public trust in the news in specific countries, such as the United Kingdom and United States, was replicated in other parts of the world. Useful insights into trust in the news around the world were provided by large international studies that used common methodologies and questions in many different countries.

The Edelman Trust published its barometer for 2020 that surveyed people in 11 different countries (Canada, China, France, Germany, India, Japan, Mexico, Saudi Arabia, South Korea, United Kingdom, United States). Surveys were conducted are various points between January and May 2020 with a sample of 13,000+ respondents. These surveys carried a number of questions designed to measure public trust in news media and journalists.

On the question of trust in their country's media, in a poll conducted in May 2020 by Edelman, over half of respondents globally (56%) expressed some trust. There were nation-to-nation variances in the extent to which traditional media were trusted, however. Trust in national media was most widely expressed in China (89%), and India (73%), and then Mexico (60%), Saudi Arabia (59%), Canada (58%), Germany (53%), South Korea (50%) and the United States (50%). Trust was least widely expressed among respondents in France (40%), the UK (40%) and Japan (37%).

Globally, nearly half the respondents surveyed by Edelman (49%) said that it had been difficult for them to find reliable and trustworthy information about the virus and its effects. Given the general uncertainty created by the pandemic, the feeling on the part of many people that they simply could not find reliable information is a serious and problematic outcome. There was enormous media coverage of the pandemic on mainstream broadcast news bulletins and daily newspapers. The mainstream news suppliers also used the Internet extensively as a platform and here also huge quantities of content were produced and posed every day about the coronavirus and the interventions being deployed or developed to tackle it. Yet for many people, so much of this information was perceived as untrustworthy.

Once again, there were international variations in finding reliable and trusted information about the coronavirus. Finding such information was most likely to be reported in China (76%) and then India (62%), as before.

They were followed by Mexico (50%) and Saudi Arabia (50%) and then the United States (47%), Japan (46%), France (45%), Germany (44%), the UK (41%), South Korea (40%) and finally Canada (30%).

Finally, Edelman produced data on the percentages of respondents who trusted different types of people to tell the truth about the pandemic. The most trusted were their doctor (80%), scientists (79%), national health officials (71%), local government leaders (67%), World Health Organization officials (60%), the leader of their country (57%), with journalists (48%) trailing in last place.

One of the biggest international investigations was conducted by the Reuters Institute for the Study of Journalism at the University of Oxford in the UK. These researchers had already established a study of international news profiles even before the pandemic. A survey already planned for January and February 2020 therefore proved timely in enabling the researchers to study news audience and their news consumption patterns just at the time when the pandemic was getting underway. The Reuters Institute teamed up with leading pollster YouGov and collected data from 42 countries. Data were obtained through an online questionnaire and virtually all the national samples exceeded 2,000 respondents selected to be representative of the wider population (Newman et al., 2020a).

Two additional surveys were conducted in 2020. One, conducted in February, looked at paying for news online and involved samples from Norway, United Kingdom and United States. The second, conducted in April, focused on the impact of the ovel coronavirus on media consumption in six countries (Argentina, Germany, Spain, South Korea, United Kingdom and United States). While the initial surveys were carried out before the pandemic had affected most of the participating countries, by April 2020, this situation had changed and all the countries taking part had experienced widespread infections and rapidly climbing hospitalisation and death rates (Newman et al., 2020a).

There was growing concern, even during the early months of the pandemic, about misinformation. In some instances, misleading statements about the new virus, its effects on people and the steps taken by government to tackle it came from the mouths of politicians. In some countries, such as the United States, public awareness, opinion and behaviour was divided in terms of political partisanship.

This polarisation was also witnessed in relation to public opinion about the news media and how well they had performed. As we will also see, many people turned to alternative sources for their information about COVID-19. Microblogging and social media sites became especially popular information sources especially among younger people. This potentially caused a bigger problem for authorities with evidence showing that reliance of these sites was associated with stronger inclinations to sign up to misinformation and conspiracy theories about the novel coronavirus, and these beliefs in turn discouraged compliance with behavioural restrictions introduced by the authorities.

In its initial January 2020 poll, The Reuters Institute study found that news in general struggled to command widespread public trust. On average, less than four in ten (38%) people across the 42 countries surveyed said they trusted the news most of the time. This was four percentage points lower than the similar finding in 2019. Even when people choose specific news suppliers, they do not invariably trust them. In this case, under half of those surveyed (46%) trusted this news in January 2020. Political polarisation undoubtedly contributed to this seemingly modest trust figure. In countries such as the United States, where the population was politically polarised after a controversial Presidential election just two months before this survey was conducted, there was low trust in most mainstream news media on the part of Republican supporters (Newman et al., 2020a).

Most people around the world (60%) said they preferred news that was politically neutral and did not lean towards or against any specific viewpoint, while far fewer (28%) wanted to consume news that presented views consistent with their own. However, more than half (52%) were comfortable with news media reporting false statements from politicians and again fewer (29%) felt that such statements should be censored.

Evidence emerged that online sources were being more widely used. Even for local news, where traditional local new media (44%) still commanded the most patronage, around one in three people (31%) on average turned to social media sources. Online news sources had achieved a status whereby many people used them alongside conventional news media, and younger people (aged 18 – 24) generally preferred to go online. Going online did not mean simply reading posts on microblogging or social media sites. Evidence also emerged than many people liked to listen to podcasts, with one in two saying that they provided "more depth and understanding" than other news sources.

In April 2020, when respondents in the UK were asked which news sources they had used in the past week, 79% mentioned social media, ahead of TV (71%), radio (35% and print media (18%). There were some slight variances between countries in claimed use of different news sources. The United States exhibited a similar pattern of reported news use over the previous week, with online media (73%) being endorsed the most followed in turn by television (60%), radio (21% and print media (16%). In South Korea, these media platforms exhibited a similar rank-order in terms of reported use over the previous week, but use of online sources (85%) was even higher and television use (65%) and print use (19%) were similar to the UK and US, but radio (14%) was less widespread (Newman et al., 2020a).

News audiences across the world turned increasingly to television as their main news source between January and April 2020 as the pandemic spread. At the same time, they switched away from online sources. In the UK, there was a 20 percentage-point shift from online sources to television. This shift was also seen in five other countries (Argentina, Germany, South Korea, Spain, United States). In the UK, the national broadcaster, the BBC, saw audiences for its bulletins increase by around 30% in march when lockdown was announced. What was also significant was that the migration towards television was especially pronounced among the under-35s who had been the keenest users of online sources.

Not all countries had a prestigious national broadcaster such as the UK's. In the United States, leading television news networks such as CNN and Fox often presented different kinds of coverage. While all major networks covered President Trump's press conferences about the pandemic, some decided not to transmit these live after the President had issue personal opinion about the virus and how to cope with it that went against prevailing medical and scientific advice.

On 12th March 2020, the government announced shielding measures. On 23rd March 2020, the lockdown restrictions were implemented. There spikes on the BC's news website at these points. Then again on 6th April 2020 when Boris Johnson was admitted to hospital with COVID-19. The Reuters Institute survey in April 2020 found that a clear majority of people across the six nations included in this study felt that the news media had done a good job in boosting public understanding about the crisis (60%) and also in informing them about the personal steps they could take to mitigate personal risk of infection. Most people also perceived the news coverage to have been measured, with only one in three on average (32%) saying that the severity of the crisis had been exaggerated. This opinion was held by somewhat more people in Argentina (41%) and the United States (38%).

There was varied public trust in information sources. When citizens across six countries (USA, UK, Germany, Spain, Argentina and South Korea) were asked which information sources they trusted, scientists and doctors (83%) were the most endorsed. They were followed by national health organisations (76%) and global health organisations (73%) comfortably ahead of news organisations (59%). Overall, across these six countries, six in ten (60%) agreed that the news media had helped them to understand the crisis and two-thirds (65%) said that these media had helped to explain to them the things they could do about the pandemic. One in three (32%) however, felt that the media had exaggerated the impact of the novel coronavirus.

People around the world turned to the media increasingly as societies were locked down during the COVID-19 pandemic. Many turned to television, despite the growing popularity of the Internet. The behavioural restrictions of lockdowns meant that many people stayed home and turned to digital interactive media to keep in touch and "see" other people through live video links. When it came to keeping up-to-date with the latest pandemic-related developments, television was generally the most trusted medium. Yet, more generally, public trust in news across the media declined in the pandemic compared with the year before. In Aril 2020, fewer than four in ten people surveyed across 42 countries by the Reuters Institute (38%) said they trusted most news most of the time, a drop of four percentage points on 2019. There were country-to-country variations with the highest level of trust in most news most of the time being recorded in Finland and Portugal (56%) and the lowest levels occurring in Taiwan (24%), France (23%) and South Korea (21%). Hong Kong also exhibited the biggest fall in public trust in the news (by 16 percentage points) to 30%. Further significant falls in trust in the news occurred in Chile (–15%), United Kingdom (–12%) and Denmark and Mexico (both –10%).

When people were asked whether they trusted most of the news most of the time, 28% indicated trust in the UK and 29% said the same in the US. Across 42 countries surveyed by the Reuters Institute's researchers, trust in this measure ranged from a high of 56% (in Finland and Portugal) to a low of 21% (South Korea).

There was also evidence of partisanship in these perceptions. Further evidence on partisan divides in public opinion about the news media will be presented later in this chapter. In the UK, in 2015, a general level of trust in the news was higher among those with right-leaning political tendencies (58%) than among those leaning politically to the left (46%). There remained a considerable gap between these two factions in 2020 (36% to 15%), but wat is most notable is the substantial decline in public trust in the news media over the five years regardless of political leaning.

In nine countries (Brazil, Denmark, France, Germany, Italy, Japan, Spain, United Kingdom, United States) nationwide samples were asked whether they preferred news that had "no point of view", that "shared your point of view" or that "challenged your point of view. Across all nine news markets, over half of respondents preferred news that offered no point of view, ranging from a low of 51% (Brazil) to a high of 80% (Germany). This preference was more widespread in the UK (76%) than in the USA (60%). The greatest volume of preferences for news that "shared your point of view" occurred in Brazil (43%), Spain (34%) and the USA (30%). This opinion was endorsed by 22% or fewer everywhere else. On news that "challenged your point of view", the greatest support occurred in France (22%) followed by Denmark (18%) with endorsement everywhere else being 13% or lower.

Lessons Learned

News about the pandemic dominated news agendas around the world. It also dominated news audiences' attention. News consumers around the world turned to the mainstream media for regular updates about the pandemic. Why? For one thing, these sources were widely regarded as authoritative and trustworthy. As international polling studies revealed, however, public trust in the news varied from country to country. Public trust in specific pandemic information sources that used the major news media to reach their publics also varied. Governments were not always trusted. Experts were generally trusted more.

News was important. Public appetite for pandemic news fluctuated as it wore on. Yet, despite a hunger for non-pandemic news that became stronger over time, while infection transmission rates remained high, the public still needed to know what government was doing to protect them. Public trust in pandemic information sources was linked to people's political allegiances and not just to their judgements about the competence and performance of their leaders in respect of managing the pandemic crisis. For some people, it did not matter what politicians asked them to do, they would only comply with the ones they had previously supported and voted for. This mindset did not help with health authorities' efforts to manage the pandemic with non-pharmaceutical interventions. It did not help when governments started to roll out their vaccination programmes when many people rejected vaccines because they were perceived as unsafe.

The varying degrees of trust in news sources was also critical because the image people had of these platforms could be conflated with their perceptions of sources using these platforms, such as government leaders and heads of public health authorities. In the UK, a number of widely publicised episodes of politicians and their advisers flouting COVID-19 rules undermined public confidence and trust in authorities (Stewart, 2020, 5th May; BBC News, 2021, 3rd February). This, in turn, did nothing to help boost public adherence to messages demanding or advising behaviour change and acceptance of restrictions on public behaviour (Fancourt et al., 2020).

Many people stayed loyal to major news providers in the trust they invested in them. As evidence from around the world showed, however, significant numbers of people were unable to do this, especially in countries such as America where judgements about the news media were shaped by partisan political allegiances. At the time of writing, more investigation is needed into why these variances in public opinion occurred and what was their eventual impact on the ways people responded to the advice and instructions they received from their governments and other authorities.

References

Aslam, F., Awan, T. M., Syed, J. H., Kashif, A., & Parveen, M. (2020) Sentiments and emotions evoked by news headlines of coronavirus disease (COVID-19) outbreak. *Humanities and Social Science Communication*, 7, 23. doi:10.1057/s41599-020-0523-3

BBC News. (2021, 3rd February) MP Margaret Ferrier appears in court accused of Covid rule breach. Retrieved from: https://www.bbc.co.uk/news/uk-scotland-scotland-politics-55924053

Christensen, S. R., Pilling, E. B., Eyring, J. B., Dickerson, G., Sloan, C. D., & Magnusson, B. M. (2020) Political and personal reactions to COVID-19 during initial weeks of social distancing in the United States. *PLoS One*, 15(9): e0239693. doi:10.1371/journal.pone.0239693

Coates, S. (2020, 24th April) Coronavirus: Britons still support lockdown despite being sadder and more anxious – poll. *Sky News*. Retrieved from: https://news.sky.com/story/coronavirus-britons-have-become-sadder-and-more-anxious-since-lockdown-poll-11977655

Coelho, C. M., Suttivan, P., Arato, N., & Zsido, A. N. (2020) On the nature of fear and anxiety triggered by COVID-19. *Frontiers in Psychology*. doi:10.3389/fpsyg.2020.581314

Dodsworth, L. (2021) *A state of fear: How the UK government weaponised fear during the COVID-19 pandemic*. London, UK: Pinter & Martin Ltd.

Edelman Trust. (2020) Edelman Trust Barometer 2020: Spring Update: Trust and the COVID-19 pandemic. Retrieved from: https://www.edelman.com/sites/g/files/aatuss191/files/2020-05/2020%20Edelman%20Trust%20Barometer%20Spring%20Update.pdf

Fancourt, D., Steptoe, A., & Wright, L. (2020) The Cummings effect: Politics, trust and behaviours during the COVID-19 pandemic. *The Lancet*, 396(10249): 464–465.

Flamingo. (2019) *How young people consume news and the implications for mainstream media*. Oxford: Reuters Institute for the Study of Journalism. Retrieved from: https://reutersinstitute.politics.ox.ac.uk/our-research/how-young-people-consume-news-and-implicationsmainstream-media

Fletcher, R., Kalogeropoulos, A., & Nielsen R. K. (2020a) *News media broadly trusted, views of UK government response to COVID-19 highly polarised*. Oxford: Reuters Institute for the Study of Journalism. Retrieved from: https://reutersinstitute.politics.ox.ac.uk/news-media-broadly-trusted-views-uk-government-response-covid-19-highly-polarised

Fletcher, R., Kalogeropoulos, A., & Nielsen, R. K. (2020b) *Trust in UK government and news media COVID-19 information down, concerns over misinformation from government and politicians up*. Oxford: Reuters Institute for the Study of Journalism. Retrieved from: https://reutersinstitute.politics.ox.ac.uk/trust-uk-government-and-news-media-covid-19-information-down-concerns-over-misinformation

Fletcher, R., Kalogeropoulos, A., & Nielsen, R. K. (2020c) *News avoidance in the UK remains high as lockdown restrictions are eased (July 28, 2020)*. Oxford, UK: Reuters Institute for the Study of Journalism, University of Oxford. Available at SSRN: https://ssrn.com/abstract=3704270

Gottfried, J., Walker, M., & Mitchell, A. (2020, 8th May) Americans' views of the news media during the COVID-19 outbreak. *Pew Research Center*. https://www.joirnalism.org/2020/05/08/americans-views-of-the-news-media-during-the-covid-19-outbreak

Greenslade, R. (2020) The British newspaper industry – another victim of the virus? In Mair, J. (Ed.) *The virus and the media: How journalism covered the pandemic.* Goring, UK: Bite-Sized Books, Chapter 3.

Gunter, B. (1987) *Poor reception: Misunderstanding and forgetting broadcast news.* Hillsdale, NJ: Lawrence Erlbaum Associates.

Gunter, B. (2015) *The cognitive impact of television news: Production attributes and information reception.* Basingstoke, UK: Palgrave Macmillan.

Jennings, W., & Curtis, C. (2020, 29th April) No, trust in the media has not collapsed because of coronavirus. YouGov.

Knight Foundation. (2020, 9th November) *American views 2020: Trust, media and democracy.* Retrieved from: https://knightfoundation.org/reports/american-views-2020-trust-media-and-democracy/

Mair, J. (Ed.) (2020a) *The virus and the media: How journalism covered the pandemic.* Goring, UK: Bite-Sized Books.

Mair, J. (2020b) The death of television news had been announced prematurely and was the BBC's demise too also? In Mair, J. (Ed.) *The virus and the media: How journalism covered the pandemic.* Goring, UK: Bite-Sized Books, Chapter 10.

Mayhew, F. (2020, 22nd April) Poll: Most say journalists not doing good job of holding govt to account during daily Covid-19 briefings. *Press Gazette.* Retrieved from: https://www.pressgazette.co.uk/poll-journalists-have-not-donea-good-job-at-covid-19-briefings-majority-of-respondents-say/

Media Lens. (2020, 18th May) An illusion of protection: The pandemic, the "criminal" government and public distrust of the media. Retrieved from: https://www.medialens.org/2020/an-illusion-of-protection-the-pandemic-the-criminal-government-and-public-distrust-of-the-media/

Mitchell, A., & Oliphant, J. B. (2020, 18th March) Americans immersed in COVID-19 news: Most think media are doing fairly well covering it. *Pew Research Center.* Retrieved from: https://www.journalism.org/2020/03/18/americans-immersed-in-covid-19-news-most-think-media-are-doing-fairly-well-covering-it/

Mitchell, A. J., Oliphant, J. B., & Shearer, E. (2020, 29th April) About seven in ten U. S. adults say they need to take breaks from Covid-19 news. *Pew Research Centre.* Retrieved from: https://www.journalism.org/2020/04/29/about-seven-in-ten-u-s-adults-say-they-need-to-take-breaks-from-covid-19-news/

Newman, N. (2020) Executive summary and key findings. In R. K. Nielsen, R. Fletcher, N. Newman, J. S. Brennen, & P. N. Howard (Eds.). *Navigating the "infodemic": How people in six countries access and rate news and information about coronavirus.* Oxford: Reuters Institute for the Study of Journalism, pp. 10–30.

Newman, N., Fletcher, R., Schulz, A., Andi, S., & Nielsen, R. K. (2020a) *Reuters Institute Digital News Report 2020.* Oxford: Reuters Institute for the Study of Journalism. Retrieved from: https://reutersinstitute.politics.ox.ac.uk/sites/default/files/2020-06/DNR_2020_FINAL.pdf

Newman, N., Fletcher, R., Schulz, A., Schulz, S., & Nielsen, R.-K. (2020b) *Digital News Report, 6, 2020-06.* Oxford, IK: University of Oxford, Reuters Institute for the Study of Journalism.

Nielsen, R. K., Kalogeropoulos, A., & Fletcher, R. (2020, 25th August) Most in the UK say news media have helped them respond to COVID-19, but a third say news coverage has made the crisis worse. Reuters Institute for the Study of Journalism. Available at SSRN: https://ssrn.com/abstract=3704276

Ofcom. (2020, April) Covid-19 news and information: Consumption and attitudes – previous results. Retrieved from: https://www.ofcom.org.uk/research-and-data/tv-radio-and-on-demand/news-media/coronavirus-news-consumption-attitudes-behaviour/previous-results

Ofcom. (2020a, July) Effects of COVID-19 on TV viewing. Retrieved from: https://www.ofcom.org.uk/__data/assets/pdf_file/0028/197731/effects-of-covid-19-on-tv-viewing.pdf

Ofcom. (2020b, July) Effects of COVID-19 on online consumption in the UK in 2020. Retrieved from: https://www.ofcom.org.uk/__data/assets/pdf_file/0027/197730/effects-of-covid-19-on-online-consumption.pdf

Ofcom. (2021a, February) Effects of COVID-19 on TV viewing. Retrieved from: https://www.ofcom.org.uk/__data/assets/pdf_file/0016/214234/covid-19-news-consumption-week-fourty-seven-barb.pdf

Ofcom. (2021b, February) Effects of COVID-19 on online consumption in the UK in 2020. Retrieved from: https://www.ofcom.org.uk/__data/assets/pdf_file/0017/214235/covid-19-news-consumption-week-fourty-seven-comscore.pdf

Roser, N., Ritchie, H., Ortiz-Ospina, E., & Hasell, J. (2020) Coronavirus pandemic (COVID-19). Our World in Data, 4.

Skinner, G., Pedley, K., & Garrett, C. (2020) *Britons think coronavirus will have harder impact for old, poor and those in cities, but beliece that society has become less divided.* London, UK: Ipsos-MORI.

Stewart, H. (2020, 5th May) Neil Ferguson: UK coronavirus adviser resigns after breaking lockdown rules. *The Guardian.* Retrieved from: https://www.theguardian.com/uk-news/2020/may/05/uk-coronavirus-adviser-prof-neil-ferguson-resigns-after-breaking-lockdown-rules

Tobitt, C. (2020, 14th April) *Press Gazette poll shows half believe trust in journalists has fallen since COVID-19 outbreak.* Press Gazette. Retrieved from: https://www.pressgazette.co.uk/press-gazette-poll-shows-half-believe-trust-in-journalism-has-fallen-since-covid-19-outbreak/

Chapter 5

News Media and Impact on Public Understanding

Huge volumes of information were in circulation about the novel coronavirus during the 2020 pandemic. There was much chatter on the Internet, with micro-blogging and social networking sites conveying expert and lay opinion about the virus, the way governments and health authorities were managing the crisis and a combination of useful and reliable factual information and fake news and conspiracy theories. Most of all, though, the mass media played a significant part in keeping people informed and in providing reassurance and emotional support during a difficult time, operating services both offline and online.

News agendas were almost entirely given over to reports about the pandemic or about events that spun off from it (Ng et al., 2021). Daily reporting of the bald statistics about the spread of the virus and death rates caused by it were counter-balanced by more humanitarian stories about volunteers helping people who were socially isolated or quarantined, survivors of COVID-19-related intensive care and those such as 99-year-old Captain (and later Colonel, Sir) Tom Morgan who walked 100 lengths of his garden before his imminent 100th birthday to raise money to support the National Health Service.

Over the years, media news researchers have reported that people often forget the news. People who watch a television news bulletin have frequently forgotten or misremembered most of its reports within hours of exposure (Gunter, 2015). Yet, in times of national crisis and uncertainty, people turn to television for up-to-date information and reassurance ((Busselle & Shrum, 2003; Schroeder & Pennington-Gray, 2015). It might then be hoped that public understanding of what was happening would also be enhanced. Certainly, the reported understanding of COVID-19 was found to influence the perceived vulnerability of people and the degree to which they took the pandemic seriously. These beliefs and attitudinal changes in turn drove people's willingness to change their behaviour to comply with coronavirus-related interventions and rules (Prasetyo et al., 2020).

DOI: 10.4324/9781003274629-5

News Media and Public Understanding

The COVID-19 outbreak presented national governments worldwide with an unprecedented emergency, not dissimilar to being on a war footing. Many governments chose to close down their societies and their economies to reduce opportunities for person-to-person spreading of the virus. For this approach to work, entire populations were required to comply with severe restrictions on their everyday behaviour and to adopt a number of other safety practices. To ensure that this happened, people needed to know what to do and be given the right incentives to comply. The principal channels for reaching populations with such appeals from the authorities were the major mass media (Bilancini et al., 2020, Capraro & Barcelo, 2020a, 2020b; Everett et al., 2020; Jordan et al., 2020; Heffner et al., 2021). In learning rapid lessons about whether this approach worked or not, we need to know through systematic and relevant forms of assessment whether it did. Did the right information get through to people? Were governments' appeals persuasive?

In determining whether media news coverage gets its information through to its audiences, we can survey people after exposure to find out whether they can answer questions accurately about the reports they have consumed. We can also test people straight away after watching or reading the news for their memory of the content. What has also emerged over many years of study of the impact of the "news" on people is that barriers to remembering and understanding media news content can be found within the news itself and especially in the way it is usually presented (Gunter, 1987, 2015).

News variously comprises verbal content in the form of spoken and written text and non-verbal content in the form of moving and still pictures, graphics and maps and other visual content. In some broadcast news, reports might be accompanied by background music which can set a particular mood. All these features can exert their own impact on audiences. The way viewers, listeners and readers react psychologically to news stories is mediated by presentational features (Sundar, 2000; Kaspar et al., 2015; Lee & Kim, 2016). Even features as subtle as the font used in printed news and the use of colour in any news format can influence the cognitive processing of information (Gerend & Sias, 2009). Each of these (and many other) variables can vary in the strength of their mediating effects on audiences' psychological reactions and also in terms of whether they trigger predominantly cognitive or emotional responses. Learning is also likely to occur when news stories can be linked back to pre-existing knowledge of viewers. Where these kinds of cognitive connections cannot be readily made, new news might either be lost or incompletely absorbed (Lazaroiu et al., 2017).

The rise in importance of the Internet as a communication system for conveying news has meant that all major news media have begun to use more interactive and dynamic forms of news presentation online and enjoy a more direct relationship with their audiences, some of whom contribute directly to the news agenda with their own content (Cairo, 2019; Liu et al., 2020).

The use of new presentational techniques simply because they are there, however, does not always improve the news if these techniques do little to enhance the information experience for news consumers (Gunter, 2015). There is evidence that more dynamic presentational techniques can promote audience liking of news and may even motivate some people to tune in more often (Michas & Berry, 2000; Chabani & Hommel, 2014; Ellahe & Hommel, 2014; Lee & Kim, 2016). Liking and learning, however, are not the same. There is plentiful research to show that when some presentation techniques are used to excess or some techniques are used together, learning can be impeded (Gunter, 1987; 2015). This applies especially to the use of certain kinds of visual images alongside verbal narratives (Findahl & Hoijer, 1976; Grimes, 1991; Lazard & Atkinson, 2015; Huang et al., 2019). Pictures can not only cause selective recall and understanding of a news story but might even create false memories of experiences that did not actually happen (Loftus & Pickrell 1995; Garry & Gerrie, 2005).

Framing and News Impact

The way a story is told is another critical feature. In this context, re-searchers have referred to a concept known as "framing". News stories present facts, but the ways in which these facts are presented can vary. Sometimes, writers will privilege some facts over others. In some instances, specific facts might even be selectively omitted. These writing techniques can be used to bias the impressions and the understanding news consumers take away from a news report. News frames can sometimes be caused by aesthetic or commercial priorities of news organisations and sometimes by political motives (Gamson & Modigliani, 1987; 1989). Frames can be used, for instance, to attribute responsibility to specific parties for the incidents or events that have been reported as well as their outcomes for those involved, which could be positive or negative (Iyengar, 1990, 1991; Goshorn & Gandy, 1995; De Hoog & Verboon, 2020).

These writing techniques can influence the psychological reactions of audiences. The way facts are packaged in the news can result in some facts standing out from others and this in turn might influence the perceptions of events and issues that are cultivated among news consumers (Entman, 1993; Scheufele, 1999; Igartua et al., 2012). Such outcomes are serious enough if they distort the public's understanding of events and issue during normal times, but they could be critical if they occur at times or major crisis or emergency (van Gorp, 2007). One psychological effect of this type of news coverage might be that people's sense of risk is enhanced along with their fear and anxiety (Kaplan, 2008; McIntyre & Gibson, 2016;

Vliegenthart & Boukes, 2018). Emotional reactions can also become attached to some of the details of news stories in relation to key actors described within those stories (Borah, 2009; Balzarotti & Ciceri, 2014; Lan et al., 2019).

News reporting of earlier pandemics showed that the media have not conventionally restricted their story-telling to the facts. They create other narratives that appear to be designed to trigger emotional responses in people. British media coverage of a Clostridium difficile outbreak in 2008 portrayed this outbreak as a conflict drawing upon wartime metaphors. Different participants in this crisis were identified and their respective roles were not simply described but also dramatized in such a way as to identify "victims" that suffered, hero figures that came to the rescue of victims and others ("villains") to whom blame could be attached for the plight of the victims (Burnett et al., 2014).

News coverage of COVID-19 was found by some analysts to portray different actors during the pandemic. One study of newspaper photographs in Finland found that children were either shown as pupils diligently studying or as enjoy the opportunities to play more if schools were closed. Slightly older youth were similarly shown as serious students or carefree party-goers. Adults also were presented in serious roles (as experts or professionals, or as people taking care of others) or as pursuing recreational activities for their own pleasure. Elderly people were shown as isolated loners.

Through news pictures, character roles were constructed as the drama of the pandemic unfolded and, in particular, distinctions were made between "heroes", "villains" and "victims". Whether these depictions reflected actual "reality" or were little more than a fabricated alternative version of real life during the pandemic that was largely a media creation could be debated. Evidence emerged that news media, which were crucial information sources for the public during the uncertain times of the pandemic, created news narratives that went beyond simply reporting the latest pandemic-related developments. Concerns were triggered if specific social groups were identified as being among the "villains" in terms of they behaved in the context of the pandemic because of the potential of this coverage to shape public opinion towards these groups (Martikainen & Sakki, 2021).

Public perceptions of risk are not invariably shaped by objective statistical probabilities of events. They can also be influenced by the prominence of events in the news (Lowry et al., 2003). News coverage can make unusual but disturbing events seem to be more frequently occurring than they really are (Romer et al., 2003; Boukes & Vliegenthart, 2017; Abrams & Greenhawt, 2020). News producers can therefore control the public agenda through these techniques (Shoemaker & Reese, 1996; Dimotrova & Stromback, 2005).

In the context of a major crisis such as a pandemic in which people are asked to restrict their movements by staying at home and only venturing out for essential purposes, governments rely on the voluntary compliance of their populations. Evidence has emerged from research into public reactions to other disasters, including the first SARS outbreak in Asia, that enhanced risk perceptions can motivate people to help others (Xie et al., 2005; Gasser & Solé, 2006).

Self-Attributed Public Knowledge of COVID News

Did people think they knew much about COVID-19. Public opinion polls indicated that many did. One survey showed that over four in five people across the UK said they had received sufficient information to know how to protect themselves from the coronavirus during the early stages of the pandemic (Davies, 2020, 23rd April). Research from the Cardiff School of Journalism, Media and Culture found that people could identify a fake COVID-19 news story, but they nonetheless still displayed gaps in their knowledge about the new virus and were not always clear about how to interpret the mass of statistical data being reported about infection and death rates (Soo et al., 2020).

In research carried out after the first lockdown had ended, between 13th and 19th August 2020, researchers at the University of Oxford found that more than half of those surveyed (56%) said they felt the news media had helped them to understand more about the pandemic. More than six in ten (61%) also said they thought the news coverage had helped to explain to them how they could respond to the crisis. In both instances, these figures showed an increase of around 10 percentage points since April 2020. Hence, over time, most of the British public had found news media coverage of the pandemic helpful to them. This still left a considerable minority, however, who did not believe this was the case. Despite some cynicism about the quality of news coverage, only one in four felt that the news media had exaggerated the pandemic both in April (25%) and August (27%). Three in ten (30%) also said they were concerned about misleading information about the pandemic being provided by the news media (Nielsen et al., 25th August).

News Media Exposure and COVID-19 Knowledge

Self-proclaimed knowledge and actual knowledge are not the same. Many people may believe they know about isues only to find that when tested more closely on their knowledge that they do not (Gunter, 1987; 2015). Evidence did emerge, however, that people who claimed to have greater exposure to news coverage about the pandemic also displayed better knowledge about it including about the steps to take to protecte themselves and others. There remained minorities of one in five or greater who still harboured misunderstandings about the pandemic and subscribed to misleading conpsiracy theories about it. Although the worst informed and the adherents to unproven conspiracy theories were in the minority, the numbers were still large enough to exceed a critical mass of 10% which was generally taken as a threshold beneath which "bad knowledge" could be phased out and above which it could still display persistance and some degree of influence (Jamieson & Albarracin, 2020).

Many different theories surfaced about SARS-CoV-2 as the pandemic progressed (Van Bavel et al., 2020). The way news messages were framed about the pandemic was found to influence public beliefs about COVID-19 including about the type of virus it was and how it came about (Bolsen et al., 2020). This type of story-telling could also trigger different public attributions of responsibility for the pandemic. Was the virus zoonotic – that it, that it jumped nturally from animals into human or had it been manufactured in a laboratory? In the early phases of the pandemic, there was much ignorance about the new virus and this created a setting in which bogus theories could and often did emerge to eplain it (Jerit et al., 2020).

News frames can shape public perceptions of events by emphasizing specific perspetives, explanations or descriptions over others. These story-telling attributes can be powerful when the truth is ambiguous or unproven (Druckman, 2001; Chong & Druckman, 2007). Framing could also be used to encourage certain types of public behaviour. In one initial pandemic control narrative, emphasized in the United Kingdom, which might be called a "civic responsibility frame", it was argued that it was incumbent upon everyone to comply with government restrictions to keep others safe and to help to ensure the health services were not overwhelmed. Effectively framed stories of this sort from credible sources can shape public beliefs and, in turn, influence public actions (Entman, 1993; Iyengar, 1991; Nisbet, 2009). The civic responsibility frame, just mentioned, was found to be effective in increasing people's intentions to behave in this kind of responsible fashion when communicated to them clearly (Jordan et al., 2020).

In some narratives, a single frame might be featured while in others there may be more than one frame given an airing. If audiences are exposed only to one argument in any narrative, when an issue might be better defined and understood when different perspectives are considered, public comprehension of specific events or issues can be distorted or unbalanced. If a single argument is also seen to derive from one respected or credible and trusted source, its potency to persuade and influence magnifies (Chong & Druckman, 2007; Bolsen & Druckman, 2018). When this happens, people's understanding of an issue and the beliefs they formulate around it, can likewise be biased (Bolsen et al., 2018; van der Linden et al., 2019).

As will become apparent with further analysis of relevant evidence, in the context of COVID-19, people around the world learned about the virus and its origins and risk-levels, together with the effectiveness and safety of specific interventions (e.g., vaccines) through exposure to different frames, some of which came from scientists, some from politicians and some from conspiracy theories of unknown source. One-sided frames could potentially bias people's impression and beliefs in the direction of the perspective emphasized in a narrative, especially among people previously largely ignorant of the issue. Similarly, if people held a different view on the issue, they might still change their mind after exposure to narratives offfering them a different but convincing, alternative, explanatory frame (Sniderman & Theriault, 2004; Druckman, 2001).

To develop a comprehensive understanding of an event such as COVID-19 therefore it is best to present people with balanced narratives, especially in mainstream news, in which different perspectives and explanations are presented and also critiqued with relevant and respected sources interrogated for relevant evidence (Bolsen & Druckman, 2018). Audiences can then choose which perspectives and arguments they find the most compelling. In a major emergency therefore it is important to monitor closely the frames that become salient in the information sources used by different communities to ensure that some people are not misled into taking poor decisions for themselves (Dietz, 2013).

Importance of Understanding for Cognitive Coping

A critical aspect of national pandemic responses comprised interventions that would change public behaviour. Achieving sustainable behaviour change in a pandemic situation could be enhanced by providing people with a supportive health-care climate, offering choice in terms of methods of protection and by understanding the practicalities of behaviour change on the ground. It was also important to create a sense that everyone is in this crisis together and therefore everyone becomes a potential stakeholder in finding and implementing solutios and a return to normality. A further important ingredient was for authorities to put out clear and consistent information and in doing so to be honest and open by acknowledging what was known and also what was unknown (Porat et al., 2020).

Learning lessons from earlier pandemics, some experts advised that policy decisions about the COVID-19 pandemic must be based on scientific evidence which should be converted into actionable knowledge and explained to the public clearly in language they can understand. Government should take steps to ensure that their citizens understood its messaging and to monitor compliance. Any public concerns needed to be picked up and addressed. Governments should seek to forge partnerships with other relevant groups and its own citizens in finding collective solutions to pandemic-related problems (Tangcharoensathien et al., 2020).

Research in China at the start of the new coronavirus outbreak conducted in early February 2020 found that having more knowledge did not emerge as having a highly significant direct impact on the public's mood state, but it was one factor that predicted a willingness to adopt more precautionary behaviours against the new virus, which in turn lifted the public's mood (Li et al., 2020).

Dutch research demonstrated that an educational video accompanied by support newspaper coverage could play an important role in encouraging people to engage in some personal protective behaviours, such as had-washing, face touching and physical distancing, but not all. Exposure to this material was positively increased hand washing motives compared to those who had not seen this it. There were still issues over whether people washed their hands long enough and on this measure the video did not improve behaviour all that much. Exposure to the video alone did not produce any hand washing influence. Compared with a non-exposure group, exposure to the combination of video and print materials was associated with improved social distancing compliance and face touching behaviour. The study showed that communications could be produced that could be effective in persuading people to comply with behavioural interventions under their own control to combat the spread of the novel coronavirus (Yousuf et al., 2020).

Lessons Learned

The mainstream broadcast and print media are important sources of news for publics around the world during normal times, but they can take on extra special significance during times of crisis. The novel coronavirus (SARS-CoV-2) pandemic that spread rapidly around the world in 2020 and persisted across 2021, was an unprecedented crisis event. Pre-pandemic research had shown that television, in particular, is the medium that most turn to at such times. In the 21st century, however, the growth of the Internet opened up many alternative sources of news information, even though the mainstream news media also had a presence there. The news does not always get through successfully to news audiences. Presentation techniques in broadcasting, for example, are focused more on enhancing entertainment value than information value. During times of crisis, however, audiences tend to be extra attentive to all news sources.

During the SARS-CoV-2 pandemic, evidence emerged that people were tuning into news sources of all kinds and especially to the major news brands which they also tended to trust the most. People who reported greater amounts of broadcast news exposure also exhibited the best knowledge about the new virus and about how their government was taking steps to bring infection transmission rates under control and protect people. At the same time, further evidence indicated that people could develop mistaken beliefs about the virus and about protective or treatment measures that could prove to be effective against it.

The news was important for the stories it told about the virus and its origins. It gave space and airtime to different theories about where the virus came from and how it had infected humans. Some theories had evidence to support them and others less so. Nevertheless, news writers offered different frameworks of interpretation and these were disseminated via mainstream news media to the public. Framing is an important aspect of news reporting. The same facts can have different impacts on people depending on the way that they are reported. In the context of SARS-CoV-2, alternative frames proposed that the virus was zoonotic (passed into humans from an animal species or that it was man-made and escaped from a laboratory. These distinct explanations of the origins of the virus affected people in different ways with some accepting one theory and others accepting the alternative.

Getting accurate, relevant and timely information about new diseases out to populations about how they can play their part can be critical in bringing a pandemic under control. Once again, the news media can be important vehicles for carrying that information quickly to lots of people. This was true during the coronavirus pandemic. Research found that many people, around the world, learned what they could do to protect themselves by tuning into the news.

Further evidence emerged that while informing people news coverage could also shape their perceptions of risk and in turn trigger unpleasant emotional responses such as anxiety and fear. This was already known about via research conducted during earlier pandemics and it was a public reaction that was apparent during the 2020 coronavirus outbreak. It was important that people understood risks from the disease and understood the steps they could take to protect themselves and others. In getting this information out, and doing so repeatedly, adverse side effects such as greater public fear might also be expected and was a price that often had to be paid.

The mainstream broadcast and print media are important sources of news for publics around the world during normal times, but they can take on extra special significance during times of crisis. The novel coronavirus (SARS-CoV-2) pandemic that spread rapidly around the world in 2020 and persisted across 2021, was an unprecedented crisis event. Pre-pandemic research had shown that television, in particular, is the medium that most turn to at such times. In the 21st century, however, the growth of the Internet opened up many alternative sources of news information, even though the mainstream news media also had a presence there. The news does not always get through successfully to news audiences. Presentation techniques in broadcasting, for example, are focused more on enhancing entertainment value than information value. During times of crisis, however, audiences tend to be extra attentive to all news sources.

During the SARS-CoV-2 pandemic, evidence emerged that people were tuning into news sources of all kinds and especially to the major news brands which they also tended to trust the most. People who reported greater amounts of news exposure also exhibited the best knowledge about the new virus and about how their government was taking steps to bring infection transmission rates under control and protect people. At the same time, further evidence indicated that people could develop mistaken beliefs about the virus and about protective or treatment measures that could prove to be effective against it.

The news was important for the stories it told about the virus and its origins. It gave space and airtime to different theories about where the virus came from and how it had infected humans. Some theories had evidence to support them and others less so. Nevertheless, news writers offered different frameworks of interpretation and these were disseminated via mainstream news media to the public. Framing is an important aspect of news reporting. The same facts can have different impacts on people depending on the way that they are reported. In the context of SARS-CoV-2, alternative frames proposed that the virus was zoonotic (passed into humans from an animal species or that it was man-made and escaped from a laboratory. These distinct explanations of the origins of the virus affected people in different ways with some accepting one theory and others accepting the alternative.

Getting accurate, relevant and timely information about new diseases out to populations about how they can play their part can be critical in bringing a pandemic under control. Once again, the news media can be important vehicles for carrying that information quickly to lots of people. This was true during the coronavirus pandemic. Research found that many people, around the world, learned what they could do to protect themselves by tuning into the news.

Further evidence emerged that while informing people news coverage could also shape their perceptions of risk and in turn trigger unpleasant emotional responses such as anxiety and fear. This was already known about via research conducted during earlier pandemics and it was a public reaction that was apparent during the 2020 coronavirus outbreak. It was important that people understood risks from the disease and understood the steps they could take to protect themselves and others. In getting this information out, and doing so repeatedly, adverse side effects such as greater public fear might also be expected and was a price that often had to be paid.

References

Abrams, E. M., & Greenhawt, M. (2020) Risk communication during COVID-19. *Journal of Allergy Clinical Immunology Practice*, 8: 1791–1794. doi:10.1016/j.jaip.2020.04.012

Adams-Prassl, A., Boneva, T., Golin, M., & Rauh, C. (2020) The impact of the coronavirus lockdown on mental health: Evidence from the US Human Capital and Economic Opportunity Working Group, Working Papers 2020-030. Retrieved from: https://ideas.repec.org/p/hka/wpaper/2020-030.html

Ajzen, I., & Fishbein, M. (1980) *Understanding attitudes and predicting social behavior.* Englewood Cliffs, NJ: Prentice-Hall.

Balzarotti, S., & Ciceri, M. R. (2014) News reports of catastrophes and viewers' fear: Threat appraisal of positively versus negatively framed events. *Media Psychology,* 17: 357–377. doi:10.1080/15213269.2013.826588

Bilancini, E., Boncinelli, L., Capraro, V., Celadin, T., & Di Paolo, R. (2020) The effect of norm-based messages on reading and understanding COVID-19 pandemic response governmental rules. *Journal of Behavioural Economics for. Policy,* 4: 45–55. doi:10.31234/osf.io/7863g

Bolsen, T., Palm, P., & Kingsland, J. T. (2020) Framing the origins of COVID-19. *Science Communication,* 42(5): 562–585. doi:10.1177/1075547020953603

Bolsen, T., Kingsland, J., & Palm, R. (2018) The impact of frames highlighting coastal flooding in the USA on climate change beliefs. *Climate Change,* 147: 359–368.

Bolsen, T., & Druckman, J. N. (2018). Do partisanship and politicization undermine the impact of a scientific consensus message about climate change? *Group Processes & Intergroup Relations,* 21(3): 389–402. doi:10.1177/1368430217737855.

Borah, P. (2009) Comparing visual framing in newspapers: Hurricane Katrina versus tsunami. *Newspaper Research Journal,* 30: 50–57. doi:10.1177/0739532 90903000106

Boukes, M., Damstra, A., & Vliegenthart, R. (2019) Media effects across time and subject: How news coverage affects two out of four attributes of consumer confidence. *Communication Research,* 48(3): 454–476. doi:10.1177/009365021 9870087

Boukes, M., & Vliegenthart, R. (2017) News consumption and its unpleasant side effect: Studying the effect of hard and soft news exposure on mental well-being over time. *Journal of Media Psychology: Theories, Methods and Applications,* 29: 137–147. doi:10.1027/1864-1105/a000224

Brossard, D., & Nisbet, M. C. (2007) Deference to scientific authority among a low information public: Understanding U.S. opinion on agricultural biotechnology. *International Journal of Public Opinion Research,* 19(1): 24–52.

Burnett, E., Johnston, B., Corlett, J., & Kearney, N. (2014) Constructing identities in the media: Newspaper coverage analysis of a major UK Clostridium difficile outbreak. *Journal of Advanced Nursing,* 70(7): 1542–1552. doi:10.1111/jan.12305

Busselle, R. W., & Shrum, L. J. (2003) Media exposure and exemplar accessibility. *Media Psychology,* 5: 255–282. doi:10.1207/S1532785XMEP0503_02

Cairo, A. (2019) *The functional art: An introduction to information graphics and visualization.* Berkeley, CA: New Riders.

Capraro, V., & Barcelo, H. (2020a) The effect of messaging and gender on intentions to wear a face covering to slow down COVID-19 transmission. *Journal of Behavioural Economics for Policy,* 4(S2): 45–55. doi:10.31234/osf.io/tg7vz

Capraro, V., & Barcelo, H. (2020b) Priming reasoning increases intentions to wear a face covering to slow down COVID-19 transmission. *arXiv*. doi:10.31234/osf.io/wtcqy

Chabani, E., & Hommel, B. (2014) Visuospatial processing in children with autism: No evidence for (training-resistant) abnormalities. *Journal of Autism and Developmental Disorders*, 44: 2230–2243. doi:10.1007/s10803-014-2107-9

Chong, D., & Drickman, J. A. (2007) Framing theory. *Annual Review of Political Science*, 10: 103–126.

Coates, S. (2020, 24th April) Coronavirus: Britons still support lockdown despite being sadder and more anxious – poll. *Sky News*. Retrieved from: https://news.sky.com/story/coronavirus-britons-still-support-lockdown-despite-being-sadder-and-more-anxious-poll-11977655.\

Davies, R. (2020, 23rd April) *Coronavirus and the social impacts on Great Britain: 23 April 2020*. Office for National Statistics. Retrieved from: https://www.ons.gov.uk/peoplepopulationandcommunity/healthandsocialcare/healthandwellbeing/bulletins/coronavirusandthesocialimpactsongreatbritain/23april2020

De Hoog, N., & Verboon, P. (2020) Is the news making us unhappy? The influence of daily news exposure on emotional states. *British Journal of Psychology*, 111: 157–173. doi:10.1111/bjop.12389

De Vreese, C. H. (2005) News framing theory and typology. *Information Design Journal + Document Design*, 13: 48–59.

Dietz, T. (2013) Bringing values and deliberation to science communication. *Proceedings of the National Academy of Sciences*, 110(Suppl 3): 14081–14087. doi:10.1073/pnas.1212740110

Dimotrova, D. V., & Stromback, J. (2005) Mission accomplished: Framing of the Iraq War in the elite newspapers in Sweden and the United States. *Gazette: The International Journal for Communication Studies*, 67(5): 399–417.

Druckman, J. N. (2001) The implications of framing effects for citizen competence. *Political Behavior*, 23: 225–256.

Ellahe, C., & Hommel, B. (2014) Effectiveness of visual and verbal prompts in training visuospatial processing skills in school age children. *Instructional Science*, 42: 1013. doi:10.1007/s11251-014-9324-7

Entman, R. M. (1993) Framing: Toward clarification of a fractured paradigm. *Journal of Communication*, 43(4): 51–58. doi:10.1111/j.1460-2466.1993.tb01304.x

Everett, J. A. C., Colombatto, C., Chituc, V., Brady, W. J., & Crockett, M. (2020) The effectiveness of moral messages on public health behavioral intentions during the COVID-19 pandemic. *PsyArXiv [Preprint]*. doi:10.31234/osf.io/9yqs8

Findahl, O., & Hoijer, B. (1976) *Fragments of reality: An experiment with news and Tv visuals*. Stockholm, Sweden: Swedish Broadcasting Corporation, *Audience and Programme Research Department*.

Fletcher, R., Kalogeropoulos, A., & Nielsen, R. K. (2020, 25th April) *News media broadly trusted as source of coronavirus information, views of UK government response highly polarised*. Reuters Institute, University of Oxford. Retrieved from: https://reutersinstitute.politics.ox.ac.uk/news-media-broadly-trusted-source-coronavirus-information-views-uk-government-response-highly

Gamson, W. A., & Modigliani, A. (1987) The changing culture of affirmative action. In R. G. Braungart, & M. M. Braungart (Eds.) *Research in political sociology* (Volume 3, pp. 137–177). Greenwich, CT: JAI press.

Gamson, W. A., & Modigliani, A. (1989) Media discourse and public opinion on nuclear power: A constructionist approach. *American Journal of Sociology*, 95: 1–37.

Garry, M., & Gerrie, M. P. (2005) When photographs create false memories. *Current Directions in Psychological Science*, 14(6): 321–325.

Gasser, G., & Solé, R. (2006) *Funding from the general public*. The International Community's Funding of the Tsunami Emergency and Relief.

Gerend, M. A., & Sias, T. (2009) Message framing and colour priming: How subtle threat cues affect persuasion. *Journal of Experimental Social Psychology*, 45: 999–1002. doi:10.1016/j.jesp.2009.04.002

Gitlin, T. (2020) Open letter to the Murdochs. *Medium.com*, April 3, 2020. https://medium.com/@journalismprofs/open-letter-to-the-murdochs-9334e775a992

Goshorn, K., & Gandy. O. H. Jr. (1995) Race-risk and responsibility: Editorial constraint in the framing of inequality. *Journal of Communication*, 45(2): 346–369.

Grimes, T. (1991) Mild auditory-visual dissonance in television news may exceed viewer attentional capacity. *Human Communication Research*, 18: 268–298.

Gross, K., & D'Ambrosio, L. (2004) Framing emotional response. *Political Psychology*, 25: 1–29.

Gunter, B. (1987) *Poor reception: Misunderstanding and forgetting broadcast news*. Hillsdale, NJ: Lawrence Erlbaum Associates.

Gunter, B. (2015) *The cognitive impact of television news: Production attributes and information reception*. Basingstoke, UK: Palgrave Macmillan.

Hameleers, M. (2020) Prospect theory in times of a pandemic: The effects of gain versus loss framing on policy preferences and emotional responses during the 2020 coronavirus outbreak. *SocArXiv*. Retrieved from: https://osf.io/prepirnts/socarxiv/7pykj/

Hanitzsch, T., Van Dalen, A., & Steindl, N. (2018) Caught in the nexus: A comparative and longitudinal analysis of public trust in the press. *The International Journal of Press/Politics*, 23(1): 3–23.

Hartley, K., & Vu, M. K. (2020) Fighting fake news in the COVID-19 era: Policy insights from an equilibrium model. *Policy Science*, 9: 1–24.

Heffner, J., Vives, M. L., & FeldmanHall, O. (2021) Emotional responses to prosocial messages increase willingness to self-isolate during the COVID-19 pandemic. *Personality and Individual Differences*, 170: 110420.

Huang, G., Li, K., & Li, H. (2019) Show, not tell: The contingency role of infographics versus text in the differential effects of message strategies on optimistic bias. *Science Communication*, 41: 732–760. doi:10.1177/1075547019888659

Igartua, J. J., Moral-Toranzo, F., & Fernández, I. (2012) Cognitive, attitudinal, and emotional effects of news frame and group cues, on processing news about immigration. *Journal of Media Psychology*, 23: 174–185. doi:10.1027/1864-1105/a000050

Iyengar, S. (1991) *Is anyone responsible? How television frame political issues*. Chicago, IL: University of Chicago Press.

Jamieson, K. H., & Albarracin, D. (2020) The relation between media consumption and misinformation at the outset of the SARS-CoV-2 pandemic in the US. *Misinformation Review*, 20 April. Retrieved from: https://misinforeview.hks.harvard.edu/article/the-relation-between-media-consumption-and-misinformation-at-the-outset-of-the-sars-cov-2-pandemic-in-the-us/

Jennings, W., & Curtis, C. (2020, 29th April) No, trust in the media has not collapsed because of coronavirus. *YouGov*. Retrieved from: https://yougov.co.uk/topics/media/articles-reports/2020/04/29/no-trust-media-has-not-collapsed-because-coronavir

Jerit, J., Paulsen, T., & Tucker, J. A. (2020) Confident and skeptical: What science misinformation patterns can teach us about the COVID-19 pandemic. *SSRN*. doi:.10.2139/ssrn.3580430

Jordan, J., Yoeli, E., & Rand, D. (2020) Don't get it or don't spread it? Comparing self-interested versus prosocially framed COVID-19 prevention messaging. *PsyArXiv [Preprint]*. doi:10.31234/osf.io/yuq7x

Kaspar, K., Wehlitz, T., von Knobelsdorff, S., Wulf, T., & von Saldern, M. A. (2015) A matter of font type: The effect of serifs on the evaluation of scientific abstracts. *International Journal of Psychology*, 50: 372–378. doi:10.1002/ijop.12160.

Kaplan, S. (2008) Framing contests: Strategy making under uncertainty. *Organization Science*, 19(5): 729–752. doi:10.1287/orsc.1070.0340

Kahneman, D., & Tversky, A. (1979) Prospect theory: An analysis of decision under risk. *Econometrica*, 47(2): 263–291.

Kekst CNC. (2020, 14th April) Covid-19 opinion tracker – edition 1. Retrieved from: https://www.kekstcnc.com/insights/covid-19-opinion-tracker-edition-1

Kekst CNC. (2020, 11th May) Covid-19 opinion tracker – edition 2. Retrieved from: https://www.kekstcnc.com/insights/covid-19-opinion-tracker-edition-2

Krause, N. M., Freiling, I., Beets, B., & Brossard, D. (2020) Fact-checking as risk communication: The multi-layered risk of misinformation in times of COVID-19. *Journal of Risk Research*. doi:10.1080/13669877.2020.1756385

Lan, J. J., Li, M., & Li, L. (2019) The occurrence and prevention of public psychological trauma in traumatic events news reports. *Psychology*, 7: 249–256. doi:10.16842/j.cnki.issn2095-5588.2019.04.006

Layard, R., Clark, A., De Neve, J.-E., Krekel, C., Fancourt, D., Hey, N., & O'Donnell, G. (2020) When to release the lockdown: A wellbeing framework for analysing costs and benefits. IZA Discussion Paper No. 13186. Retrieved from: https://papers.ssrn.com/sol3/papers.cfm?abstract_id=3590884

Lazard, A., & Atkinson, L. (2015) Putting environmental infographics center stage: The role of visuals at the elaboration likelihood model's critical point of persuasion. *Science Communication*, 37: 6–33. doi:10.1177/1075547014555997

Lazaroiu, G., Pera, A., Stefanescu-Mihaila, R. G., Bratu, S., & Mircica, N. (2017) The cognitive information effect of televised news. *Frontiers of Psychology*, 8: 165. doi:10.3389/jpsyg.2017.01165

Lecheler, S., de Vreese, C. H., & Slothuus, R. (2009) Issue importance as a moderator of framing effects. *Communication Research*, 36(3): 400–425. doi:10.1177/0093650209333028

Lee, E. J., & Kim, Y. W. (2016) Effects of infographics on news elaboration, acquisition, and evaluation: Prior knowledge and issue involvement as moderators. *New Media and Society*, 18: 1579–1598. doi:10.1177/1461444814567982

Lerner, J. S., & Keltner, D. (2001) Fear, anger, and risk. *Journal of Personality and Social Psychology*, 81: 146–159.

Li, J.-B., Wang, A., Dou, K., & Wang, L.-X. (2020) Chinese public's knowledge, perceived severity and perceived controllability of the COVID-19 and reactions, social participation and precautionary behaviour: A national survey. Retrieved from: https://www.researchgate.net/publication/33950638

Liu, Q., Zheng, Z., Zheng, J., Chen, Q., Liu, G., Chen, S., Chu, B., Zhu, H., Akinwunmi, B., Huang, J., Zhang, C. J. P., & Ming, W.-K. (2020) Health communication through news media during the early stage of the COVID-19 outbreak in China: Digital topic modeling approach. *Journal of Medicine and Internet Research*, 22(4): e19118. doi:10.2196/19118

Loftus, E., & Pickrell, J. E. (1995) The formation of false memories. *Psychiatric Annals*, 25: 720–725.

Lowry, D. T., Nio, T. C. J., & Leitner, D. W. (2003) Setting the public fear agenda: A longitudinal analysis of network TV crime reporting, public perceptions of crime, and FBI crime statistics. *Journal of Communication*, 53: 61–73. doi: 10.1111/j.1460-2466.2003.tb03005.x

Martikainen, J., & Sakki, I. (2021) How newspaper images position different groups of people in relation to the COVID-19 pandemic: A social representations approach. *Journal of Community and Applied Social Psychology*, 4. doi:10.1002/casp.2515

McIntyre, K. E., & Gibson, R. (2016) Positive news makes readers feel good: A silver-lining approach to negative news can attract audiences. *Southern Communication Journal*, 81(5).

Meyerowitz, B. E., & Chaiken, S. (1987) The effect of message framing on breast self-examination attitudes, intentions, and behavior. *Journal of Personality and Social Psychology*, 52(3): 500–510.

Mheidy, N., & Fares, J. (2020) Leveraging media and health communication strtegies to overcome the COVID-19 infodemic. *Journal of Public Health Policy*, 41(4): 410–420.

Michas, I. C., & Berry, D. C. (2000) Learning a procedural task: Effectiveness of multimedia presentations. *Applied Cognitive Psychology*, 14: 555–575. doi:10.1002/1099-0720(200011/12)14:6<555::AID-ACP677>3.0.CO;2-4

Moscadelli, A., Albora, G., Biamonte, M. A., Giorgetti, D., Innocenzio, M., Paoli, S., Loini, C., Bonanni, P., & Bonaccorsi, G. (2020) Fake news and Covid-19 in Italy: Results of a quantitative observational study. *International Journal of Environmental Research and Public Health*, 17(16): 5850. doi:10.3390/ijerph17165750

Nabi, R. L. (2003) Exploring the framing effects of emotion: Do discrete emotions differentially influence information accessibility, information seeking, and policy preference? *Communication Research*, 30: 224–247.

Newman, N., Fletcher, R., Kalogeropoulos, A., & Nielsen, R. K. (2019) *Reuters Institute Digital News Report 2019*. Oxford: Reuters Institute for the Study of Journalism.

Ng, R., Chow, T. Y. J., & Yang, W. (2021) News media narratives of Covid-19 across 20 countries: Early global convergence and later regional divergence. *PLoS*

One. Retrieved from: https://journals.plos.org/plosone/article?id=10.1371/journal.pone.0256358

Nielsen, R. K., Kalogeropoulos, A., & Fletcher, R. (2020, 25th August) *Most in the UK say news media have helped them respond to COVID-19, but a third say news coverage has made the crisis worse*. Oxford: Reuters Institute for the Study of Journalism. Retrieved from: https://reutersinstitute.politics.ox.ac.uk/most-uk-say-news-media-have-helped-them-respond-covid-19-third-say-news-coverage-has-made-crisis

Nielsen, R. K., Fletcher, R., Newman, N., Brennen, J. S., & Howard, P. N. (2020) *Navigating the "Infodemic": How People in Six Countries Access and Rate News and Information about Coronavirus*. Oxford: Reuters Institute for the Study of Journalism.

Nisbet, M. L. (2009) Framing science: A new paradigm in public engagement. In L. Kahlor, & P. Stout (Eds.) News Agendas in Science Communication. London, UK: Routledge.

Pew Research Center. (2019a) Many Americans say made-up news is a problem that needs to be fixed. https://www.journalism.org/2019/06/05/many-americans-say-made-up-news-is-a-critical-problem-that-needs-to-be-fixed/

Pew Research Center. (2019b) Republicans far more likely than Democrats to say fact-checkers tend to favor one side. https://www.pewresearch.org/fact-tank/2019/06/27/republicans-far-more-likely-than-democrats-to-say-fact-checkers-tend-to-favor-one-side/

Pew Research Center. (2020) Explore the data. Retrieved from: https://www.pewresearch.org/pathways-2020/covidcover2/main_source_of_election_news/us_adults/

Porat, T., Nyrup, R., Calvo, R. A., Pudyal, P., & Ford, E. (2020) Public health and risk communication during COVID-19-enhancing psychological needs to promote sustainable behavior change. *Frontiers in Public Health*, 8: 573397. doi: 10.3389/fpubh.2020.573397

Prasetyo, Y. T., Castillo, A. M., Salonga, L. J., Sia, J. A., & Seneta, J. A. (2020) Factors affecting perceived effectiveness of COVID-19 prevention measures among Filipinos during enhanced community quarantine in Luzon, Philippines: Integrating protection motivation theory and extended theory of planned behavior. *International Journal of Infectious Diseases*, 99: 312–323.

Quattrone, G. A., & Tversky, A. (1984) Causal versus diagnostic contingencies: On selfdeception and on the voter's illusion. *Journal of Personality and Social Psychology*, 46(2): 237–248. doi:10.1037/0022-3514.46.2.237

Renn, O. (1992) Concepts of risk: A classification. In S. Krimsky, & D. Golding (Eds.) *Social theories of risk* (pp. 53–79). Westport, CT: Praeger.

Requarth, T. (2020) Please, let's stop the epidemic of armchair epidemiology. *Slate*. Retrieved from: https://slate.com/technology/2020/03/armchair-epidemiology-coronavirus.html

Romer, D., Jamieson, K. H., & Aday, S. (2003) Television news and the cultivation of fear of crime. *Journal of Communication*, 53: 88–104. doi:10.1111/j.1460-2466.2003.tb03007.x

Roser, M., Ritchie, H., Ortiz-Ospina, E., & Hasell, J. (2020) Coronavirus Disease (COVID-19). *Our World in Data*. Retrieved from: https://ourworldindata.org/coronavirus

Roseman, I. J. (1991) Appraisal determinants of discrete emotions. *Cognition and Emotion*, 5(3): 161–200. doi:10.1080/02699939108411034

Rothman, A. J., & Salovey, P. (1997) Shaping perceptions to motivate healthy behavior: The role of message framing. *Psychological Bulletin*, 12: 3–19.

Sanders, M., Stockdale, E. Hume, S., & John, P. (2020) Loss aversion fails to replicate in the coronavirus pandemic: Evidence from an online experiment. *Economic Letters*. doi:10.1016/j.econlet.2020.109433

Scheufele, D. A. (1999) Framing as a theory of media effects. *Journal of Communication*, 49: 103–122. doi:10.1111/j.1460-2466.1999.tb02784.x

Scheufele, D. A., & Krause, N. M. (2019) Science audiences, misinformation, and fake news. *Proceedings of the National Academy of Sciences*, 116(16): 7662–7669. doi:10.1073/pnas.1805871115

Schroeder, A., & Pennington-Gray, L. (2015) The role of social media in internationl tourists' decision-making. *Journal of Trauvel Research*, 54(5).

Shoemaker, P. J., & Reese, S. D. (1996) *Mediating the message* (2nd Ed.). White Plains, NY: Logman.

Siegrist, M. (2000) The influence of trust and perceptions of risks and benefits on the acceptance of gene technology. *Risk Analysis*, 20(2): 195–203. doi:10.1111/0272-4332.202020

Skinner, G., Pedley, K., & Garrett, C. (2020, 29th April) Journalists seen to be doing a better job of holding the Government to account on coronavirus than MPs and the Opposition. *Ipsos-MORI*. Retrieved from: https://www.ipsos.com/ipsos-mori/en-uk/journalists-seen-be-doing-better-job-holding-government-account-coronavirus-mps-and-opposition

Sniderman, P. M., & Theriault, S. M. (2004) The structure of political argument and the logic of issue framing. In P. M., Siderman, & S. M., Theriault (Eds.) *Studies in public opinion*. Princetone, NJ: Pirnceton University Press. doi:10.1515/9780691188386-007

Soo, N., Morani, M., Kyriakidou, D., & Cushion, S. (2020, 28th April) Research suggests UK public can spot fake news about COVID-19 but don't realise the UK's death toll is far higher than in many other countries. *LSE Blog*. Retrieved from: https://blogs.lse.ac.uk/covid19/2020/04/28/research-suggests-uk-public-can-spot-fake-news-about-covid-19-but-dont-realise-the-uks-death-toll-is-far-higher-than-in-many-other-countries/

Southwell, B. G., Thorson, E., & Sheble, L., eds. (2018) *Misinformation and mass audiences*. Austin, TX: University of Texas Press.

Survation. (2020, 30th April) Survation COVID-19 public attitude tracker. Retrieved from: https://www.survation.com/survation-covid-19-public-attitude-tracker/

Sundar, S. S. (2000) Multimedia effects on processing and perception of online news: A study of picture, audio and video downloads. *Journalism & Mass Communication Quarterly*, 77(3).

Sweney, M. (2020, 7th May) Coronoavirus sparks debate over trust in media despite record audience figures. *The Guardian*. Retrieved from: https://www.theguardian.com/media/2020/may/07/public-trust-in-uk-journalism-eroding-amid-coronavirus-polls-suggest

Tangcharoensathien, V., Calleja, N., Nguyen, T., Purnat, T., D'Agostino, M., Garcia-Saiso, S., Landry, M., Rashidian, A., Hamilton, C., AbdAllah, A., Ggiga, I., Hill, A., Hougendoubler, D., van Andel, J., Nunn, M., Brooks, I., Sacco, P. L., De Domenico, M., Mai, P., Gruzd, A., Philippe, A., & Briand, S. (2020) Framework for managing the COVID-19 infodemic: Methods and results of an online, crowdsourced WHO technical consultation. *Journal of Medicine and Internet Research*, 22(6): e19659. doi:10.2196/19659

Tufekci, Z. (2020) Don't believe the COVID-19 models. *The Atlantic*. Retrieved from: https://www.theatlantic.com/technology/archive/2020/04/coronavirus-models-arent-supposed-be-right/609271/?fbclid=IwAR3Sz117_0qniVmCbkWV1JxP1OtiNW-m2XCfhRrf2aisM5W6RfMBBt3X1_Q8

Tversky, A., & Kahneman, D. (1981) The framing of decisions and the psychology of choice. *Science*, 211(4481): 453–458. doi:10.1126/science.7455683

Van Gorp, B. (2008) The constructionist approach to framing: Bringing culture back in. *Journal of Communication*, 57: 60–78.

Van Bavel, J. J., Baicker, K., Boggio, P. S., Capraro, V., Cichocka, A., Cikara, M., Crockett, M. J., Crum, A. J., Douglas, K. M., Druckman, J. N., Drury, J., Dube, O., Ellemers, N., Finkel, E. J., Fowler, J. H., Gelfand, M., Han, S., Haslam, S. A., Jetten, J., Kitayama, S., Mobbs, D., Napper, L. E., Packer, D. J., Pennycook, G., Peters, E., Petty, R. E., Rand, D. G., Reicher, S. D., Schnall, S., Shariff, A., Skitka, L. J., Smith, S. S., Sunstein, C. R., Tabri, N., Tucker, J. A., Linden, S. V., Lange, P. V., Weeden, K. A., Wohl, M. J. A., Zaki, J., Zion, S. R., & Willer, R. (2020). Using social and behavioural science to support COVID-19 pandemic response. *Nature Human Behaviour*, 4(5): 460–471. doi:10.1038/s41562-020-0884-z.

Van Gorp, B. (2007) The constructionist approach to framing: Bringing culture back. *Journal of Communication*, 57(1): 60–78. doi:10.1111/j.1460-2466. 2006.00329.x

van der Linden, S., Leiserowitz, A., & Maibach, E. (2019). The gateway belief model: A large-scale replication. *Journal of Environmental Psychology*, 62: 49–58. doi:10.1016/j.jenvp.2019.01.009.

Vliegenthart, R., & Boukes, M. (2018) On the street and/or on Twitter? The use of "every day" sources in economic news coverage by online and offline outlets. *Digital J*, 6: 829–846. doi:10.1080/21670811.2018.1497449

Waldrop, T., Alsup, D., & McLaughlin, E. (2020) Fearing coronavirus, Arizona man dies after taking a form of chloroquine used to treat aquariums. *CNN.com*. https://www.cnn.com/2020/03/23/health/arizona-coronavirus-chloroquine-death/index.html

Xie, X., Zheng, R., Xie, D., & Wang, H. (2005) Analysis on psychological panic phenomenon of SARS. *Acta Scientific: National University of Pekkinen*, 41: 628–639.

Yousuf, H., Corbin, J., Sweep, G., Hofstra, M., Scherder, E., van Gorp, E., Zwetsloot, P. P., Zhao, J., van Rossum, B., Jiang, T., Lindemans, J.-W., Narula, J., & Hofstra, L. (2020) Association of a public health campaign about coronavirus disease 2019 promoted by news media and a social influencer with self-reported personal hygiene and physical distancing in The Netherlands. *JAMA Network Open*, 3(7): e2014323. doi:10.1001/jamanetworkopen.2020.14323

Chapter 6

The Internet and Public Perceptions of the Pandemic

The Internet was widely used during the pandemic both as a direct extension of mainstream news outputs, via news providers' websites and also for its distinctive information sources provided by excusive online news proviers, government sites, health authority sites and from a multitude of other sources, with some of unproven authenticity. We will return in Chapter 7 to the topic of misinformation and conspiracy theories that have benefited considerably from the open communications systems of the Internet. For now, attention is turned to the way the Internet was used and how it may have shaped public perceptions of the pandemic.

The Internet is not a single entity. It is a platform on which many different kinds of sites or information sources reside. Among the biggest and most inlfuential are the biggest of the microblogging and social networking sites. These include such well-known brands as Facebook, Instagram, Pinterest, Tik Tok, Twitter and YouTube. These "sites" are actually massive, open (for registered users) networks that enable individuals and organisations to present content – both verbal and pictorial – on a virtually unlimited scale with the potential to reach massive audiences.

There was an increase in the use of mainstream media news during the pandemic from publics eager to find out all they could about the new virus and also about how they could protect themselves from it. After a time, the public's information appetites turned towards finding out when the pandmeic would end and life would return to normal and, in the meantime, keeping up with constaantly changing lockdown rules of behaviour. As the pandemic progessed, the Internet became the platform that conveyed timely and varied information about the etiology of the new coronavirus, its symptoms, impact, treatment and prevention. As information about the virus profilerated on traditonal media and online media and the pandemic triggered many national governments and public health authorities to restrict people's movements, more and more people turned to the Internet for information and advice, rather than simply being reliant on the mainstream news (Kouzy et al., 2020). Google searches using terms such as "wash hands" also increased as some governments initially opted for light-touch

DOI: 10.4324/9781003274629-6

interventions (Lin et al., 2020). While vast amounts of useful information could be found online, it was also an environment in which much misinformation circulated (Cuan-Baltazar et al., 2020).

In some parts of the world, and for some population sub-groups, the Internet was a primary source of COVID-19 information. Evidence emerged from Taiwan, for example, that people in general turned to the Internet, but medical and health professionals in particular found that specialist content about the pandemic was helpful to them in their work. In the absence of face-to-face briefings, the Internet provided information from different expert sources that was regularly updated and gave them greater self-confidence in difficult and uncertin times. For the population at large and for healthcare workers in Taiwan, information online was widely used to help them cope and to provide reassurance and alleviate worries (Wang et al., 2020).

Attention to Social Networks during the Pandemic

Social media have emerged as one of the major sources of news and information and command the attention of billons of users worldwide. Data for 2020, the year of pandemic, showed that there were 5.4 billion Internet users and 3.8 billion users of social networking sites (Kemp, 2020). Social media allow users and those in authority over them to interact more directly. Hey can also empower ordinary members of the public by giving them access to a mass communication platform over which they can reach potentially massive audiences (Gokalp et al., 2020). There is evidence that social media sites can raise public awareness of major issues and that they can be used to disseminate important information rapidly to large numbers of people during times of crisis (Shah et al., 2019).

There is further evidence that because social media empower ordinary citizens by giving them access to large audiences to which they can voice their opinions, decision-makers are more likely to react to lobbying on these platforms (Kaya et al., 2020). The communicative power of social media sites has also drawn political parties to them as campaigning tools (Nulty et al., 2016). Lobbying groups championing specific causes in spheres such as climate change, and gender and ethnic equality have also found that social media provide access to massive audiences at little cost (Maes et al., 2019; Varghese, 2019). Traditional media can still provide mass audiences but access is controlled by their internal editorial gatekeepers, whereas on social networking sites users have more immediate and direct control over the communications process.

These online communication platforms have considerable utility during times of new disease outbreaks. They can be used to distribute public health information to let people know about emergent epidemics and the risks they present, as well as advice on how people can safeguard themselves

(Fung et al., 2016). These sites can also be used by health authorities to provide early insights into the emergence of new epidemics. People often search for information about symptoms online and any dramatic upsurge in specific searches using specific search terms can act as early warning signals of potentially new diseases before they are registered by health authorities dependent upon people already showing advanced symptoms (Kaya & Sağsan, 2015; Avery, 2017). At the same time, social networking sites have bene identified as primary sources of misleading and false information about health issues (Wang et al., 2019). Given the growing significance of social media sites as information sources therefore concerns about information quality and authenticity in these domains deserves serious attention.

Many people were found to turn to these sites for information about the COVID-19 pandemic. This was especially true of younger people. The content sought out by users of these sites included expert information, regular news updates and opportunities to engage intteractively in discussions with others about the new coronavirus, the pandemic and their government's interventions to control it. This environment runs alongside the mainstream news media and has surpassed the tranditional media in scale and reach. Although, micro-blogging and social networking sites are communicatinos environments that have a relatively short history, having mostly emerged during the first two decades of the 21st century, they have acquired considerable currency for many people as information and advice sources. People become switched on them with especial acuity during times of crisis and disaster (Gonzalez-Padilla & Tortolero-Blanco, 2020). The COVID-19 pandemic represents one of the biggest such events. There was a rapid burst of searches on the Internet, especilaly around social media platforms in China as the pandemic took hold there in early 2020 (Abd-Alrazaq et al., 2020; Li et al., 2020).

Social networking sites have also been known to have a special pull on their users to maintain open communications channels with their family members and friends. They also provide places to relieve boredom, achieve relief from stress and seek social sustenance and emotional support at times that cause personal anxiety or depression. The pandemic became a time of social isolation for many people and such social deprivation proved to be distressing for many. Personal, face-to-face meetings between people in each other's homes were banned for extensive periods, especially for those deemed to be most "at-risk" from COVID-19 infection and remote meetings became normative as a partial solution (Brooks et al., 2020).

Evidence emerged around the world that many people turned to social networking sites for COVID-related information. Many were aware that these sites can convey fake news about the pandemic but this did not deter them from seeking out sources they did trust on these sites. People's use of these sites was also found to differ from normal times as they were turning to their online social networks for information from trusted sources and also for more general support and social contact as behavioural restrictions imposed on their everyday lives started to bite (Kaya, 2020).

Online Information Dissemination

Online social networking platforms were seen by experts as having potentially an important role to play in getting information out to mass public quickly. At the start of the COVID-19 pandemic in 2020, nearly three billion people used these sites (Clement, 2020). They were also platforms used by many specialist organisations in medicine and public health. Social media could get news out to their users as speedily and extensively as mainstream media news organisations. They also engendered direct interactions between information suppliers and information consumers, who could also exchange roles on these sites (Merchant, 2020).

The open nature of social media sites meant that information about the pandemic that was false and misleading could gain equal traction to that from official and expert sources. Conspiracy theories about the pandemic and about government interventions to control it abounded on social media. These sites also had built-in self-controlling and information counterbalancing features whereby false claims and reports could be challenged and discredited.

The ability to move seamlessly from mass communication to interpersonal communication on these sites also meant that they enabled users to take information in mass circulation and discuss its relevance to themselves with people they knew well and trusted. These networks of online social contacts (some of which also existed in the offline world) provided support systems during a time of great uncertainty. Social media users could learn from each other as well as from official sources and the major news media and the mass information outputs over which they would normally have little or no control could be re-cast through online discussions with friends (Merchant & Lurie, 2020). These more interactive social dialogues could help also to provide fresh perspective on the risks associated with this new disease (Merchant et al., 2019).

Evidence emerged to show that social networking sites proved to be effective at spreading important information about personal protection both for members of the public and those working in specialist front-line jobs where they care for us at close quarters daily. Specialists could share experiences as well as information about availability and sources of equipment and about protocols through these online channels. Many different contributors meant that these communications networks had built-in quality control systems to ensure that any advice or other information being given out was validated by multiple checkers (Emanuel et al., 2020).

The most widely used micro-blogging and social networking sites could disseminate information rapidly to large numbers of people without being slowed by the kinds of gatekeeping editorial processes that characterised the mainstream news media. Specialists could establish information exchange networks with other specialists. Patients could do likewise with other patients. While information spread through an online network, in reaching recipients around the world, it would also get translated along the way into multiple languages, rendering the information even more accessible and to wider communities (Chan et al., 2020).

The rapid dissemination of information could be critical when it concerned essential preventive advice. At the start of the pandemic, little was known about the novel coronavirus and this placed everyone on a steep learning curve. This ignorance created a huge appetite for information. One study found that the 100 most viewed videos on YouTube accessed with the word "coronavirus" had accumulated more than 165 million views by 5th March 2020. Most of these videos (85%) had been originated by major news channels which illustrated the centrality of these organisations to early information dissemination to the public. Even so, the quality of information contained in many of these videos was problematic. Most (nearly 90%) focused on deaths reportedly caused by COVID-19, but fewer than one in three covered advice about preventive measures and fewer than one in two explained the symptoms people should look out for in determining whether they had become infected (Basch et al., 2020).

Although the major social networking sites had the advantage of being able to circulate information quickly to large numbers of people, checks on information quality were not always of the highest order. Earlier reference was made to some degree of self-checking of content by the networks of people across which information flowed. This process did not always occur. When it did, critiques were not always accurate or balanced. These open communications systems therefore could allow inaccurate and deliberately misleading information to gain currency as authentic and trustworthy knowledge.

Online networks also have built-in systems of information monitoring. They use these devices to make recommendations about content that an individual might find to be of interest based on their previous content consumption habits. These "bubble filters" are underwritten by algorithms that constantly compile online behaviour data about each user (Pariser, 2011; Holone, 2016). While these services can offer shortcuts to selected content, they might constrain the range of information an individual consumes because they do not consider more diverse content that could be useful in broadening the individual's perspective on an issue.

Another outcome of over-reliance on micro-blogging and social networking sites is that they often contain highly emotional content that dramatizes events and issues and can give rise to warped risk perceptions and associated fears to an unnecessary degree. If maintained over time, these communications and their immediate effects could build to have longer-term adverse health consequences for those exposed to it. Research emerged from China that found more than half the 1200+ people surveyed estimated that the new coronanvirus epidemic had had a oderate to severe psychological impact on them. Significant amounts of stress were reportedly experienced and heightened anxiety (Wang et al., 2020). Similar findings had emerged following the first SARS outbreak in China in 2003 (Mak et al., 2009).

The global pandemic generated huge volumes of public conversations and debates about COVID-19 and the different ways that governments and health authorities handled the crisi it caused. There was also a surge in scientific research and analysis across a range of disciplines inlcuding biological and medical, physical and behavioural sciences (Van Bavel et al., 2020). Many new research studies were produced and their findings placed in the pulbic domain at a pace not normally seen. This also meant that a great deal of new research was "published" before being checked by usual peer review processes.

This vast "infomedic" produced a swathe of potential new knowledge but also an informaiton overload with large amounts of new science being openly discussed as valid and reliable new knowledge before it had been thorughly checked and critiqued. Some research commentators advised caution over the way such research was used and some suggested quick-check procedures to assess the veracity of new findings before they were used to reinforce new pandemic intervention policies (Mheidy & Fares, 2020).

In the online world, vast amounts of information also flowed about COVID-19, some of which derived from trusted sources, while other information derived from other sources whose credibility and agendas could not always be verified. The online world, especially through social media sites, could also provide infrastructures for spontaneous support communities to become established in response to specific COVID-related developments. They could also cultivate communities built upon unsubstantiated suspicions and false accusations about the origins of the pandemic, the nature of the virus, the reasons why governments imposed extreme behavioural restrictions and about the ingedients and effects of vaccines.

With limited amounts of gatekeeping, which served as information quality controllers, information could spread like wildfire across the Internet that presented misleading or fictional claims about the pandemic. Often, the sources of that informaiton seemed genuine, authentic and authoritative. Closer inspection of the claims being made and the evidence (or lack of) being presented could reveal that all was not well with these messages (Freckelton, 2020). Not everyone swallowed these messages. A few did however. When false claims worked against public policies designed to protect people, they could become both worrying and dangerous. Hence, while the online world was once trumpeted as a domain in which information avalability across all parts of society will become equalised and "democratised", according to some critics, this had not happened during the 2020 COVID-19 pandemic (Viswanath et al., 2020).

Online Chatter and COVID Awareness and Attitude

The mainstream media played a major role in keeping the public informed about the latest pandemic developments including infection and death rates and most importantly steps being taken by government to combat the spread of the novel coronavirus. At the same time, there was an explosion of chatter over the major online social networks such as Facebook, Instagram, Twitter, What's App, YouTube and others (Cinelli et al., 2020). Given the fluid conditions created by the pandemic where new developments occurred multiple times daily, these online communications forums were able to keep their users right up-to-date more frequently sometimes than the mainstream broadcast news bulletins. Moreover, the online chatter derived from many more diverse sources than just the major media organisations. Yet, there were risks here in that not all of these sources were reliable or accurate. Engaging with other people online, initially through regular social media channels and then increasingly via video-links facilitated most of all by the sudden emergence of Zoom, provided the best available substitutes to face-to-face interactions as increasingly severe government restrictions prohibited people meeting others not from their own household.

The online chatter can also provide advance insights into the spreading of a new disease when epidemics arise when people talk online about their symptoms or search on specific topics known to be linked to specific health conditions (Jahanbin & Rahmanian, 2020; Medford et al., 2020; Singh et al., 2020).

Analysis of chatter about new epidemics or pandemics on online social networks can reveal the salience of an issue and how wide-ranging is public concern about these events. In the case of the novel coronavirus in 2020, this chatter not only indicated what people knew about hatter, for example, was found to cover multiple topics about the new virus and subsequently about the way their government had responded to it once large numbers of people had started to become infected (Medford et al., 2020; Sharma et al., 2020).

Chen et al. (2021) examined tweets posted between 22nd January and 5th June 2020 that had, according to available geographical identifiers, been originated in Belgium, France, Germany and Luxembourg. They looked at daily case data for COVID-19 and tweet volumes over this period. The two variables were found to be strongly inter-correlated. Daily discussions revealed that there was concern about anti-contagion and treatment measures even before infection levels had peaked and also about the extent and way that daily life had bene disrupted. Chatter about a pandemic such as COVID-19 can get ahead of volume of cases and might, in reporting case known to those tweeting offered some prescience to what is to come. Further evidence had also shown that when social network sites were used to convey anti-contagion policies, they could affect the spread of COVID-19 (Courtemanche et al., 2020; Dergiades et al., 2020; Hsiang, Allen, Annan-Phan, Bell, Bolliger, Chong, Druckenmiller, Huang, Hultgren, Krasovich et al., 2020).

The impact of chatter on Twitter can be good or bad. Where online conversations draw upon government policies and advice designed to mitigate the spread of the virus and are harmonious with them, they could magnify the impetus for behaviour change in a positive way. Where these conversations are swayed by ill-informed theories about the virus and encourage people to ignore the guidance of government and health authorities, they can disrupt attempts to control the pandemic (Hsiang, Allen, Annan-Phan, Bell, Bolliger, Chong, Druckenmiller, Huang, Hultgren, Krasovich et al., 2020; Park, Park, & Chong, 2020).

One interesting analysis of Twitter activity in Belgium, France, Germany and Luxembourg revealed that conversations about COVID-19 varied across the early period of the pandemic internationally, when it had not yet really infiltrated these countries and then later on when it had done so. Analysis of the sentiments being expressed in the early tweeting indicated a degree of "optimistic bias"! whereby many people were not immediately fully convinced that their country would be seriously impacted (Chen et al., 2021). This might then have caused many people to be slow to take the forthcoming pandemic seriously and to pay little heed to initial messages from government designed to mitigate the spread of the new disease (Paek et al., 2008; Sharot, 2011; Smith et al., 2016).

Twitter and Public Attitudes to COVID Interventions

Countries varied in their approaches to tackling the COVID-19 pandemic. Some deployed many non-pharmaceutical interventions and did so swiftly, while others used these measures more hesitantly and acted only after some delay, and a few used only limited restrictions of this type on public behaviour. Public reactions to their governments' responses to the pandemic also varied and were, not surprisingly, shaped by the success with which the national response brought the pandemic under control and limited the number of people that died from COVID-19. This variance in response could be tracked in different ways. Public opinion polls provide the conventional method of ascertaining populations' attitudes to their goverments and their country's current status. Analysis of online commentary, for example on Twitter, has emerged as another technique that is sensitive to the current mood of the people.

One Twitter analysis that covered over three-quarters of a million tweets about COVID-19 in six countries (Autralia, Canada, Ireland, New Zealand,

United Kingdom and United States) found that the volume of chatter about COVID-19 and the nature of that chatter varied between countries (Doogan et al., 2020). Much greater attention was devoted to discussing non-pharmaceutical interventions (NPIs) in Australian and New Zealand than in the United States. Chatter covered topics such as personal protection, social distancing, testing and tracing, public gathering restrictions, lockdown, travel restrictions and workplace closures. Less restrictive non-pharmaceutial interventions received support across many countres and more restrictive interventions were less well received in some countries than in others. Where there was a more positive public response to the nature and timeliness of NPIs, compliance tended to be greater.

Lessons Learned

The Internet has become a widely used information source. Its ubiquity has rendered its use almost normative in many countries. Younger generations especially have frequently rated it as more important to them for information about what is happening in the world than television. It is also a setting in which the trends in people's concerns can be detected very early and even before journalists working for major news media are aware of them. During the 2020 SARS-CoV-2 pandemic, while many governments were still determining what their strategies would be to tackle the pandemic, should it become a problem, there were already signs that many in the public were ahead of the game given search patterns on Google using terms related to the virus and related protective measures.

Evidence emerged from the Far East of early online searches by health professionals who had become concerned about the new virus reported by authorities in mainland China. These searches sought information about how those on the frontline could deal with this news disease and about the risks it posed to those on the frontline in health services.

The Internet is not a single entity. It is a technology platform that houses many different sources of information. These sources reside on computer storage facilities in different locations and can be accessed through other computer interfaces. Micro-blogging and social networking sites had become prevalent over the 10–15 years before the 2020 pandemic. Billions of people now tuned into them for information from a wide range of sources. They acted as information broadcasters. In addition, they housed discussion forums and interpersonal communications networks that individuals could use to "talk" to other individuals.

Stories could circulate rapidly in these settings. This meant that these sites could be extremely helpful to governments and health authorities seeking to get important messages out to large numbers of people quickly following timeframes under the control of message sources. The problems posed by this setting were that they could also be used by sources that had no authority or credibility and that would sometimes represent disreputable interest groups with destructive rather than constructive agendas.

Social networking sites such as Facebook and YouTube and microblogging sites such as Twitter and other equivalents on mainland China were found to have been extensively used by authorities to get important health messages out to the public. Although mainstream media also proved useful in this context, online media could be even better with younger people. These messages could be repeatedly transmitted and might then trigger much additional "chatter" in these settings that would help to reinforce the original messages. Sometimes, of course, the additional chatter distorted core messages or provided sources of alternative viewpoints.

The constant updating of "facts" in online chatter forums enabled their users to maintain a continuous flow of information about the pandemic. These sources would often provide pandemic-related information that was not reported by major news providers. By tuning into these forums, researchers were also able to get a different perspective on public opinion about the pandemic and about the way their government and health authorities were managing it. Different interest groups also frequently appeared with their opinions. Hence, as well as representing an alternative to the mainstream as a news channel, the Internet also provided alternative methods for monitoring public opinion.

Some research showed, of course, that inaccurate and misleading information would abound on some online sites. These sources could be influential beacons of public opinion among their regular users. At the same time, however, analysis of chatter on microblogging sites (such as Twitter) had revealed that national populations responded differently to the use of non-pharmaceutical interventions. Some countries welcomed these interventions even when they were severe. Others did not. It was important to understand how people were reacting because these responses to different restrictions on their was related to people's willingness to comply with them.

References

Abd-Alrazaq, A., Alhuwail, D., Househ, M., Hamdi, M., & Shah, Z. (2020) Top concerns of tweeters during the COVID-19 pandemic: Infoveillance Study. *Journal of Medicine and Internet Research*, 22: e19016.

Avery, E. (2017) Public information officers' social media monitoring during the Zika virus crisis, a global health threat surrounded by public uncertainty. *Public Relations Review*, 43(3): 468–476. doi:10.1016/j.pubrev.2017.02.018

Brooks, S. K., Webster, R. K., Smith, L. E., Woodland, L., Wessely, S., Greenberg, N., & Rubin, G.J. (2020) The psychological impact of quarantine and how to reduce it: Rapid review of the evidence. *Lancet*, 395(10227): 912–920. doi:10.1016/S0140-6736(20)30460-8

Basch, C. H., Hillyer, G. C., Meleo-Erwin, Z. C., Jaime, C., Mohlman, J., & Basch, C. E. (2020) Preventive behaviors conveyed on YouTube to mitigate transmission of COVID-19: Cross-sectional study. *JMIR Public Health Surveillance*, 2020(6): e18807. Erratum in: *JMIR Public Health Surveillance*, 6: e19601.

Cuan-Baltazar, J., Muñoz-Perez, M. J., Robledo-Vega, C., Pérez-Zepeda, M. F., & Soto-Vega, E. (2020 April 9) Misinformation of COVID-19 on the internet: Infodemiology study. *JMIR Public Health Surveill*, 6(2): e18444. doi:10.2196/1 8444. https://publichealth.jmir.org/2020/2/e18444/

Chan, A. K. M., Nickson, C. P., Rudolph, J. W., Lee, A., & Joynt, G. M. (2020) Social media for rapid knowledge dissemination: Early experience from the COVID-19 pandemic. *Anaesthesia*, 12: 1579–1582. doi:10.1111/anae.15057

Chen, E., Lerman, K., & Ferrara, E. (2020) Tracking social media discourse about the COVID-19 pandemic: Development of a public coronavirus Twitter data set. *JMIR Public Health and Surveillance*, 6(2): e19273. doi:10.2196/19273

Cinelli, M., Quattrociocchi, W., Galeazzi, A., Valensise, C. M., Brugnoli, E., Schmidt, A. L., Zola, P., Zollo, F., & Scala, A. (2020) The COVID-19 social media infodemic. *Scientific Reports*, 16598. doi:10.1038/s41598-020-73510-5

Clement, J. (2020) Number of global social media users 2010-2021. *Statistica web site*. https://www.statistica.com/statistics/278414/number-of-worldwide-social-network-users

Courtemanche, C., Garuccio, J., Le, A., Pinkston, J., & Yelowitz, A. (2020) Strong social distancing measures in the United States reduced the COVID-19 growth rate. *Health Affairs*, 39(7): 1237–1246. doi:10.1377/hlthaff.2020.00608

Dergiades, T., Milas, C., Mossialos, E., & Panagiotidis, T. (2020) Effectiveness of government policies in response to the COVID-19 outbreak. *SSRN*. Available at SSRN: https://ssrn.com/abstract=3602004. doi:10.2139/ssrn.3602004

Doogan, C., Buntine, W., Linger, H., & Brunt, S. (2020) Public perceptions and attitudes toward COVID-19 nonpharmaceutical interventions across six countries: A topic modeling analysis of Twitter data. *Journal of Medical Internet Research*, 22(9): e21419. doi:10.2196/21419

Emanuel, E. J., Persad, G., Upshur, R., Thome, B., Parker, M., Glickman, A., Zhang, C., Boyle, C., Smith, M., & Phillips, J. P. (2020) Fair allocation of scarce medical resources in the time of Covid-19. *New England Journal of Medicine*, 382(21): 2049–2055. doi:10.1056/NEJMsb2005114

Freckelton, Q. C. I. (2020) COVID-19: Fear, quackery, false representations and the law. *International Journal of Law and Psychiatry*, 72: 101611. doi:10.1016/j.ijlp.2020.101611

Fung, I., Duke, C., Finch, K., Snook, K., Tseng, P., & Hernandez A. (2016) Ebola virus disease and social media: A systematic review. *American Journal of Infection Control*, 44(12): 1660–1671. doi:10.1016/j.ajic.2016.05.011

Gokalp, B., Karkin, N., & Çalhan, H. S. (2020) The political use of social networking sites in Turkey: A systematic literature analysis. In Boateng R. (Ed.) *Handbook of research on managing information systems in developing economies*. IGI Global, pp. 503–521.

Gonzalez-Padilla, D. A., & Tortolero-Blanco, L. (2020) Social media influence in the COVID-19 pandemic. *International Brazilian Journal of Urology*, 46(suppl. 1): 120–124. doi:10.1590/S1677-5538.IBJU.2020.S121

Holone, H. (2016) The filter bubble and its effect on online personal health information. *Croatian Medical Journal*, 57: 298–301.

Hsiang, S., Allen, D., Annan-Phan, S., Bell, K., Bolliger, I., Chong, T., Druckenmiller, H., Huang, L. Y., Hultgren, A., Krasovich, E., Lau, P., Lee, J., Rolf, E., Tseng, J., & Wu, T. (2020) The effect of large-scale anti-contagion policies on the COVID-19 pandemic. Nature, 584(7820), 262–267. doi: 10.1038/s41586-020-2404-8

Jahanbin, K., & Rahmanian, V. (2020) Using twitter and web news mining to predict COVID-19 outbreak. *Asian Pacific Journal of Tropical Medicine*, 13(8): 378–380.

Kaya, T. (2020) The changes in the effects of social media use on Cypriots due to COVID-19 pandemic. *Technology and Society*, 63: 101380. doi:10.1016/techsoc.2020.101380

Kaya, T., & Sağsan, M. (2015) The impact of tacit knowledge capacity on social media: An empirical research on physicians in north Cyprus. Proceedings of the 12th International Conference on Intellectual Capital, Knowledge Management & Organisational Learning (ICICKM 2015), 15-16 November 2015. Bangkok, Thailand.

Kaya, T., Sagsan, M., Medeni, T., Medeni, T., & Yildiz, M. (2020) Qualitative analysis to determine decision-makers' attitudes towards e-government services in a de-facto state. *Journal of Information and Communication Ethics and Society*, in press.

Kemp, S. (2020, 30th January) Digital 2020: 3.8 billion people use social media. We Are Social.

Kouzy, R., Abi Jaoude, J., Kraitem, A., El Alam, M. B., Karam, B., Adib, E., Zarka, J., Traboulsi, C., Akl, E. W., & Baddour, K. (2020) Coronavirus goes viral: Quantifying the COVID-19 misinformation epidemic on Twitter. *Cureus*, 13, 12(3): e7255. doi: 10.7759/cureus.7255. http://europepmc.org/abstract/MED/32292669

Li, C., Chen, L. J., Chen, X., Zhang, M., Pang, C. P., & Chen, H. (2020) Retrospective analysis of the possibility of predicting the COVID-19 outbreak from Internet searches and social media data, China, 2020. *European Surveillance*, 25: 2000199.

Lin, Y., Liu, C., & Chiu, Y. (2020) Google searches for the keywords of "wash hands" predict the speed of national spread of COVID-19 outbreak among 21 countries. *Brain, Behavior and Immunity*, 10: 1–3. doi:10.1016/j.bbi.2020.04.020. http://europepmc.org/abstract/MED/32283286

Maes, C., Schreurs, L., Van Oosten, J., & Vandenbosch, L. (2019) #(Me)too much? The role of sexualizing online media in adolescents' resistance towards the me-too-movement and acceptance of rape myths. *Journal of Adolescence*, 77: 59–69. doi:10.1016/j.adolescence.2019.10.005

Mak, I. W., Chu, C. M., Pan, P. C., You, M. G., & Chan, V. L. (2009) Long-term psychiatric morbidities among SARS survivors. *General Hospital Psychiatry*, 31: 318–326.

Medford, R. J., Saleh, S. N., Sumarsono, A., Perl, T. M., & Lehmann, C. U. (2020) An "infodemic": Leveraging high-volume twitter data to understand early public sentiment for the coronavirus disease 2019 outbreak. *Open Forum Infectious Diseases*, 7(7): ofaa258. doi:10.1093/ofid/ofaa258

Merchant, R. M. (2020) Evaluating the potential role of social media in preventive health care. *JAMA*, 323(5): 411–412.

Merchant, R. M., Asch, D. A., Crutchley, P., Ungar, L. H., Guntuku, S. C., Eichstaedt, J. C., Hill, S., Padrez, K., Smith, R. J., & Schwartz, H. A. (2019) Evaluating the predictability of medical conditions from social media posts. *PLoS One*, 14(6): e0215476. doi:10.1371/journal.pone.0215476.

Merchant, R. M., & Lurie, N. (2020, 23rd March) Social media and emergency preparedness in response novel coronavirus. *JAMA*, 323(20), 2011–2012.

Mheidy, N., & Fares, J. (2020) Leveraging media and health communication strategies to overcome the COVID-19 infodemic. *Journal of Public Health Policy*, 41(4): 410–420.

Nulty P., Theocharis Y., Popa S., Parnet O., & Benoit K. (2016) Social media and political communication in the 2014 elections to the European Parliament. *Election Studies*, 44: 429–444. doi:10.1016/j.electstud.2016.04.014

Paek, H. J., Hilyard, K., Freimuth, V. S., Barge, J. K., & Mindlin, M. (2008) Public support for government actions during a flu pandemic: Lessons learned from a statewide survey. *Health Promotion Practice*, 9(4): 60S–72S. doi:10.1177/1524 839908322114

Pariser, E. (2011) *The filter bubble: What the Internet is hiding from you*(pp. 294). New York: Penguin Press.

Park, H. W., Park, S., & Chong, M. (2020) Conversations and Medical News Frames on Twitter: Infodemiological Study on COVID-19 in South Korea. Journal of Medical Internet Research, 22(5), e18897. https://doi.org/10.2196/18897

Shah Z., Chu J., Feng B., Qaisar S., Ghani U., & Hassan Z. (2019) If you care, I care: Perceived social support and public engagement via SNSs during crises. *Technology in Society*, 59: 101195. doi:10.1016/j.techsoc.2019.101195

Singh, L., Bansal, S., Bode, L., Budak, C. , Vanasdall, R., Vrage, E. , & Wang, Y. (2020) A first look at COVID-19 information and misinformation sharing on Twitter. ArXiv.

Sharma, K. , Seo, S., Meng, C., Rambhata, S., & Liu, Y. (2020) COVID-19 on social media: Analysing misinformation in Twitter conversations. ArXiv.

Sharot, T. (2011) The Optimism Bias. New York, NY: Pantheon Books.

Smith, M., Broniatowski, D. A., Paul, M. J., & Dredze, M. (2016) Toward a real-time measurement of public epidemic awareness: monitoring influenza awareness through twitter. In: AAAI Spring Symposium on Observational Studies through Social Media and Other Human Generated Content. Washington, DC: George Washington University.

Statista. (2020) Global digital population as of January 2020. Retrieved from: https://www.statista.com/statistics/617136/digital-population-worldwide/

Van Bavel, J. J., Baicker, K., Boggio, P. S., Capraro, V., Cichocka, A., Cikara, M., Crockett, M. J., Crum, A. J., Douglas, K. M., Druckman, J. N., Drury, J., Dube, O., Ellemers, N., Finkel, E. J., Fowler, J. H., Gelfand, M., Han, S., Haslam, S. A., Jetten, J., Kitayama, S., Mobbs, D., Napper, L. E., Packer, D. J., Pennycook, G., Peters, E., Petty, R. E., Rand, D. G., Reicher, S. D., Schnall, S., Shariff, A., Skitka, L. J., Smith, S. S., Sunstein, C. R., Tabri, N., Tucker, J. A., Linden, S. V., Lange, P. V., Weeden, K. A., Wohl, M. J. A., Zaki, J., Zion, S. R., & Willer, R. (2020) Using social and behavioural science to support COVID-19 pandemic response. *Nature and Human Behaviour*, 4(5): 460–471. doi:10.1038/s41562-020-0884-z.E

Varghese S. (2019) How kids organized one of the world's largest climate protests. *Wired*. Retrieved from: https://www.wired.co.uk/article/climate-change-strike-protest-children-social-media

Viswanath, K., Lee, E. W. J., & Pinnameneni, R. (2020) We need the lens of equity in COVID-19 communication. *Health Communication*, 35(14): 1743–1746.

Wang, C., Pan, R., Wan, X., Tan, Y., Xu, L., & Ho, C. S., et al. (2020) Immediate psychological responses and associated factors during the initial stage of the 2019 coronavirus disease (COVID-19) epidemic among the general population in China. *International Journal of Environmental Research and Public Health*, 17: 1729.

Wang, P. W., Lu, W. H., Ko, N. Y., Chen, Y. L., Li, D. J., Chang, Y. P., & Yen, C. F. (2020) COVID-19-related information sources and the relationship with confidence in people coping with COVID-19: Facebook survey study in Taiwan. *Journal of Medical Internet Research*, 22(6): e20021. doi:10.2196/20021.

Wang Y., McKee M., Torbica A., & Stuckler D. (2019) Systematic literature review on the spread of health-related misinformation on social media. *Social Science and Medicine*, 240: 112552. doi:10.1016/j.socscimed.2019.112552

Chapter 7

Misleading Pandemic Information and the Public

COVID-19 dominated news coverage around the world for many months. There was also a huge amount of chatter online about it. While people understandably had a hunger for as much information as possible about this new virus and the latest status of the pandemic in their part of the world, there was also a great deal of false information in circulation (Allcott & Gentzkow, 2017; Allen et al., 2020; Frenkel et al., 2020). Differences of opinion emerged driven by partisanship and conspiracy theories. The strategies of governments often also appeared to change direction as new "science" was constantly being generated (Lewandowsky et al., 2012; Berinsky, 2017). Sometimes it was necessary for the true science to counter false claims (Swire & Ecker, 2018; Wood & Porter, 2018; Wittenberg & Berinsky, 2020).

In perpetrating effective health campaigns, it is essential that people know about and understand the relevant facts that derive from *bone fide* medical and scientific research and treatments. Although it is important to question the evidence to be confident in it, the circulation of misinformation simply causes confusion. It is important therefore for governments and health authorities to know how best to get knowledge across to the public and also to head off any false information before it gains traction. Active debunking of false claims forms one part of this process (Van der Linden et al., 2017).

Research during the pandemic confirmed the impact fake news can have on public confidence in authorities. Participants installed a browser extension tracking their online behaviour between survey waves. Participants' browsing behaviour was used to measure their exposure to fake news sites. Greater exposure to fake news online was related to lower trust in the mainstream media. Fakes news exposure was also associated with greater political trust. However, this effect was actually restricted for moderates and conservatives whereas it was for strong liberals, where it was also related to lower political trust (Ognyanova et al., 2020).

DOI: 10.4324/9781003274629-7

Bias in Media Coverage

Misleading and biased news coverage could result in the public being misinformed about the pandemic (Motta et al., 2020; Tasnim et al., 2020; Simonov et al., 2020). This could cause public misunderstanding of critical issues and might even undermine their ability or willingness to comply with behavioural restrictions implemented to protect the public at large (Mota et al., 2020).

False narratives about COVID-19, also referred to as "infodemics", grew at an astonishing rate during the pandemic (Kouzy et al., 2020). Rather than challenging the facts in order to test and verify them, this wave of misinformation more often undermined the aims of lockdowns and other restrictions on people's behaviour, by creating doubts about their purpose and veracity. Where the public no longer trust authorities and officialdom, they are rendered less willing to comply with the rules and regulations emanating from those sources. When this happens, the effectiveness of already damaging restrictions can be weakened or neutralised which means that the impact of the new virus could be magnified and that the pandemic persist for longer. As the pandemic lengthens, so its collateral damage also grows (Brennan et al., 2020; Mheidly & Fares, 2020; Orso, et al., 2020; Zandifar & Badrfam, 2020). Severe and extensive mental health consequences will feature among the most damaging of these.

Misleading messages about COVID-19 could lead to personally high-risk behaviour. The US President, Donald Trump, suggested at one point that if disinfectant could be used to destroy the virus (on surfaces) perhaps it could be drunk by people infected with the virus. During May and June 2020, 15 cases were reported of methanol poisoning caused by people drinking disinfectant (Liu et al., 2020; Reihani et al., 2021; Yamey & Gonsalves, 2020; Yip et al., 2020). Despite the reckless nature of some of these comments by politicians, some people were taken in by them (Chary et al., 2021; Finset et al., 2020).

The downside of COVID-19 infodemics is that they can distract public attention away from official advice about behavioural restrictions designed to offer protection against infection. Public health messages will combine advice on coping with COVID-19 and also maintaining a healthy lifestyle more generally, that will, in turn, offer some generic protection against illness. The mainstream news media have a major part to play in getting the right information out to people on a mass scale and in a timely way. The media invest considerable resources in news coverage that is supportive of broader public health objectives. Medical experts and scientists are the primary sources of specialist advice, but the media can make their complex messages more digestible for members of the public most of whom lack detailed understanding of medicine and science (Fauci et al., 2020).

The vast amount of information that flowed through the major mass media and the online networks that many people also engaged with, inevitably resulted in some degree of confusion and misunderstanding where different advice came from different sources. This was not simply a problem of information *overload*, but also one of informational *confusion*. When official advice was countered or challenged by discrepant information received by people through their online social networks, misunderstanding could occur that also resulted in unhelpful and potentially harmful consequences (The Lancet, 2020; Wu et al., 2020).

Research covering the first five months of 2020 reported, significant volumes of misinformation as being distributed by the mainstream media with frequent examples of poor fact-checking (Evanega et al., 2020). Exposure to media coverage of the pandemic was related to public fear levels. Furthermore, inaccurate or misleading information about COVID-19 was found to have persistent effects on people's mental health (Ahmad & Murad, 2020). While there were plenty of conspiracy theories in circulation online, mainstream news media by giving them further attention (Rovetta & Bhagavathula, 2020; Su et al., 2020; Wen et al., 2020; Zheng et al., 2020).

In the United States, trust in news about COVID-19 varied with people's political allegiances. Concerns among some people, especially Republican supporters, about so-called "fake news" meant that there was already an established distrust of most news media. This distrust did not exist to the same degree or extent among Democratic Party supporters. Yet, the widespread mistrust of the media clearly undermined their ability to play a constructive role in helping the authorities to impose effective behavioural restrictions (Bunker, 2020; Okan et al., 2020).

Conspiracy Theories

Another phenomenon that had the potential to sow further seeds of confusion were a range of so-called "conspiracy theories" that emerged, mostly via websites, about the causes and effects of COVID-19, about the efficacy of certain treatments using existing drugs and other substances and about the safety of new vaccines that were being developed to protect people against this new virus.

One theory claimed that the SARS-CoV-2 originated in a science laboratory in China where it was being developed as a bioweapon. Other theories focused on treatments and cures for the new virus and argued for alternative medical treatments over conventional medicine (McLaughlin, 2020). None of these theories could be substantiated. Their emergence derived from a need for people to offer explanations for new phenomena, especially when they posed a threat (Leman & Cinnirella, 2013; Drinkwater et al., 2012; Dagnall, Drinkwater, Parker, Donovan & Parton, 2015;

van Prooijen, 2018). Conspiracies might also be created by people seeking to cause mischief through the spread of false accusations or alternative "truths". Some research has linked this behaviour to psychopathology, that is, they are the work of unstable personalities (Swami et al., 2017).

Conspiract Theories – Explanations

Conspiracy theories present explanations of events that reject official reasons or causes and frame them instead as disguised plots by powerful forces to influence and shape the mindsets and behaviour of peoplefor their prsonal benefit (Bale, 2007). Thus, apparently altruistic, constructive and beneficial actions ostensibly presented as being in everyone's best interests are, in fact, nothing of the sort. The "benefits" are fabricated or will be much less than indicated, and the real reasons behind the actions are to further the vested interests of the few (Douglas et al., 2016). Conspiracies have been part of everyday public debate for a long time, but in the 21st century, the rapid evolution of communications technologies has facilitated the rate at which they spread (van Prooijen & Douglas, 2017). In fact, the Internet, bogging and micro-blogging and social networking sites have all acted as catalysts for conspiracy theories, some of which would not have taken off without these ubiquitous communications systems (Douglas et al., 2016).

Conspiracy theories are especially likely to occur during times of crisis. Emergency and uncertainty. These might inlcude financial meltdowns, natural disasters, terrorist attacks, war, as well as pandemics. One purpose they serve for those signing up to them is that they offer an explanation for unexplained events and a model of understanding in times of great uncertainty (van Prooijen & Douglas, 2017). It seems, in fact, that the greater the uncertainty of a crisis situation, the more people are willing to embrace theories that might seem plausible on the surface, but are untrue. When confronted with uncertainty, human beings will naturally experience anxiety and this will heighten their senses to risk, which they may begin to see everywhere. If this uncertainty prevails, it can create considerable psychological discomfort and our response is to find coping mechanisms based in explanations of external circumstances over which we feel we have no control (Bale, 2007; van Prooijen, 2019). Even though a conspiracy theory is not grounded in fact and presents a wholly or mostly false or mislieading narrative, it does servethe purpose of giving anxious people something to hang on to to explain what is happening to them and the world around them.

Another factor that comes into play on these occasions is the degree to which the public trust their government and others in authority. If this trust is generally weak or beecomes temporarily compromised because of the behaviour of those in power in a partcular moment in a crisis, then a climate is created in which conspiracy theories can flourish. If you combine generalised anxiety borne out of uncertainty stemming from an national crisis with an underlying lack of trust in government, the challenge for government in controlling the public's behaviour becomes even greater. Scientific evidence has emerged that it is associated with political cynicism, a distrust of authority and generalised feelings of alienation from the mainstream in governance (Bruder et al., 2013; Chichocka et al., 2016).

Conspiracy theorists will feed off this public distrust of authorities and offer an outward air of integrity which then makes their theories more palatable even though they may not always appear to be plausible. Under different circumstances, many of people would probably reflect on conspiracies and question their plausibility, which might be easy to find when scratching beneath the surface with the explanations thet provide for crisis situations. In times of real uncertainty, however, emotional reactions might run high and overpower cognitive rationality leading to a less critical acceptance of outlandish alternative worldviews (Oleksy et al., 2021).

One approach to the study of the impact of "fake news" or "misinformation" about COVID-19 on what people think about this virus, the pandemic and the different interventions deployed by governments to protect their populations has been to investigate whether the COVID-19 news exerts similar influences to those observed for political fake news. News stories that appear genuine and authentic but are in fact made up can shape public opinion about specific events, issues, institutions and organisations or individuals (e.g., politicians) that are based on inaccurate and fabricated representations of those entities (Lazer et al., 2018).

As we have seen already, in some settings, including the consumption of mainstream news, the reception of news narratives and their "truths" can be mediated by partisanship. If a news narrative is judged to be supportive of their pre-existing beliefs on the part of its consumers, they will accept uncritically the things it tells them. If the narrative is judged to present views or impressions that run contrary to the individual's own perspectives, it will be rejected. (Kahan et al., 2017; Shin & Thorson, 2017).

Evidence has emerged that fake news stories and conspiracy theories can circulate and become credible as explanation of COVID-19 because of a degree of complacency and lack of due attention to detail on the part of media audiences. When American adults were presented with narratives about the coronavirus and asked to discern true from false content, their accuracy in doing so depended upon whether the researchers had directed their attention towards critiquing the information given or whether they were simply asked to decide whether they would share a news story with others on their social media site. When people's attention was steered towards thinking carefully about whether a news story was credible and accurate, they took a more forensic approach to judging it. Otherwise, left to their own devices or encouraged to think about a news story in a different way, they did not. Inserting a reminder to people to consider the accuracy of the story, regardless of the original orientation towards the story (that is, judging its accuracy or simply its likely appeal to others), also increased significantly the tendency of social media users to think more carefully about its informational veracity (Pennycook et al., 2020).

The Role of Different Media in the Spread of Conspiracies

The mass media and online social networks represent major information sources for the public. The mainstream news – as we have seen already – played a significant role in circulating regular updates about the status of the new virus in different communities and of medical and scientific developments designed to combat its spread. Growing numbers of people also turn to the so-called "social media", that is, microblogging sites (e.g., Twitter) and social networking sites (e.g., Facebook, Instagram, YouTube) as information sources. Conspiracies will generally be challenged in the mainstream, but frequently find communities of support in the online world where public chatter does not have to pass through the restrictive editorial gatekeeping characteristic of the major mass media.

A documentary film called *Plandemic* was released on 4th May 2020 and spread rapdily via social media such as Twitter and YouTube. The film examined a number of conspiracy theories about COVID-19 concerning its origins, nature and infectivity and also questioned the effficacy and safety or vaccines. At a time when the pandemic was spreading rapdily around the world, leading many countries to severely restrict the everyday activities of their populations, it was imperative that accurate and timely information could be circulated to encourage people to comply with behavioural restrictions and to accept and act up the information being provided by the authorities. Any information campaign that worked against this agenda could be disruptive and potentially harmful. Despite its production values and appearance of being informed by experts, *Plandemic* promoted unsubstantiated claims about COVID-19 and the agenda behind the rapid deelopment of vaccines (Alba, 2020). It attempted to sow public distrust in the authorities and mistrust in the information they provided. The documentary played on many public uncertainties to create greater confusion and to disrupt legitimate attempts to bring the virus under contro (Frenkel et al., 2020).

By the 7th May, the film was removed by YouTube because it denied or countered World Health Organization guidance and advice and also breached the codes of many social media platforms. A further instalment of the film was released on 18th August 2020, but largely failed to attract much attention and was mostly blocked from social media platforms. Analysis of behaviour on Twitter found that the film continued to have influence on public ideas about COVID-19 and associared vaccines. It also encouraged personalised attacks on specific experts who had attained a public profiles during the pandemic and key spokespersons advising the public about it. There was also a wave of tweets that attempted to counter the effects of this documentary, directly challenging its misinformation, as well as monitoring appearances by various conspiracy theories online to challlenge them through fact-checking exercises and finding out who were the people and organisations behind this misleading narratives (Lapin, 2020).

In terms of Twitter chatter about COVID conspiracies, this increased dramatically over the first week or so after the initial part was released in May 2020, before falling away very quickly. This chatter was both supprtive of the conspiracies presented in *Plandemic* and were negative towards it. In fact, even though there were anti-government sentiments in wide circlation after the film's initial release, these sentiments had already been prevalent before then. Tweets targeted specific personalities more after the film's release, but opinion on the site was polarised between the film's supporters and opponents (Kearney et al., 2020).

Another analysis of Twitter activity about this theory showed that just over one third of a sample of tweets (35%) promulgated this conspiracy theory and around one third (32%) denounced it. The remaining tweets made reference to the issue without presenting a firm opinion or position on the issue (33%). Two-thirds (65%) of the tweets about this theory, however, derived from people who had identified as non-supporters of the theory. Only a minority of those tweeting about the theory apparently believed it, and yet they were still quite vocal and attracted the attention of many others. What this study showed was that the views of the few can become significantly magnified on sites such as Twitter and even though much of the comment might be negative, it nonetheless allows a false news story to gain considerable traction and public attention (Ahmed et al., 2020).

A survey of 2501 adults in England and found that half (50%) showed evidence of COVID-19 conspiracy thinking. One in four (25%) showed some level of endorsement. 15% showed consistent endorsemnt and 10% were firmly signed up to these theories. Higher levels of conspiracy theory endorsement were associated with lower levels of compliance with government guidelines, less willingness to take antibody tests or to get vaccinated. Conspiracy theory adherents tended to be more suspcious and paranoid and engaged in sustaining a climate of conspiracy (Freeman et al., 2020).

Fake News, Conspiracy Theories and Public Raction

One of the main reasons why the identification and control of unproven or false information about COVID-19 was so important was illustrated by research showing that exposure to this material could trigger unhelpful psychological reactions in populations. Misinformation about COVID-19 can generate misconceptions about the virus and fear responses that are unpleasant and capable of undermining behavioural compliance with non-pharmaceutical interventions. When people sign up to these theories, they then seem less likely to engage with health protective behaviours as recommended by government and health authorities (Allington et al., 2020).

Perceived threat and ability to cope with the pandemic are important reactions among members of the public because these mental states will also shape people's behaviour. Misinformation about COVID-19 can generate misconceptions about the virus and fear responses that are unpleasant and capable of undermining behavioural compliance with non-pharmaceutical interventions. A study of people in the United States, Kuwait and South Korea found that perceived threat from COVID-19 was greater among those who sought out more information about it from various sources, and especially from social media. Greater perceived threat from COVID-19 and a stronger perceived ability to cope with it were also positively related to propensity to adhere to social distancing rules. Paying more attention to relevant information sources also improved people's knowledge about what was going on and this also strengthened their willingness to comply with social distancing restrictions. These effects were sgnificant in all the countries investigated, but were strongest in the United States (Al-Hasan et al., 2020).

Evidence emerged from health-care workers that the tendency to believe in conspiracy theories about the novel coronanvirus such as it was intentionally developed in a laboratory was closely associated with greater propensity to experience syptoms of psychological distress and anxiety (Chen et al., 2020).

Research carried out with a nationwide sample of adults (aged 18+) in the United Kingdom in the final week of March 2020 found that a significant minority of people (46%) clamed to have come across false or misleading information about COVID-19. The youngest respondents, aged 18 to 24 years (58%) were much more likely than the oldest aged 65+ (33%) to say this. Most of those seeing misinformation (55%) did nothing about it, while minorities said they checked details with the BBC's website (15%), with family and friends (13%) or with a fact-checking source (10%) (Ofcom, 2020, April).

Social Media Use and Belief in Conspiracy Theories

Conspiracy theories are important in understanding public compliance and non-compliance with behavioural restrictions of the kind that are imposed in pandemic lockdowns and also in relation to the uptake of behaviour designed to combat the pandemic such as getting vaccinated. There is mounting evidence that people who believe in conspiracy theories exhibit greater reluctance to adopt health-protective behaviours. This phenomenon often undermines campaigns to persuade people to get vaccinated (Grebe & Nattrass, 2011; Dunn et al., 2017). This evidence has led some researchers to surmise that similar conspiracy theory effects could impact upon people's willingness to get vaccinated against COVID-19 (Allington & Dhavan, 2020; Freeman et al., 2020).

Conspiracy theories can be especially prevalent on major social media sites such as Facebook and YouTube. Users of these sites have found them to be effective platforms for the dissemination of misinformation (Buchanan & Beckett, 2014; Pathak et al., 2015; Oi-Yee Li et al., 2020). While some countries impose regulations on public broadcasters to guard against unfounded conspiracy theories, social media platforms are not controlled in the same way. They have largely escaped local and national regulatory systems and the codes of practice they impose. This means that misleading content can flow freely on sites such as Facebook and Twitter (Brennan et al., 2020).

Research then emerged to indicated that unregulated social media platforms can present risks to health campaigns when they publish theories that undermine the behaviours these campaigns try to cultivate. A series of surveys by Daniel Allington and his colleagues found that COVID-19 conspiracy theory beliefs tended to discourage COVID-19 health protective behaviour uptake. Furthermore, the propensity to hold conspiracy beliefs was found to be positively related to frequency of use of social media sites (Allington et al., 2020).

Conspiracy theories that were found to be particularly strengthened by more regular social media use included the belief that the coronavirus may not exist, that it is not as lethal as some reports claim and that its symptoms may not even be caused by the coronavirus. Across three separate surveys, however, this research did not always confirm these findings. In one survey, for example, frequency of checking on your social media site for COVID-related updates was unrelated to willingness to adopt some health-protective behaviours against COVID-19, but was related to a weaker propensity to avoid seeing other people outside the home or not to remain at home to work even though it was possible to do so. What did become fairly apparent from across all the surveys conducted here was a general tendency for greater social media use (especially when linked to tracking COVID-19 updates) to be significantly associated with greater belief in conspiracy theories about the novel coronavirus and for holding those beliefs to be significantly linked to a weaker willingness to comply with health protective behaviours to combat this new disease.

Countering Conspiracies

Misinformation can produce public misunderstanding about COVID-19 and that in turn might result in inappropriate coping behaviour or even outright rejection of behavioural restrictions designed to combat the spread of the virus. Misinformation effects had been studied widely even before the pandemic. Tackling this problem generally entails more than simply

rejecting fake stories or comsiracy theories as wrong and involves produ-
cing and circulating counter-messages that set the record straight by systematically debunking false truths. This approahc can be effective, but
adherents to conspiracy theories about major societal events can in turn
generate further arguments to justify their own position and resist any influences of misinformation debunking messages (Chan et al., 2017).

Studies or previous pandemics had shown that media coverage of them
could inform people of the nature of the disease, how to catch it, what its
symptoms might be and what to do if infected. Media coverage of new
disease outbreaks, however, can also have other effects that might not always be anticipated and are not necessarily helpful to public health authorities seeking to mobilise populations effectively to play their part in
tackling the spread of an infectious disease. Sometimes, media coverage
intended to help people can also give rise to exaggerated perceptions of
personal risk and disproportionate anxiety reactions. Such responses can
work against getting people always to do the right thing during a pandemic
or when coming out of it (Garfin et al., 2020).

This phenomenon of misinformation resilience was observed with earlier
health issues. A Zika outbreak in Brazil was explained by an untrue claims
that it was being spread by genetically modified mosquitos, a view that
persisted despite scientists saying there was no evidence to support it
(Heukelbach et al., 2016). Resistance to vaccination against measles,
mumps and rubella has persisted in the United States and parts of Europe
despite the research supprting the claim that this vaccine can trigger autism
being discredited.

In many cases, adherents to these conspiracy theories are harmless, but
sometimes they are not. A potentially damaging spin-off from them can
occur when members of the wider population begin to question whether to
take a vaccine because conspiracy theorists have spread untrue stories about
its safety. It is possible to counter this phenomenon and even to inoculate
people cognitively against unfounded conspiracy theories.

The problem is that the more widely these conspiracy theories spread, the
more traction they gain among believers (McCauley & Jacques, 1979; van
Prooijen & Douglas, 2017). If these theories are the only ones available,
then they are more likely to be believed. Conspiracy theories can also
generate animosity towards other groups when they are perceived as responsible (Marchlewska et al., 2019). These theories can prove to be a
major problem when they discourage people from following scientific advice once it has become available. This phenomenon is particularly relevant
with vaccine use where "anti-vaxxer" campaigns discourage people from
taking advantage of these preventative treatments.

Such fake news stories were particularly unhelpful at a time of an international health crisis when rapidly changing circumstances and government interventions were confusing enough for ordinary people to keep up

with. Such fakery was sometimes based on ill-informed rumour and mischief making and sometimes by misinterpretations of the facts underpinned by exaggerated risk perceptions and fears.

This misinformation might be filtered by gatekeepers in the mainstream media, but mass audiences can be easily reached via micro-blogging and social media sites. It therefore become incumbent on the companies that operate the biggest online social networks and search engines to help to combat the spread of unhelpful misinformation that undermines the messaging of governments. The actions of these companies can potentially have a big impact on combating counter-productive fakery (Hartley & Vu, 2020). The need for proactivity by major social media companies was underlined by research showing that in the presence of initially confused government messaging about the new coronavirus and public risk, fake news stories were quickly able to take hold as people sought greater certainty (Moscadelli et al., 2020).

Countering misinformation can be difficult when the arguments that surround it have been extensively rehearsed by their supporters along with their reasons for rejecting counterarguments presented as an antidote (Lewandowsky et al., 2012; Lewandowsky et al., 2015). The complexities of memory processes mean that simply lining up counterarguments will not invariaby be sufficient to debunk misinformation because even the counterarguments will cause the original misinformed arguments to be rehearsed and considered again. Which message or position is adopted will depend upon the relative degree of elaboration of arguments constructed around it (Kahneman, 2003; Petty & Brinol, 2010; Arceneaux et al., 2013).

If any new arguments surface to support preexisting misinformation, even when they also are not reinforced by scientific evidence, their preence might still strengthen conspiracy or fake narratives and reduce the impact of debunking arguments (Arceneaux, 2012; Johnson-Laird, 2013). To be effective therefore, debunking messages must be powerful and compelling and overshadow any misinformation circulating at the same time (Schwarz et al., 2007; Jerit, 2008). Counter messages grounded in simplistic arguments that misinformation is incorrect will not be sufficiently compelling to prove effective (Johnson & Siefert, 1994).

A detailed analysis of relevant published studies found that merely repeating misinformation messages eventually failed to yield dividends and would not striengthen their original arguments. Yet, in the presence of debunking messages, the misinformation these messages were designed to weaken might become reinforced if those debunking messages triggered new elaboration of reasons to continue supporting conspiracy theories or other false or unsubstantiated explanations of specific phenomena (Chan et al., 2017).

In one interesting intervention, researchers got participants to critique a non-COVID new story in terms of its accuracy and believability before being given the opportunity to forward on misinformation about COVID-19 that had been circulating on social media sites. Control participants were not given this or any other intervention. Afterwards, those who had critiqued a different news story were nearly three times more likely than controls to want to share verified, truthful information rather than false information about COVID-19 (Pennycook et al., 2020). Further research showed that countering conspiracy theories might also be important in a health context given that adherents to COVID-19 conspiracy theories were less likely to maintain health-protective behaviours such as hand-washing and social distancing (Allington et al., 2020).

COVID Conspiracies: Conclusions

Conspiracies surrounding COVID-19 have provided explanations for the virus outbreak itself and its genesis and also a perspective on the efficacy and safety of COVID-related vaccines. The virus is widely believed to have originated in Wuhan, China which is where it was first recorded. Exactly where it come from is less certain. One explanation suggested that it circulated in thw wet markets in Wuhan where many exotic ainimal species were sold as food or for health and well-being products. Another (non-conspiracy) theory was that it originated in a science laboratory that secialised in research into viruses of this kind.

One conspiracy theory circulated that it was deliberately developed by scientists in China, not to further scientific and medical knowledge, but as a biological weapon. The Chinese government, meanwhile, orchestrated its own conspiracy theory that the novel coronasvirus did not originate in their country at all, but was brought in by foreign visitors. Another conspiracy theory believed that COVID-19 was caused by 5G mobile phone signals and was an attempt by large businesses and government to control people's behaviour.

So widespread and so serious were emergent conspiracy theories, even during the early phases on the pandemic that the World Health Organization was promoted to to issue a statement which defined misleading chatter, which was spreadin like wildfire via the Internet, as an "infodemic" that posed every bit as much trouble for the world as the pandemic itself. The online world was permeated with fake news stories about the origins of the coronavirus, how it spread, its symptoms and how it could be treated. It also mischieviously attributed all kinds of false motives to governments, big corporations and other powerful organisations in relation to the pandemic (Pennycook et al., 2020; Van Bavel et al., 2020).

Analysis of conspiracy theories has found that they can take the form of a generalised orientation or position towards the world leading to conspiracies to be perceived in many different contexts and settings (Bruder et al., 2013). Having a generally suspicious view of the world where goverments and authorities are universally distrusted can result in sceptics signing up to disparate conspiracy theories that seem to have nolongical connection to each other (Wood et al., 2012).

Other conspiracy theorists tend to fixate on a single issue and persistently challenge government policies about it. In some instances, such challenges derive from a broad distrust of government and on other occasions it might be linked specifcially to opposition to the political party in government. In other words, if a theory was espoused by your ingroup, you support it, but if comes from an outgroup, it automatically gets rejected and displaced by some else, no matter how good the original theory might have been (Cichocka et al., 2015).

In the context of COVID-19, conspiracy theorists proposed that the virus was either a hoax or was developed as a biological weapon. Each of these theories was found to have different social consequences and could generate different reactions from people in terms of their own attitudes towards the virus and the behavioural restrictions associated with it. In one instance, the existence of the virus was challenged, despite the widespread evidence that large numbers of people appeared to be getting ill from it. In the other case, there was no disute about the fact of the virus, but its origins were described in a very specific fashion which had some credibility but very little hard evidence to substantiate it (Imhoff & Lamberty, 2020). Conspiracy theories might present the virus as a threat, but not in the way popularly defined. As such, these theories often invited people to adopt a contrary position to the advice of government and also brought their adherents into direct dispute with scientists. Some of these alternative theories were simply a reaction to government and stemmed from a deep distrust in the authorities and politicians.

In other cases, they represented a form of anti-science which rejected existing scentific facts and even rejected science per se (van der Linden, 2015; van Prooijen, 2019). More specifically, many medical conspiracy theories rejected vaccines not simply on the grounds of their efficacy and safety, but also because they believed they were driven by a hidden agenda of public control (Bogart et al., 1999; Setbon & Raude, 2010; Lamberty & Imhoff, 2018).

These theories posed a real threat in themselves to the exent that they persuaded sections of the public not to comply with governments' behavioural restrictions designed to slow the spread of the virus or to accept forms of treatment or protection through vaccines. The only potentially positive consequence of conspiracy theories is that they can stop the public from blindly following government advice without ever questioning its validity and efficacy (Swami & Coles, 2010). Hence, by raising the possibility of an alternative worldview, no matter how outlandish it may seem, conspiracy theorising raises the possibility that the government might not always be on tp of a crisis, do not always get things right and might not always be totally honest with people.

Problems arise when conspiracy theorists themselves are notivated by mischief making and causing trouble for the sake of it. Sometimes also these theories are driven by hostility on the part of extremist activists towards the political mainstream or towards specific institutions to which they are opposed and about which they have a grievance (Bilewicz & Sędek, 2015; Jolley et al., 2019). In these contexts, conspiracy theories are driven by a need to orchestrate widespread reaction to the actions of targets of such hostility (Jolley & Paterson, 2020).

These theories also feed another public appetite to find sources to blame for a crisis, especially one where they have personally suffered negative consequences. In a situation in which most people feel they have no control and where future uncertainty is high, feelings can run high. In the pandemic, many people were affected not because they became ill or knew someone who had, but because of the disruption caused to their lives by government interventions.

Although these interventions were well-intentioned, there were debates about whether the right interventions had bene deployed in the nest way at the right times. There were questions raided about what was already known in advance aboyt how to deal with situations such as the COVID-19 crisis and whether they ought to have been more advance preparation and protection in place.

When the world spirals out of control, psychologists invoke the teoriy of compensatory control whereby people try to find explanation for uncertain circumstances to make some sense out of what is happening. This process inevitably results in part in peple looking for someone to hold responsible where things have obviously gone wrong (Kay et al., 2009).

In the scramble to find explanations fast, all available theories might be perused including ones that are not based in the truth. When people feel that their lives are spiralling out of control, they can either sink completely and go under or confront the challenges throw at them and try to understand them in order to find effective solutions. Conspsiracy theories can provide available and convenient explanations of events in crises when no other sensible explanations are immediately to hand. It is incumbent upon those in authority therefore to be aware of this psychological phenomenon so that it can devise a strategy for countering it. This means that if government takes the decision to take control over people lives to protect by closing down society and the national economy, it must not simply offer compensation, but also demonstrate a united front among political leaders and their advisers to produce consistent messaging to explain to the public precisely and comprehensively the nature of the problems facing everyone.

References

Ahmad, A. R., & Murad, H. R. (2020) The impact of social media on panic during the covid-19 pandemic in Iraqi Kurdistan: Online questionnaire study. *Journal of Medical Internet Research*, 22(5): e19556.

Ahmed, W., Vidal-Alaball, J., Downing, J., & Lopez, S. F. (2020) COVID-19 and the 5G conspiracy theory: Social network analysis of twitter data. *Journal of Medical Internet Research*, 22(5).

Alba, D. (2020, 9th May) *Virus conspiracists elevate a new champion. The New York Times.* Retrieved from: https://www.nytimes.com/2020/05/09/technology/plandemic-judy-mikovitz-coronavirus

Al-Hasan, A., Khuntia, J., & Yim, D. (2020) Threat, coping, and social distance adherence during COVID-19: Cross-continental comparison using an online cross-sectional survey. *Journal of Medical Internet Research*, 22(11): e23019. doi:10.2196/23019.

Allcott, H., & Gentzkow, M. (2017) Social media and fake news in the 2016 election. *Journal of Economic Perspectives*, 31: 211–236.

Allen, J., Howland, B., Mobius, M., Rothschild, D., & Watts, D. J. (2020) Evaluating the fake news problem at the scale of the information ecosystem. *Science Advances*, 1: eaay3539.

Allington, D., & Dhavan, N. (2020) The relationship between conspiracy beliefs and compliance with public health guidance with regard to COVID-19. Working paper published by the Center for Countering Digital Hate, London. Retrieved from: https://kclpure.kcl.ac.uk/portal/files/127048253/Allington_and_Dhavan_2020.pdf

Allington, D., Duffy, B., Wesseley, S., Dhavan, N., & Rubin, J. K. (2020) Health-rpotective behaviour, social media usage and conspiracy belief during the COVID-19 public health emergency. *Psychological Medicine*, 1–7. doi:10.1017/S003329172000224X

Arceneaux, K., Johndon, M., & Cryderman, J. (2013) Communication, persuasion, and the conditioning value of selective exposure: Like minds may unite and divide but they mostly tune out. *Journal of Political Communication*, 30: 213–231.

Arceneaux, K. (2012) Cognitive biases and the strengths of olitical arguments. *American Journal of Political Science*, 56(2): 271–285.

Bale, J. M. (2007) Political paranoia vs. political realism: On distinguishing between bogus conspiracy theories and genuine conspiratorial politics. *Patterns of Prejudice*, 41(1): 45–60.

Berinsky, A. J. (2017) Rumors and health care reform: Experiments in political misinformation. *British Journal of Political Science*, 47: 241–262.

Bilewicz, M., & Sędek, G. (2015) Conspiracy stereotypes. Their sociopsychological antecedents and consequences. In M. Bilewicz, A. Cichocka, & W. Soral (Eds.) *The psychology of conspiracy*. London, UK: Routledge.

Bogart, L. M., Wagner, G., Galvan, F. H., & Banks, D. (1999) Conspiracy beliefs about HIV are related to antiretroviral treatment nonadherence among African American men with HIV. *Journal of Acquired Immune Deficiency Syndromes*, 53(5): 648.

Brennan, J. S., Simon, F. M., & Nielsen, R. K. (2020) Beyond (mis)representation: Visuals in COVID-19 misinformation. *The International Journal of Press/Politics*, 26(1).

Bruder, M., Haffke, P., Neave, N., Nouripanah, N., & Imhoff R. (2013) Measuring individual differences in generic beliefs in conspiracy theories across cultures: Conspiracy mentality questionnaire. *Frontiers in Psychology*, 4: 225. doi:10.3389/fpsyg.2013.00225

Buchanan, R., & Beckett, R. D. (2014) Assessment of vaccination-related information for consumers available on Facebook. *Health Information and Libraries Journal*, 31(3): 227–234.

Bunker, D. (2020) Who do you trust? The digital destruction of shared situational awareness and the COVID-19 infodemic. *International Journal of Information Management*, 55: 102201– 102201. doi:10.1016/j.ijinfomgt.2020.102201

Chan, M. S., Jones, C. R., Jamieson, K. H., & Albarracin, D. (2017) Debunking: A meta-analysis of the psychological effiacy of messages countering misinformation. *Psychological Science*, 28(11): 1531–1546.

Chary, M. A., Overbeek, D. L., Papadimoulis, A., Sheroff, A., & Burns, M. M. (2021) Geospatial correlation between COVID-19 health misinformation and poisoning with household cleaners in the Greater Boston Area. *Clinical Toxicology (Philadelphia)*, 59(4): 320–325. doi:10.1080/15563650.2020.1811297

Chen, X., Zhang, S. X., Jahanshahi, A. A., Alvarez-Risco, A., Dai, H., Li, J., & Ibarra, V. G. (2020) Belief in a COVID-19 conspiracy theory as a predictor of mental and well-being of health-care workers in Ecuador: Cross-sectional study. *JMIR Public Health Surveillance*, 6(3): e20737. doi:10.2196/20737

Chichocka, A., Marchlowski, M., Golec de Zavala, A., & Olechowski, M. (2016) 'They will not control us': Ingroup positivity and belief in intergroup conspiracies. *British Journal of Psychology*, 107(3): 556–576.

Cichocka, A., Marchlewska, M., Golec de Zavala, A., Olechowski, M. (2015) "They will not control us": Ingroup positivity and belief in intergroup conspiracies. *British Journal of Psychology*, 107(3): 556–576. doi:10.1111/bjop.12158

Dagnall, N., Drinkwater, K., Parker, A., Denovan, A., & Parton, M. (2015) "Conspiracy Theory and Cognitive Style: A Worldview." Frontiers in Psychology 6:206. https://doi.org/10.3389/fpsyg.2015.00206

Denovan, A., Dagnall, N., Drinkwater, K., & Parker, A. (2018) Latent profile analysis of schizotypy and paranormal belief: Associations with probabilistic reasoning performance. *Frontiers in Psychology*, 9, Article 35. doi:10.3389/fpsyg.2018.00035

Douglas, K. M., Sutton, R. M., Callan, M. J., Dawtry, R. J., & Harvey, A. J. (2016) Someone is pulling the strings: Hypersensitive agency detection and belief in conspiracy theories. *Thinking & Reasoning*, 22(1): 57–77. doi:10.1080/13546783.2015.1051586

Drinkwater, K., Dagnall, N., & Parker, A. (2012) Reality testing, conspiracy theories and paranormal beliefs. *Journal of Parapsychology*, 76(1): 57–77.

Dunn, A. G., Surian, D., Leask, J., Dey, A., Mandl, K. D., & Coiera, E. (2017) Mapping information exposure on social media to explain differences in HPV vaccine coverage in the United States. *Vaccine*, 35: 3033–3040.

Evanega, S., Lynas, M., Adams, J., & Smolenyck, K. (2020) *Coronavirus misinformation: Quantifying sources and themes in the COVID-19 "infodemic"*. Ithaca: Cornell University.

Fauci, A. S., Lane, H. C., & Redfield, R. R. (2020) Covid-19 – navigating the uncharted. *New England Journal of Medicine*, 382(13): 1268–1269.

Finset, A., Bosworth, H., Butow, P., Gulbrandsen, P., Hulsman, R. L., Pieterse, A. H., Street, R., Tschoetschel, R., & van Weert, J. (2020) Effective health communication – a key factor in fighting the COVID-19 pandemic. *Patient Education and Counseling*, 103(5): 873–876. doi:10.1016/j.pec.2020.03.027

Freeman, D., Waite, F., Rosebrock, L., Petit, A., Causier, C., East, A., Jenner, L., Teale, A. L., Carr, L., Mulhall, S., Bold, E., & Lambe, S. (2020) Coronavirus conspiracy beliefs, mistrust, and compliance with government guidelines in England. *Psychological Medicine*, 52(2): 251–263. doi:10.1017/s0033291720001890

Frenkel, S., Alba, D., & Zhong, R. (2020) *Surge of virus misinformation stumps Facebook and Twitter. The New York Times.* https://www.nytimes.com/2020/03/08/technology/coronavirus-misinformation-social-media.html

Garfin, D. R., Silver, R. C., & Holman, E. A. (2020) The novel coronavirus (COVID-19) outbreak: Amplification of public health consequences by media exposure. *Health Psychology*, 39(5): 355–357.

Goertzel, T. (2010) Conspiracy theories in science. *European Molecular Biology Organization Reports*, 11: 493–499.

Grebe, E., & Nattrass, N. (2011) AIDS conspiracy beliefs and unsafe sex in Cape Town. *AIDS and Behavior*, 16(3): 761–773.

Hartley, K., & Vu, M. K. (2020) Fighting fake news in the COVID-19 era: Policy insights from an equilibrium model. *Policy Science*, 9: 1–24.

Heukelbach, J., Alencar, C. H., Kelvin, A. A., de Oliveira, W. K., & Pamplona de Góes Cavalcanti, L. (2016) Zika virus outbreak in Brazil. *Journal of Infection in Developing Countries*, 10(2): 116–120. doi:10.3855/jidc.8217

Imhoff, R., & Lamberty, P. (2020) A bioweapon or a hoax? The link between distinct conspiracy beliefs about the coronavirus disease (COVID-19) outbreak and pandemic behavior. *Social Psychological and Personality Science*, 11(8): 1110–1118. doi:10.1177/1948550620934692

Jerit, J. (2008) Issue framing and engagement: Rhetorical strategy in public policy debates. *Political Behaviour*, 30: 1–24.

Johnson, H. M., & Siefert, C. M. (1994) Sources of the continued influence effect: When misinformation in memory affects later references. *Journal of Experimental Psychology: Human Learning, Memory and Cognition*, 20: 1420–1436.

Johnson-Laird, P. N. (2013) Mental models and consistency. In B. Gawronski, & S. Fritz (Eds.) *Cognitive consistency: A unifying concept in social psychology* (pp. 225–244). New York, NY: Guilford Press.

Jolley, D., Meleady, R., & Douglas, K. M. (2019) Exposure to intergroup conspiracy theories promotes prejudice which spreads across groups. *British Journal of Psychology*, 111(6): 1–19. doi:10.1111/bjop.12385

Jolley, D., & Paterson, J. L. (2020) Pylons ablaze: Examining the role of 5G COVID-19 conspiracy beliefs and support for violence. *British Journal of Social Psychology*, 58(3): 628–640.

Kahan, D. M., Peters, E., Dawson, E., & Slovic, P. (2017) Motivated numeracy and enlightened self-government. *Behavioural Public Policy*, 1: 54–86.

Kahneman, D. (2003) A perspective on judgment and choice: Mapping bounded rationality. *American Psychologist*, 58: 697–720.

Kay, A. C., Whitson, J. A., Gaucher, D., & Galinsky, A. D. (2009) Compensatory control: Achieving order through the mind, our institutions, and the heavens. *Current Directions in Psychological Science*, 18(5): 264–268. doi:10.1111/j.1467-8721.2009.01649.x

Kearney, M. D., Chiang, S. C., & Massey, P. M. (2020, 9th October) The Twitter origins and evolution of the COVID-19 "plandemic" conspiracy theory. Mis\information Review. Retrieved from: https://misinforeview.hks.harvard.edu/article/the-twitter-origins-and-evolution-of-the-covid-19-plandemic-conspiracy-theory/

Kouzy, R., Abi Jaoude, J., Kraitem, A., El Alam, M. B., Karam, B., Adib, E., Zarka, J., Traboulsi, C., Akl, E. W., & Baddour, K. (2020) Coronavirus goes viral: Quantifying the COVID-19 misinformation epidemic on twitter. Cureus, 12(3): e7255. doi:10.7759/cureus.7255

Lamberty, P., & Imhoff, R. (2018) Powerful pharma and its marginalized alternatives? Social Psychology, 49: 255–270.

Lapin, T. (2020, 8th May) Social media networks scarmbling to remove viral 'Plandemic' conspiracy video. New York Post. Retrieved from: https://www.nypost.com/2020/07/07/social-media-networks-scrambling-to-remove-viral-conspiracy-video

Lazer, D. M. J., Baum, M. A., Benkler, Y., Berinsky, A. J., Greenhill, K. M., Menzer, F., Metzger, M. J., Nyhan, B., Pennycock, G., Rothschild, D., Schudson M., Sloman, S. A., Sunstein, C. R., Thorson, E. A., Waats, D. J., & Zittrain, J. L. (2018) The science of fake news. Science, 359(6380): 1094–1096.

Leman, P. J., & Cinnirella, M. (2013) Beliefs in conspiracy theories and the need for cognitive closure. Frontiers in psychology, 4: 378. doi:10.3389/fpsyg.2013.00378

Lewandowsky, S., Cook, J., Oberauer, K., Brophy, S., Lloyd, E. A., & Marriott, M. (2015) Recurrent fury: Conspiratorial discourse in the blgosphere triggered by research on the role of conspiracist ideation in climate denial. Journal of Social and Political Psychology, 3: 161–197.

Lewandowsky, S., Ecker, U. K. H., Seifert, C. M., Schwarz, N. & Cook, J. (2012) Misinformation and its correction: Continued influence and successful debiasing. Psychological. Science in the Public Interest, 13: 106–131.

Liu, M., Caputi, T. L., Dredze, M., Kesselheim, A. S., & Ayers, J. W. (2020) Internet searches for unproven COVID-19 therapies in the United States. JAMA Internal Medicine, 180(8): 1116–1118.

Marchlewska, M., Cichocka, A., Łozowski, F., Górska, P., & Winiewski, M. (2019) In search of an imaginary enemy: Catholic collective narcissism and the endorsement of gender conspiracy beliefs. Journal of Social Psychology, 159(6): 766–779. doi:10.1080/00224545.2019.1586637

McCauley, C., & Jacques, S. (1979) The popularity of conspiracy theories of presidential assassination: A Bayesian analysis. Journal of Personality and Social Psychology, 37(5): 637–644. doi:10.1037/0022-3514.37.5.637

McLaughlin, A. (2020, 23rd June) Investigating the most convincing COVID-19 conspiracy theories. Kings College London.

Mheidly, N., & Fares, J. (2020) Leveraging media and health communication strategies to overcome the COVID-19 infodemic. Journal of Public Health Policy, 41(4): 410–420. doi:10.1057/s41271-020-00247-w

Moscadelli, A., Albora, G., Biamonte, M. A., Giorgetti, D., Innocenzio, M., Paoli, S., Lorini, C., Bonanni, P., & Bonaccorsi, G. (2020) Fake news and Covid-19 in Italy: Results of a quantitative observational study. International Journal of

Environmental Research and Public Health, 17(16): 5850. doi:10.3390/ijerph1
7165850

Mota, N. B., Weissheimer, J., Ribeiro, M., de Paiva, M., Avilla-Souza, J.,
Simabucuru, G., Chaves, M. F., Cecchi, L., Cirne, J., Cecchi, G., Rodrigues, C.,
Copelli, M., & Ribeiro, S. (2020) Dreaming during the Covid-19 pandemic:
Computational assessment of dream reports reveals mental suffering related to
fear of contagion. *PLoS ONE*, 15(11): e0242903. doi:10.1371/journal.
pone.0242903

Motta, M., Stecula, D., & Farhart, C. (2020) How right-leaning media coverage of
COVID-19 facilitated the spread of misinformation in the early stages of the
pandemic in the U.S. *Canadian Journal of Political Science. Revue Canadienne De
Science Politique.* 1–8. doi:10.1017/S0008423920000396

Ofcom. (2020) April COVID-19 news and information: Consumption and attitudes. *Office of Communications*. Retrieved from: https://www.ofcom.org.uk/__
data/assets/pdf_file/0031/194377/covid-19-news-consumption-weeks-one-to-
three-findings.pdf

Ognyanova, K., Wilson, D., Lazer, R. E., & Robertson, C. (2020) Misinformation
in action: Fake news exposure is linked to lower trust in media, higher trust in
government when your side is in power. *The Harvard Kennedy School
Misinformation Review*, 1(4). Retrieved from: https://misinforeview.hks.harvard.
edu/wp-content/uploads/2020/06/Misinformation-in-action-Ognyanova-et-al-
2020.pdf

Oi-Yee Li, H., Bailey, A., Huynh, D., & Chan, J. (2020) Youtube as a source of
information on COVID-19: A pandemic of misinformation? *BMJ Global Health*,
5: e002604.

Okan, O., Bollweg, T. M., Berens, E. M., Hurrelmann, K., Bauer, U., & Schaeffer, D.
(2020) Coronavirus-related health literacy: A cross-sectional study in adults during
the COVID-19 infodemic in Germany. *International Journal of Environmental
Research and Public Health*, 17(15): 5503. doi:10.3390/ijerph17155503

Oleksy, T., Wnuk, A., Maison, D., & Lys, A. (2021) Content matters. Different
predictors and social consequences of general and government-related conspiracy
theories on COVID-19. *Personality and Individual Differences*, 168: 110289.
doi:10.1016/j.paid.2020.110289

Orso, D., Federici, N., Copetti, R., Vetrugno, L., & Bove, T. (2020) Infodemic and
the spread of fake news in the COVID-19-era. *European Journal of Emergence
Medicine*, 27(5): 327–328. doi:10.1097/MEJ.0000000000000713

Pathak, R., Poudel, D. R., Karmacharya, P., Pathak, A., Aryal, M. R., Mahmood,
M., & Donata, A. (2015) Youtube as a source of information on Ebola virus
disease. *North American Journal of Medical Sciences*, 7(7): 306–309.

Pennycook, G., McPhetres, J., Zhang, Y., Lu, J. G., & Rand, D. G. (2020) Fighting
COVID-19 misinformation on social media: Experimental evidence for a scalable
accuracy-nudge intervention. *Psychological Science*, 31(7): 770–780.

Petty, R. E., & Brinol, P. (2010) Attitufe change. In R. F. Baumeister, & E. J. Finkel
(Eds.) *Advanced social psychology: The state of the science* (pp. 217–259).
Oxford, UK: Oxford University Press.

Reihani, H., Ghassemi, M., Mazer-Amirshahi, M., Aljohani, B., & Pourmand, A.
(2021) Non-evidenced based treatment: An unintended cause of morbidity and

mortality related to COVID-19. *American Journal of Emergency Medicine*, p. S0735–6757(20)30317-X.

Rovetta, A., & Bhagavathula, A. S. (2020) COVID-19-related web search behaviors and infodemic attitudes in Italy: Infodemiological study. *JMIR Public Health Surveillance*, 6(2): e19374.

Schwarz, N., Sanna, L. J., Skurnik, I., & Yoon, C. (2007) Metacognitive experiences and the intricacies of setting people straight: Implications for debiasing and public information campaigns, *Advances in Experimental Social Psychology*, 39: 127–161.

Setbon, M., & Raude, J. (2010) Factors in vaccination intention against the pandemic influenza A/H1N1. *European Journal of Public Health*, 20(5): 490–494.

Shin, J., & Thorson, K. (2017) Partisan selective sharing: The biased diffusion of fact-checking messages on social media. *Journal of Communication*, 67: 233–255.

Simonov, A., Sacher, S. K., Dub, J.-P. H., & Biswas, S. (2020) The persuasive effect of Fox News: Non-compliance with social distancing during the covid-19 pandemic. *National Bureau of Economic Research*. Working Paper 27237. Retrieved from: http://www.nber.org/papers/w27237

Su Z., McDonnell, D., Ahmad, J., Cheshmehzangi, A., Li, X., Meyer, K., Cai, Y., Yang, L., & Xiang, Y. T. (2020) Time to stop the use of "Wuhan virus", "China virus" or "Chinese virus" across the scientific community. *BMJ Global Health*, 5(9): e003746. doi:10.1136/bmjgh-2020-003746

Swami, V., Barron, D., Weis, L., Voracek, M., Stieger, S., & Furnham, A. (2017) An examination of the factorial and convergent validity of four measures of conspiracist ideation, with recommendations for researchers. *PLoS One*, 12(2): e0172617. doi:10.1371/journal.pone.0172617

Swami, V., & Coles, R. (2010) The truth is out there: Belief in conspiracy theories. *The Psychologist*. 23(7): 560–563.

Swire, B., & Ecker, U. K. H. (2018) Misinformation and its correction: Cognitive mechanisms and recommendations for mass communication. In B. G. Southwell, E. A. Thorson, & L. Sheble (Eds.) *Misinformation and mass audiences* (pp. 195–2011). Austin, TX: University of Texas Press.

Tasnim, S., Hossain, M. M., & Mazumder, H. (2020) Impact of rumors and misinformation on COVID-19 in social media. *Journal of Preventive Medicine and Public Health*, 53(3): 171–174. doi:10.3961/jpmph.20.094

The Lancet. (2020) COVID-19: Fighting panic with information. *Lancet*, 95(10224): 537.

Van Bavel, J. J. V., Baicker, K., Boggio, P. S., Capraro, V., Cichocka, A., Cikara, M., Crockett, M. J., Crum, A. J., Douglas, K. M., Druckman, J. N., Drury, J., Dube, O., Ellemers, N., Finkel, E. J., Fowler, J. H., Gelfand, M., Han, S., Haslam, S. A., Jetten, J., Kitayama, S., Mobbs, D., Napper, L. E., Packer, D. J., Pennycook, G., Peters, E., Petty, R. E., Rand, D. G., Reicher, S. D., Schnall, S., Shariff, A., Skitka, L. J., Smith, S. S., Sunstein, C. R., Tabri, N., Tucker, J. A., Linden, S. V., Lange, P. V., Weeden, K. A., Wohl, M. J. A., Zaki, J., Zion, S. R., & Willer, R. (2020) Using social and behavioural science to support COVID-19 pandemic response. *Nature and Human Behaviour*, 4(5): 460–471. doi:10.1038/s41562-020-0884-z

Van der Linden, S., Leiserowitz, A., Rosenthal, S., & Maibach, E. (2017) Inoculating the public against misinformation about climate change. *Global Challenges*, 1: 1600008.

van der Linden, S. (2015) The conspiracy-effect: Exposure to conspiracy theories (about global warming) decreases pro-social behavior and science acceptance. *Personality and Individual Differences*, 87, 171–173. doi:10.1016/j.paid.2015.07.045

van Prooijen, J. W. (2018) Empowerment as a tool to reduce belief in conspiracy theories. In J. E. Uscinski (Ed.) *Conspiracy theories and the people who believe them*. Oxford, UK: Oxford University Press.

van Prooijen, J. W. (2019) An existential threat model of conspiracy theories. *European Psychologis*, 25(1): 1–10. doi:10.1027/1016-9040/a000381

van Prooijen, J. W., & Douglas, K. M. (2017) Conspiracy theories as part of history: The role of societal crisis situations. *Memory Studies*, 10(3): 323–333. doi:10. 1177/1750698017701615

Wen, J., Aston, J., Liu, X., & Ying, T. (2020) Effects of misleading media coverage on public health crisis: A case of the 2019 novel coronavirus outbreak in China. *Anatolia*, 31(2): 331–336.

Wittenberg, C., & Berinsky, A. J. (2020) Misinformation and its correction. In N. Persily, & J. A. Tucker (Eds.) *Social media and democracy: The state of the field*. Cambridge: UK Cambridge University Press.

Wood, M. J., Douglas, K. M., & Sutton, R. M. (2012) Dead and alive: Beliefs in contradictory conspiracy theories. *Social Psychological and Personality Science*, 3(6): 767–773. doi:10.1177/1948550611434786

Wood, T., & Porter, E. (2018) The elusive backfire effect: mass attitudes' steadfast factual adherence. *Political Behaviour*, 41: 135–163.

Wu, A. W., Connors, C., & Everly, G. S. (2020) COVID-19: Peer support and crisis communication strategies to promote institutional resilience. *Annals of Internal Medicine*, 172(12): 822–823.

Yamey, G., & Gonsalves, G. (2020) Donald Trump: A political determinant of COVID-19. *BMJ*, 369: m1643.

Yip, L., Bixler, D., Brooks, D. E., Clarke, K. R., Datta, S. D., Dudley, S., Komatsu, K. K., Lind, J. N., Mayette, A., Melgar, M., Pindyck, T., Schmit, K. M., Seifert, S. A., Shirazi, F. M., Smolinske, S. C., Warrick, B. J., & Chang, A. (2020) Serious adverse health events, including death, associated with ingesting alcohol-based hand sanitizers containing methanol — arizona and New Mexico, May–June 2020. *MMWR. Morbidity and Mortality Weekly Report*, 69(32): 1070–1073. doi:10.15585/mmwr.mm6932e1.

Zandifar, A., & Badrfam, R. (2020) Iranian mental health during the COVID-19 epidemic. *Asian Journal of Psychiatry*, 51: 101990.

Zheng, Y., Goh, E., & Wen, J. (2020) The effects of misleading media reports about COVID-19 on Chinese tourists' mental health: A perspective article. *Anatolia*, 31(2): 337–340.

Chapter 8

Media, Risk Perceptions and Fear

When news first surfaced about the emergence of a new virus in central China that was initially described as causing pneumonia-like symptoms, many people in other parts of the world did not immediately see this outbreak as a direct threat. By March 2020, however, the mood began to change as cases surfaced in the United Kingdom and then across other parts of Europe and other parts of the world. The viral cause and the new disease itself were given names (SARS-CoV-2 and COVID-19). The World Health Organization classified the spread of this new virus as a "pandemic", signalling a very serious threat (Cucinotta & Vanelli, 2020).

The British government took a light-touch approach to managing the pandemic. The public were advised to take some precautions such as washing their hands more often especially after having been put and about in places where they may have touched surfaces, to avoid touching their faces and to keep away, as much as possible, from really crowded places. All this changed when scientific modelling was presented to the government by one group of expert advisors warning that without more stringent interventions to control public behaviour, this new virus could cause up to 500,000 deaths (Imai et al., 2020).

While people remained relatively relaxed about the new coronavirus up to that point, the public mood changed dramatically when the British Prime Minister, Boris Johnson, appeared on television on 21st March 2020 and instructed people to stay home, announcing a major lockdown of society from 23rd March 2020. Suddenly, it became clear that something highly significant was happening and this was a genuine crisis that would affect virtually everyone. Media coverage resonated with messages that the pandemic represented a major national crisis event. Media coverage of specific traumatic crises and events can also generate public fear (Holman et al., 2014). The same was true for this latest pandemic. Certainly, public opinion polls at this time indicated that people were getting increasingly worried about the pandemic. When YouGov asked the British public about catching the coronavirus, one in four (24%) said they were "very" or "somewhat" scared of this on 1st March 2020, and this figure progressively

DOI: 10.4324/9781003274629-8

increased over the next month, reaching 38% on the 13th March, 48% on 20th March and 61% by 27th March, just after lockdown was implemented (YouGov, 2021, 21st March).

Risks and fears we already known to be bound up together. It is perceived risk rather than actual statistical risk that is the critical cognitive factor in this context. As people perceive greater risks to themselves from a specific source or phenomenon, so their fear will grow as well (Slovic, 1987; Langford et al., 2000). Perceived risk is affected by the level of uncertainty associated with an event or situation (Zhang et al., 2020). The COVID-19 pandemic created considerable uncertainty for the entire world. Understandably therefore it generated considerable actual risk and perceived risk.

News Framing and Public Risk Perceptions

Understanding the impact of news media and other information sources on the public's perceptions of personal risks from COVID-19 was important because realistic appraisal of risks might play a part in motivating public compliance with draconian restrictions on their movements. At the same time, exaggerated calculations of these risks might lead to powerful fear responses that in the longer term might prove difficult to shake as lockdown rules were relaxed and society tried to return to normal

A survey of pharmacists found that their perceptions of risk did vary by specific demographic factors, such as their gender, where they lived and whether they had children, but also, over and above these factors, by the amount of media coverage of the pandemic they saw. Heavier exposure to media coverage was associated with greater perception of risk from the coronavirus (Karasneh et al., 2021). What this research did not reveal, however, were reasons why media exposure was related to risk perceptions.

The way that the news presents risks can be critical to how much it influences members of the audience will make their own risk assessments on the basis of that information. Researchers found that specific frames, or perspectives tended to characterise news coverage of the pandemic and also chatter about it on micro-blogging and social networking sites. Some perspectives presented the new virus and the pandemic as a "war", while others focused on family life and the disruption of relationships, and yet others focused variously on the crisis primarily as a health issue versus an economic issue, a social issue or even a signal of the deterioration of western democracies (see Poirier et al., 2020; Wicke & Bolognesi, 2020).

Loss frames were believed to trigger more willingness to adopt riskier crisis solutions and gain frames encouraged more caution. Messages that contain threats might have more traction in the initial stages of the crisis to frighten people into compliance with tough new controls over their behaviour. In the coronavirus pandemic context, this initially amounted to staying indoors as much as possible and passively accepting closures of different spaces in which people would normally expect to mix with others. Messages from authorities, however, also need to give people some hope. Initially, the hope might be that the extreme closures of activities and spaces will be short-lived. Against that backdrop therefore a widespread willingness on the part of the public voluntarily to comply with these restrictions will be strong. If promises are made that the "end is in sight" only subsequently to be dashed when they have offered false hope, the public mood might change and the willingness to comply with yet further extreme restrictions could weaken.

It is also important to acknowledge that the effects of (gain versus loss) framing do not operate in a psychological vacuum. How much people care about an issue and how relevant it is for them can make attitudes about the issue more readily accessible. Under these conditions, people become more alert to information about the issue which they also absorb more richly. Having done this, they are then much less sensitive to framing effects. Whether messages issued by authorities about a crisis focus on the alleged benefits of interventions or the losses that might otherwise occur, it has also been found that those committed to an issue and who are often better informed about it, will hold attitudes that are less sensitive to the influences of message frames (Lecheler et al., 2009).

Hamerleers and van der Meer (2020) surveyed people in the United States and The Netherlands to investigate their support for different choice options regarding the coronavirus. The research was theoretically influenced by Prospect Theory which predicted that the prospect of losing something would lead people to choose higher risk solutions and the prospect of making a gain would motivate them to choose lower risk options. When confronted with losing something, people would also experience stronger and more negative emotional reactions, in particular, feeling frustration and powerless. These negative emotions added to the drive to take more risks in seeking to avert losses. In the context of the coronavirus therefore being presented with the prospect of losing something, support for stricter preventative interventions was more likely to emerge. People in the survey were given either a gain framed or loss-framed messages about the coronavirus. The exact wording of these two versions of the message are shown in the Box 8.1 below.

Respondents were given three further items to which they reacted on seven-point, agree-disagree scales: "It is important to lock down our country to prevent the spread of the virus further"; "We need to take even more extreme measures to fight the coronavirus"; and "I am afraid that we don't do enough to prevent the virus from spreading". Respondents were then also asked about the emotions they experienced when thinking about the impact of the coronavirus.

Support for the risk-aversive programme A was greater among respondents exposed to the "gain frame" (64%) with lesser support among those exposed to the "loss frame" (36%). For Programme B, there was

---

Box 8.1   Gain Frame and Loss Frame

Gain Frame "Recently, there have been a number of concerns about the treatment and spread of the coronavirus in the US/the Netherlands – and there are many different opinions and perspectives on how we should deal with it. What if, hypothetically speaking, there are two potential strategies to deal with the outbreak: Program A and program B. Program A has the consequence that 65% of all contaminated people can be saved. Program B has a 65% likelihood to save all contaminated people, and a 35% likelihood to save none of the contaminated people."

Loss Fame "Recently, there have been a number of concerns about the treatment and spread of the Corona virus in the US/the Netherlands – and there are many different opinions and perspectives on how we should deal with it. What if, hypothetically speaking, there are two potential strategies to deal with the outbreak: Program A and program B. Program A has the consequence that 35% of all contaminated people will die. Program B has a 65% likelihood that none of the contaminated people will die, and a 35% likelihood that all of the contaminated people will die."

Source: Hamerleers & van der Meer, 2020.

---

much more extensive support among those given the "loss frame" (76%) than among those given the "gain frame" (24%). Hence, framing a solution to the coronavirus crisis in terms of *losing lives* strengthened support for a risky option that had a good chance of saving all people, but also came with the risk that possibly none would be saved. When pacing emphasis on how many people will be *saved* (as opposed to lost), people were more likely to opt for a more cautious or low risk option to protect people. When framed this way, the participants were disinclined to take unnecessary risk in that in trying to save everyone, you end up saving no one.

The research showed only a small effect of a gain frame over a loss frame on public support for strict governmental interventions. Hence, procuring public endorsement of specific protective measures is not affected greatly one way or the other by emphasizing gains or losses being delivered. Promising gains as opposed to alleviating losses also failed in this study to influence respondents' levels of hope. There was some indication, however, that focusing on loss generated greater frustration and anger in participants than did emphasizing gains. Perception of powerlessness and fear levels were not influenced by message framing.

Elsewhere, research has failed to replicate the "loss aversion" effect. In one study, participants recruited in mid-May 2020 were presented with two scenarios and then were asked to make a series of judgements about when different parts of society should be opened up as well as their intentions to comply with government guidelines (Sanders et al., 2020). The two scenarios offered a gain option and a loss option:

Gain: As many as 100,000 people could be saved by a well-managed extension to the lockdown.

Loss: As many as 100,000 people could die without a well-managed extension to the lockdown.

The researchers found no significant impacts of loss aversion on any of three outcome measures. People seeing the loss frame were slightly, but not significantly, more likely to favour faster easing of lockdown restrictions and were less likely to comply with these restrictions. Exposure to the loss frame resulted in participants being significantly more likely to favour opening schools later than did participants who saw the gain-framed message.

The nature of the frame (whether loss or gain) was not significant in relation to how soon participants thought the government should re-open restaurants, hairdressers, offices, international travel and large gatherings or end the furlough scheme of social distancing requirements. The findings here were not consistent with earlier literature, in showing that being shown a loss frame or a gain frame relating to COVID-19 risk did not influence most judgments about when specific interventions ought to be relaxed.

In this study, participants were required to make just one judgment about whether to extend the lockdown. They were not asked about the economic and social consequences of lockdown extension. A general consideration of the efficacy of continued lockdown might have been strengthened by thinking about its relevance to saving people's lives and protecting the NHS, which government repeatedly asked the public to do. There were, however, important economic and social impact considerations of lockdown that were much closer to home. Taking these considerations into account may well have changed the results of this study (Adams-Pressl et al., 2020; Layard et al., 2020).

News Exposure and Emotional Reactions to the Pandemic

Wahl-Jorgensen (2020) argued that that in times of crisis, media news coverage can set agendas for public debate. The media do not invariably enhance public understanding, but it can draw people's attention to specific issues and perspectives on those issues. The novel coronavirus outbreak at the start of 2020 received far more media coverage than the Ebola epidemic in 2018, even though Ebola was a far more deadly disease. She tracked early news coverage of the coronavirus in January and February 2020 and located 9,387 stories about it. Of these, 1,066 stories mentioned the word "fear" or semantically-related words. In other words, there was extensive use of emotive language in relation to the emerging pandemic, with soe articles explicitly referring to the new disease as a "killer". This reference was used despite the fact that although some people died early in the outbreak in Wuhan, China, more generally, only a small minority of those infected were at this degree of risk.

Wahl-Jorgensen also found that many news stories adopted a local angle and reported on fears that the new virus had triggered in specific communities. A range of differently sourced "fears" were typically mentioned. These included a fear of the disease itself. In addition, there were fears caused by the side-effects of the pandemic which included the closure of businesses and loss of income or employment as people were advised by their authorities to stay home. The "killer" references had been used with the first SARS virus outbreak in 2003, which was mostly restricted to the far East. Emotive news coverage was also registered concerning the H1N1 influenza epidemic of 2009.

What also made a different kind of interesting comparison was the typical media coverage given to seasonal influenza which, most years, kills several hundred thousand people. Yet, during the same period monitored by Wahl-Jorgensen (2020), just 488 articles were found across the world's newspapers. Only around one-tenth of these stories made references to fear or other similar emotional reactions among communities affected.

Fear might prove to be an effective motivation to elicit initial behavioural compliance on a mass scale. If it persists, however, it might cultivate perceptions of life being unduly characterised by uncertainty and risks and being beyond individuals' own control. This reaction could cause frustration leading to anger. Anger could encourage individuals to feel that they can take control again, but only via destructive rather than constructive actions. It might be far healthier all round therefore for those in authority to give people a sense of control through hope rather than fear. This is more likely to be achieved by offering solutions that are regarded as feasible by individuals and this means getting the balance of positive and negative outcome options right (Roseman, 1991; Nabi, 2003).

A survey was conducted with 4991 people in China between 12th and 11th February 2020 during a period when the novel coronavirus was spreading rapidly across the country (Liu et al., 2020). On 30th January 2020, the World Health Organization had already declared this new outbreak a public health emergency of international concern. This survey addressed issues of early public risk perception and anxiety about this new disease. Principally, however, the study investigated the relationship between reported media exposure and public thoughts and feelings about COVID-19. At the time of the survey, relatively few of the respondents

(6%) said they knew someone who had been infected and one in three (32%) were aware of reported cases in their area. Among the sources of information mentioned were WeChat, a popular Chinese social media site (63%), television (61%), TikTok, a video sharing site (45%), other people (42%), Weibo, a Twitter-like micro-blogging site (39%), newspapers (16%) and radio (9%).

Greater anxiety about COVID19 was higher among young people and better educated people, and also among those who knew someone who had caught the virus and lived in an area where more cases had been reported. Greater anxiety was also related directly to greater perceived risk from COVID-19 both to oneself and to others. Further analyses, however, showed only a weak connection between relevant news media exposure and anxiety about COVID-19 (Liu et al., 2020).

Research conducted during the earliest stage of the pandemic in Wuhan, China at the end of January and early February 2020 found that reported anxiety levels and reported anxiety with depression levels among an adult sample were significantly greater among heavier users of social media sites. These relationships remained significant after statistical controls were introduced for different population characteristics and historical health status (Gao et al., 2020).

The uncertainty that can be created by a new crisis can trigger anxiety and fear in populations and also heightens their sensitivity to news that keeps them informed about latest crisis developments but also may help them to understand more about it so that they can devise personal coping mechanisms. The public anxiety that occurred during the 2020 COVID-19 pandemic was driven by information tat the virus as infectious an could spread easily, that it was spread widely (and quickly), that some people could become very ill with it and that the medical profession had no known effective treatment for or protection against it. Research with people in different parts of the world confirmed that these issues were uppermost in their minds and undoubtedly made them feel more fearful. In some places, this feeling of being lacking control over a potentially dangerous situation drove people to panic. This reaction could be fuelled by news coverage and also by information people acquired through online sources such as micro-blogging and social networking sites.

Research in China during the COVID-19 pandemic showed that the more people were conscious of and thought about the negative consequences of COVID-19, the more anxious they felt and more their sense of panic intensified (Xu & Sattar, 2020). How much people panicked was also linked to how and where they got their information about the new virus. At the time of this Chinese research (February 2020), news coverage and online information flows about COVID-19 were at their peak. Use of official media and other social media were associated with public concern about the pandemic. This outcome is not surprising given that at the time the virus was spreading out of control and this was widely reported and discussed in mainstream and online media. Many people turned to multiple information sources to find out as much as they could about the new disease but this behaviour only served to heighten their anxieties. While the mainstream media in China focused on official information produced by the government and its health authorities, the popular commercial social networking sites circulated more open discussions about the virus including false and misleading information.

What were perceived as not just more open information flows but because of that more honest one attracted a great deal of attention. Yet the absence of editorial controls meant that information quality and accuracy were not checked on these sites and the content they provided could exaggerate or distort facts about the virus and the pandemic. Users of these social networking sites also engaged in spreading chatter between themselves and friends leading to further fresh interpretations of the original messages about the virus. As with the spread of rumours some of the original details of a story could be lost or changed almost beyond recognition as on person after another placed their own spin on it before passing it on to someone else. Official media outlets could gain trust be substantiating "facts" with relevant evidence and countering false or misleading narratives.

This research further showed that increased reliance of official information sources was related to a gradual and progressive decrease in anxiety and panic. Users of unofficial sources on their preferred social media sites in contrast exhibited greater levels of panic as their reliance of these sites increased. The unofficial media, however, were found often to move information around faster than the official media. This could lead to those reliant on unofficial sources for their COVID-19 information developing greater mistrust of information from the slowing-moving official sources (Xu & Sattar, 2020).

Research has examined relationships between exposure to traditional and online media exposure and public fear of coronavirus. In one study, a Fear of Coronavirus Questionnaire was developed to measure people's anxieties about COVID-19 (Mertens et al., 2020). This instrument comprised a list of statements, each of which was accompanied by a five-point Likert-type response scale ("strongly disagree = 1 to strongly agree = 5). Illustrative items are: "I am very worried about the coronavirus"; "I am taking precautions to prevent infection (e.g., washing hands, avoiding contact with people, avoiding door handles)"; "I am constantly following all news updates regarding the virus".

Media exposure was measured with a series of questions that covered different types of media information sources. Respondents were asked if they had "looked up any extra information regarding the coronavirus outbreak?". They responded here with a simple "yes" or "no". They were then which information sources they had consulted. The options here comprised: regular "newspapers/websites/TV news"; "social media (Facebook, Instagram, Twitter, etc)"; "professional websites" meaning those posted by health and medical professionals, institutions and other specialists; online searches via major search engines such as Google; family and friends and other sources which they could specify. They were then asked to use a five-point scale again to indicate the extent to which they paid attention to various information sources.

The expectation that media exposure might trigger anxiety or fear responses was reinforced by earlier research showing that exposure to media coverage of traumatic events could render those exposed more fearful about the events and their wider consequences (Holman et al., 2014). Research connected to earlier pandemics had also shown that exposure to media coverage of new disease outbreaks featured among a suite of variables that could trigger fear in the public (Van den Bulck & Custers, 2009). Fear responses were also especially profound among people who had an intolerance for uncertainty (Carleton, 2016).

Van den Bulck and Custers (2009) obtained data from 23 European countries and found for each additional hour of television viewing there was a 16% increase in the proportion of people worried about the H5N1 avian influenza virus in 2004 when there had apparently been a marked increase in news coverage of this new virus. The key viewing measure was average hours per day of television watching as measured by each country's national audience measurement service using "people meter" methodology. This combined automatic logging of when TV sets in households were switched on with each householder's individual records of when they were physically present in front of an active set. Despite claims that it could be used as a proxy for televised news exposure, this general measure of amount of daily viewing could have been made up exclusively of non-news programmes. An alternative explanation of the findings could be that more anxious people watched more TV as a distraction.

Returning to Mertens et al. (2020), they found that fear of COVID-19 was predicted by having a low tolerance of uncertainty, being a worrier and being anxious about one's own health. The status of someone's general health, their worries about the safety of their family and the degree to which they felt they had control over the situation were further predictors. The use of different information sources and their impact of coronavirus fear responses was examined in two stages. When specific information sources were analysed in relation to fear individually, the findings showed that reported use of regular media, social media, websites posted by professionals and interpersonal interactions with family and friends were all significantly linked to greater fear of coronavirus.

Then, all these variables were combined together with non-media variables such as intolerance for uncertainty, general health worries, health status and demographics, were examined together as predictors of fear of coronavirus in a multiple regression analysis. This analysis accounted overall for 37% of the variance in fear responses. This meant that the predictor variables measured by this study did not provide a complete explanation of why some people exhibited more coronavirus fear than did others. Within this analysis, reported use of regular media outlets and of social media as pandemic information sources still had a significant link to fear of coronavirus, along with concern about risks for loved ones and general health anxiety. The other information sources were no longer major predictors of coronavirus fear (Mertens et al., 2020). On a note of caution here, the measurement of exposure to information sources used in this study was crude. Binary responses (i.e., "yes" versus "no") fail to differentiate between degrees of exposure and also coronavirus information quality variances across the multiple information sources available within a specific medium (e.g., television or newspapers).

Variances in News Storytelling and Public Response

We have considered how populations have reacted to media coverage of COVID-19 through post-exposure questioning of their perceptions of the pandemic and fears generated from these cognitive responses. The evidence considered to this point was based mostly on data about overall exposure levels to media outputs. As we saw in earlier chapters, however, the coverage given to the pandemic in the mainstream news media and on micro-blogging and social networking sites access via the Internet could vary. News stories can focus on positive news about the pandemic or negative news. Most of the attention focused on negative news, especially during the early stages of the pandemic and of later fresh waves of infection. The mainstream news can present verbal narratives and also visual images to convey essential information. These different elements of news storytelling can convey different meanings and impressions to audiences and demand different levels of attention.

Within the narratives or scripts of news reports different perspectives might be used to convey the same facts by different news providers. These differing news "frames" can create alternative realities in respect of the understanding about specific events and issues that different audience members take away with them, a psychological process known as "priming". Hence, the production methods selected by news editors can make a significant difference to the audience experience even when the same events are being reported by different news providers. These features if the news can in turn trigger varying cognitive, emotional and behavioural responses in audience members.

In the context of live news coverage, priming effects can amplify the impact of news reports or specific parts of them resulting in shifts in risk perceptions (e.g., making them greater), emotional feelings (e.g., fear) and behavioural intention (e.g., willingness to comply with lockdown restrictions). When these techniques are deployed retrospectively in news that has gone, all these effects are weaker (Wen et al., 2021).

News Coverage and Discrimination

News coverage takes on even greater significance for nations' populations around the world at times of crisis. People turn to the major news media for timely, relevant and trustworthy information about extreme events that are emotionally upsetting to them. This interest can grow exponentially when their own lives are directly impacted. Even with one-off disasters such as an earthquake, a tsunami, a terrorist atrocity or a financial crash, the public's attention to the news becomes more acutely focused. Up to the end of the 20th century, publics around the world were dependent on the major mass news media for explanation and reassurance on these occasions. In the 21st century, people could turn to other sources that were just as widely available via the Internet. This platform was occupied by major news media, but also by many new news suppliers and also by interpersonal gossip, but on a mass scale. "Citizen journalism" operating via weblogs and micro-blogging sites together with online social communities, known popularly as "social networking" or "social media" sites now figure just as prominently as relied upon information sources (Schultz et al., 2011).

The COVID-19 pandemic represented the biggest global crisis since the Second World War. Initially, perceived as an internal problem for China, where the virus was first noticed, the rest of the world quickly learned that this was an issue that would concern everybody. Some critical commentators labelled the virus as a symptom of shortcomings in China and this led to discriminatory remarks about Oriental people living in or visiting countries in the West. Such discrimination was unhelpful and could be potentially damaging not just for the reputation of China but also for individuals caught up on the receiving end of racially divisive behaviour. Past research had shown that media coverage of these "frames" could catalyse and crystallize discriminatory language and attitudes among ethnic groups targeted in this way with damaging mental health consequences for those victimised (Rodriguez-Seijas et al., 2015).

Media coverage presenting unsubstantiated and misleading explanations of the origins of the new virus spread problematic ideas about it that caused local populations to display discriminatory behaviour towards people from China visiting the places where they lived. Even Chinese immigrants who had lived in an overseas territory for more than a generation and ran established businesses there found themselves on the receiving end of discrimination as the novel coronavirus was conceived to be a specifically Chinese problem.

This prejudice extended to Chinese people who had never visited China having been born and brought up elsewhere. Local populations turned away from Chinese businesses and steered clear of fellow citizens who were Chinese across Australia, Europe and North America and even in parts of Asia. Chinese children were shunned in western schools. Chinese guests were turned away from western hotels. Chinese visitors were even refused entry to restaurants in neighbouring Asian countries such as Japan, South Korea and Vietnam (Wen et al., 2020).

Lessons Learned

As the new coronavirus invaded more and more countries and infected rapidly growing numbers of people, official briefings repeatedly reminded people of the risks of catching COVID-19 and emphasised death rates from the virus. This messaging not only raised public risk awareness, it also triggered powerful fear responses. As we saw in earlier discussions, among the vast volume of information generated about the pandemic, much was distorted or untrue. This posed a challenge for the authorities and mainstream news media in terms of getting the truth across – or at least messages that had some semblance of scientific justification and support.

Further evidence reviewed in this chapter showed that more measured narratives that presented factual content that could be checked, especially if it was originated by official sources that commanded the public's trust, could give people reassurance. This outcome was important in the context of removing anxieties and fears that could present psychological barriers to a return to normality. If "normality" was perceived as dangerous because perceptions of potential risks remained prevalent and top-of-the-mind for many people, accompanying fears could motivate them to reject relaxation of behavioural restrictions which they believed to be necessary going forward to provide protection.

Such risk perceptions could also become attached to groups of "others", differentiated from individuals' own communities or tribes. This would then result in prejudicial and discriminatory ideas and impressions of others that often got the blame for ongoing risks in society from the coronavirus. Such reactions might then lead to other negative orientations towards such targets giving rise to further tensions across societies. It is critical for governments, experts, the media and the public to be cognizant of these unfortunate psychological legacies of the pandemic and to work hard to prevent their occurrence or to dismantle these prejudices when they do arise.

References

Adams-Prassl, A., Boneva, T., Golin, M., & Rauh, C. (2020) Inequality in the impact of the coronavirus shock: Evidence from real time survey. *Journal of Public Economics*, 189: 104245. doi:10.1016/j.pubeco.2020.104245

BBC News. (2020, 3rd October) Coronavirus: "I really worried we might lose PM" Dominic Raab says. Retrieved from: https://www.bbc.co.uk/news/uk-politics-54402615

Carleton, R. N. (2016) Into the unknown: A review and synthesis of contemporary models involving uncertainty. *Journal of Anxiety Disorders*, 39: 30–43.

Cucinotta, D., & Vanelli, M. (2020) WHO declares COVID-19 a pandemic. *Acta Biomedica*, 91(1): 157–160.

Gao, J., Zheng, P., Jia, Y., Chen, H., Mao, Y., Chen, S., Wang, Y., Fu, H. , & Dai, J. (2020) Mental health problems and social media exposure during COVID-19 outbreak. *PLoS ONE*, 15(4): e0231924. doi:10.1371/journal.pone.0231924

Hameleers, M., & Van der Meer, T. G. L. A. (2020) Misinformation and polarization in a high-choice media environment: How effective are political fact-checkers? *Communication Research*, 47(2): 227–250. doi:10.1177/009365021 8819671

Holman, E. A., Garfin, D. R., & Silver, R. C. (2014) Media's role in broadcasting acute stress following the Boston Marathon bombings. *Proceedings of the National Academy of Sciences of the United States of America*, 111(1): 93–98.

Imai, N., Gaythorpe, K. A. M., Abbott, S., Bhatia, S., van Elsland, S., Prem, K., Liu, Y., & Ferguson, N. M. (2020) Adoption and impact of non-pharmaceutical interventions for COVID-19 [version 1: peer review: 1; 1 approved, 3 approved with reservations]. *Wellcome Open Research*. Available at: https://wellcomeopenresearch.org/articles/5-59/v1

Karasneh, R., Al-Azzam, S., Muflih, S., Soudah, O., Hawamdeh, S., & Khader, Y. (2021) Media's effect on shaping knowledge, awareness risk perceptions and communication practices of pandemic COVID-19 among pharmacists. *Research in Social and Administrative Pharmacy*, 17(1): 1897–1902. doi:10.1016/j.sapharm.2020.04.027

Langford, I. H., Day, R. J., Georgiou, S., & Bateman, I. J. (2000) *A cognitive social psychological model for predicting individual risk perceptions and preferences.* Norwich, UK: CSERGE GEC Working Paper.

Layard, R., Clark, A., De Neve, J.-E., Krekel, C., Fancourt, D., Hey, N., & O'Donnell, G. (2020, April) When to release the lockdown: A wellbeing framework for analysing costs and benefits. Occasional Paper 49. *Centre for Economic Performance, London School of Economics and Political Science*. Retrieved from: https://eprints.lse.ac.uk/104276/1/Layard_when_to_release_the_lockdown_published.pdf

Lecheler, S., de Vreese, C., & Slothus, R. (2009) Issue importance as a moderator of framing effect. *Communication Research*, 36(3): 400–425.

Liu, M., Zhang, H., & Huang, H. (2020) Media exposure to COVID-19 information, risk perception, social and geographical proximity, and self-rated anxiety in China. *BMC Public Health*, 20, Article no. 1649(2020) Retrieved from: https://bmcpublichealth.biomedcentral.com/articles/10.1186/s12889-020-09761-8

Mertens, G., Gerritsen, L., Duijndanm, S., Salermink, E., & Engelhard, I. M. (2020) Fear of coronavirus (COVID-19): Predictors of an online study conducted in March 2020. *Journal of Anxiety Disorders*, 74, 102258.

Nabi, R. L. (2003) Exploring the framing effects of emotion: Do discrete emotions differentially influence information accessibility, information seeking and policy preferences. *Communication Research*, 30(2): 224–247.

Poirier, W., Ouellet, C., Rancourt, M. A., Bechard, J., & Dufresne, Y. (2020) (Un) covering the COVID-19 pandemic: Framing analysis of the crisis in Canada. *Canadian Journal of Political Science*, 53: 365–371.

Rodriguez-Seijas, C., Stohl, M., Hasin, D., & Eaton, N. (2015) Transdiagnostic factors and mediation of the relationship between perceived racial discrimination and mental disorders. *JAMA Psychiatry*, 72(7): 706–713.

Roseman, I. J. (1991) Appraisal determinants of discrete emotion. *Cognition and Emotion*, 5(3): 161–200.

Sanders, M., Stockdale, E., Hume, S., & John, P. (2020) Loss aversion fails to replicate in the coronavirus pandemic: Evidence from an online experiment. *Economic Letters*, 199: 109433. doi:10.1016/j.econlet.2020.109433

Schultz, F., Utz, S., & Goritz, A. (2011) Is the medium the message? Perceptions of and reactions to crisis communication on twitter, blogs and traditional media. *Public Relation Review*, 37(1): 20–27.

Slovic, P. (1987) Perception of risk. *Science*, 236: 280–285.

Van den Bulck, J., & Custers, K. (2009) Television exposure is related to fear of avian flu, an Ecological Study across 23 member states of the European Union. *European Journal of Public Health*, 19(4): 370–374.

Wahl-Jorgensen, K. (2020, 14th February) Coronavirus: How media coverage of epidemics often stokes fear and panic. *The Conversation*. https://www.theconversation.com/coronavirus-how-media-coverage-of-epidemics-often-stokes-fear-and-panic-131844

Wen, F., Ye, H., Wang, Y., Xu, Y., & Zuo, B. (2021) Icing on the cake: "Amplification effect" of innovative information form in news reports about COVID-19. *Frontiers of Psychology*, 12: 600523. doi:10.3389/fpsyg.2021.600523

Wen, J., Aston, J., Liu, X., & Ying, T. (2020) Effects of misleading media coverage on public health crisis: A case of the 2019 novel coronavirus outbreak in China. *Anatolia: An International Journal of Tourism and Hospitality Research*, 31(2). Retrieved from: https://www.tandfonline.com/doi/full/10.1080/13032917.2020.1730621

Wicke, P., & Bolognesi, M. M. (2020) Framing COVID-19: How we conceptualise and discuss the pandemic on Twitter. *PLoS One*, 15(9): e0240010. doi:10.1371/journal.pone.0240010

Xu, T., & Sattar, U. (2020) Conceptualizing COVID-19 and public panic with the moderating role of media use and uncertainty in China: An empirical framework. *Healthcare (Basel)*, 8(3): 249. doi:10.3390/healthcare8030249

YouGov. (2021, 21st March) COVID-19 fears. Retrieved from: https://yougov.co.uk/topics/international/articles-reports/2020/03/17/fear-catching-covid-19

Zhang, L., Li, H., & Chen, K. (2020) Effective risk communication for public health emergency: Reflection on the COVID-19 (2019-nCoV) outbreak in Wuhan, China. *Healthcare*, 8: 64.

Chapter 9

Media and Behavioural Compliance

Before the COVID-19 pandemic, the mainstream media were known to provide effective channels for disseminating important health information (Wakefield et al., 2010). Governments can quickly reach much of their populations through broadcast media and print media provide more detailed upon which people can reflect. Analysis of news coverage of pandemics had previously shown storytelling that followed a specific pattern. With reports of rising infection levels, the volume of airtime and space devoted to a pandemic increased. Then, as infection levels started to fall, so too did the amount of news coverage. Research carried out in China, for example, at the time of the 2009 A/H1N1 influenza epidemic illustrated this pattern of news coverage. The media coverage of the outbreak in the Shaanxi province of China where it initially occurred rose as the epidemic took hold and then switched off as it subsided (Xiao et al., 2015).

News coverage can wax and wane with an infectious disease. What may strengthen this outcome is when news reporting focuses not purely on the absolute number of cases but on the rate of change in cases. Reports showing the disease rising or falling could have the strongest impact on people during these health emergencies. Rising hospitalisation rates emerged as an especially powerful news narrative in relation to the attentiveness of the public (Yu et al., 2020).

Further evidence has indicated that it is also the seriousness of the news that can enhance its impact in situations of crisis where public behaviour modification is needed. Once again, research from China linked to the 2009 A/H1N1 influenza epidemic showed that the amount of news, not just on mainstream media, but also on news web sites, that covered the epidemic had an impact on the public's awareness of the epidemic and shifted specific attitudes towards being supportive of taking specific protective steps. What really made a difference, however, was not simply increasing the news coverage, but reports of cases needing hospitalisation. In other words, when news gave the impression that growing numbers of people were not simply getting infected but also became ill enough to need hospital care, then people in general really start to take notice (Yan et al., 2016).

DOI: 10.4324/9781003274629-9

The same research team reported that people's awareness of the 2009 influenza epidemic initially grew as the disease itself spread in four provinces where it initially broke out. After a time, user awareness and case numbers displayed an inverse relationship as people turned away from consuming information about the viral outbreak within those provinces. Then, when a new twist in the story occurred with the influenza spreading afresh to other parts of China, public awareness was again positively correlated with numbers of cases (which also presumably derived in part from the coverage they received in the news). There was also evidence that the main topics of interest to the public shifted over time. Initially, people wanted to know about the diagnosis of the disease, its symptoms, its mortality rate and whether it would mutate. Over the next few months, people sought information more often about treatment and infection prevention (Xie et al., 2014).

Media, Risk Availability and Behavioural Compliance

The almost routine focus of the news media on loss of life from coronavirus during the 2020 pandemic and an impression, in the early stages of the pandemic, that the virus was out of control created the psychological climate for people to welcome extreme action by their governments to bring the problem under control. Whether people become risk-seeking or risk-averse under these exceptional circumstances can depend on how the potential solutions are presented to them. When losses are given prominence, they will be more willing to take chances, but when gains or benefits are emphasized, they will be more likely to prefer cautious solutions. (Meyerowitz & Chaiken, 1987; Quattrone & Tversky, 1988). While the news media may indeed stay true to what they might claim to be their core value of objectivity, this does not invariably render "factual selectivity" as illegitimate

The many unknowns about the virus even among the experts and authorities meant that the public also could not be expected to feel confident about dealing with this new disease. The dependency of the public on the media was reinforced by the constantly changing conditions surrounding the new virus. The daily reporting of growing numbers of infected cases, hospitalisations and deaths exacerbated feelings of uncertainty which in turn generated anxiety and fear (Boukes et al., 2019). Under these conditions, the way the media framed the pandemic could shape public understanding of what was going on more immediately and more powerfully than usual (Entman, 1993; Scheufele, 1999; De Vreese, 2005). The media can offer people ways of interpreting and making sense of what is going on. This cognitive support becomes increasingly significant during times of great uncertainty (Entman, 1993; Druckman, 2001; De Vreese, 2005).

News Relevance and Public Behaviour

As it spread around the world, much of the attention of mainstream news providers focused initially on death and hospitalisation rates and on how ordinary people were coping with not b being allowed to see loved ones on their death beds, being socially deprived, losing their jobs and not knowing when the crisis would end. Evidence accumulated from around world that people were experiencing personal risk from this new disease and that the lack of knowledge about this risk meant that they were also feeling heightened anxiety (Liao et al., 2021). The relentless flow of pandemic stories on the news contributed towards these psychological reactions. Early evidence of this emerged from China where the pandemic started and which therefore was ahead of the rest of the world in coping with the new virus (Dong & Zheng, 2020). These outcomes were not surprising and had been observed in relation to previous large-scale crises (Yamashita, 2012).

Oosterhoff and Palmer (2020) conducted an online self-completion survey between 20th and 22nd March 2020 of American adolescents aged 13 to 18 years. Questions were asked about their monitoring of the news, their social distancing, disinfecting and hoarding behaviours. Further measures were taken of respondents' social values including social responsibility, social trust and self-interest. A majority of these teens (70%) said they did not personally follow social distancing practices, but most (88%) said they engaged in at least one disinfecting practice many times a day. Three out of four (75%) were monitoring the news for the latest information about COVID-19. Those scoring higher on social responsibility tended to claim to disinfect more often and also monitored COVID news more often. Those driven by self-interest were less likely than average to observe social distancing practices and were more likely to hoard.

Further research showed that the more coverage an epidemic (within a single country) or pandemic (across more than one country) received in the news, the more people's risk perceptions increased and alongside this also the more they worried (Dong & Zheng, 2020; Brooks et al., 2020; Khosravi, 2020; Olagoke et al., 2020).

At times such as these people's sensitivities to crisis-related information are heightened and this means that their reactions to the information they receive can become more acute. Bad news will cause them much more severe psychological reactions than they would experience to similar news during normal times. Equally, good news might prove to be more effective at bringing out the best in people. Many people display greater empathy towards others at such times and this might motivate them to be more likely to engage in voluntary work to help others (Glik, 2007; Greenaway & Cruwys, 2019).

Another behavioural impact of such extreme circumstances, when people experience a heightened sense of personal risk is that they also show greater willingness to comply with the advice of authorities to play their part in bringing a dangerous situation under control (Glik, 2007; Vaughan & Tinker, 2009). As people come to perceive greater personal risk, often as a result of the information received through major news media, they become more acutely attuned to their own security and that of their family members. In recognising also that by playing their part in complying with pandemic-related restrictions on their movements, they are demonstrating a sense of civic responsibility. Further to this, it might be recognised that it is only if everyone adopts this same attitude that the pandemic will eventually be defeated and life would return to normal (Vaughan & Tinker, 2009). Pre-pandemic evidence also showed that repeated media risk messages might motivate at least some of the non-compliers to follow official advice on how to behave under crisis conditions (Buck & Ferrer, 2012).

Working against this impact that news coverage of the pandemic was the fact that amongst the maelstrom of information swirling around on the mainstream media and the Internet were messages that openly encouraged people to reject behavioural restrictions or interventions (e.g., getting vaccinated). Often these messages were backed up by fake claims about the pandemic (Tasnim et al., 2020). Fake news stories had the potential to undermine public confidence in governments and health authorities, politicians and experts and also in people's confidence in their own abilities to cope with a crisis (Ali, 2020; Jalali & Mohammadi, 2020).

Research in China during the early stages of the pandemic (24th to 28th February 2020) shed further light on the impact of rumours about pandemics on public attitudes and behavioural intentions around COVID-19 (Liao & Wang, 2021). The amount of pandemic-related information in circulation made a difference to the public's anxiety levels and their attitudes towards preventative measures imposed by public health authorities. The clearer the factual information people received, the more inclined they were to accept restrictions on their behaviour in a positive light and comply with them. The more often they were exposed to misleading or ambiguous information and rumours about the pandemic, they less likely they were to accept what authorities were telling them. If misleading information created greater uncertainty and anxiety, which was more pronounced in some people than others, this further reinforced the public's questioning of the advice and regulations they received from authorities.

The lesson learned from this study was that it is extremely important at times of crisis of this kind that authorities issue timely and relevant information to the public that has clarity and credibility. When rumours were in circulation that had little basis in truth or science, and authorities allowed time for their influence to take hold, these false narratives could shape the public's reaction to the pandemic and to the advice they subsequently received from their health authorities. Compliant behaviour on the part of the public was dependent upon people holding supportive attitudes towards the interventions being imposed upon them by their government and health authorities. Such attitudes could be weakened by false narratives.

Getting the right information out to the public can help them to formulate realistic rather than exaggerated subjective risk estimates. Failing to do this can result in uncertainty among the public that triggers fear responses that further strengthens any adverse effects of false narratives (Khosravi, 2020). In China, Liao & Wang (2021) found that many people had been exposed to information about the COVID-19 from a wide range of sources in the mainstream media and over the Internet. This also meant the possibility of exposure to many different perspectives about the new virus. Further evidence emerged that the Chinese public were widely supportive of their authorities' protection measures during a particularly critical stage of the COVID-19 epidemic. The more they had been exposed to official messages about the new disease, the more compliant with the restrictions they were likely to be. These findings were consistent with earlier research into public reactions to major disasters (Greenaway & Cruwys, 2019).

As a further nuance to the findings, the impact of rumours can depend upon the types of rumours to which people are exposed. There was what some researchers have called "dread" rumours which talk about negative outcomes and "wish" rumours that focus on possible solutions to a crisis and give people hope (Bordia & Difonzo, 2004), Dread rumours can promote public fear and hope rumours have the opposite effect. Hence in relation the COVID-19, dread rumours focused on death levels and inferred health risks, while wish rumours focused more on progress made in the development of vaccines and medical therapies (Jiang, 2020). With losses being given more weight than gains in risk assessments, it could be hypothesized here that much media coverage during the early stages of the pandemic could have cultivated an exaggerated sense of risk.

Local media news has been found to have a potential impact on the way people respond to a pandemic. In in the United States, where the country is criss-crossed with numerous local television stations, people were found to turn to these news outputs, but their influence on public opinion depended on their style coverage (Kim et al., 2020). Much local broadcast news in the United States has been labelled as "urban-centric". Much of the news presented derives from events taking place in major urban centres in the region or locality being served. More rural areas tend to attract less coverage. This can lead some people living in rural locations to question the relevance of the coverage for them. In the context of the pandemic, however, there was a lot of attention given to the behaviour of people in larger towns and cities because it was in these more crowded areas that people were most at risk of infection from the new coronavirus. As such, people in urban areas tended to engage readily in social distancing and other protective behaviours. The trick was to make local televised news relevant also to rural dwellers. When local news audiences are receptive to this news, it can have powerful and positive effects on public behaviour (King et al., 2017).

Further American research found that people living in rural areas served by local television news from stations in large urban centres tended to be less approving of their news coverage on average than were those served by stations located in smaller urban centres. There was further evidence that people became increasingly less approving of local television news coverage when urban centres from which those services derived were more impacted by COVID-19. This could well have been because the more specific cities were affected by the coronavirus., the more this was talked about in the news. Rural areas tended to be much less impacted by coronavirus because of their sparser populations. Urban dwellers and recipients of news from those centres tended to be more compliant with COVID restrictions such as social distancing advice than were rural dwellers for whom local televised news held little relevance. People in general were more likely to comply when their locality had legally enforced "stay at home" orders imposed upon it. Even so, experience of restriction reinforcing televised news still exerted its own individual impact on behavioural compliance (Kim et al., 2020).

Narrative Frames and Public Behaviour

The narrative frames about COVID-19 that were created by news coverage and by chatter on social media sites served to inform (or misinform) public understanding about the new coronavirus and about the interventions implemented by government to tackle the pandemic. At the same time, they could also potentially shape public behaviour. People's understanding of issues will tend to mingle with their beliefs and attitudes about these things as well and together these internal and therefore largely unseen cognitive reactions can determine behavioural intentions and then in turn overt behaviour.

For specific individuals, certain frames can be elevated into a position of dominance. For others, different frames that offer different perspectives or explanation for events or outcomes might be considered. When this happens, two or more frames might work together to determine subsequent behaviour or they might cancel each other out (Bolsen et al., 2020). In the context of COVID-19, therefore, it was possible that when people were exposed to different "frames" or explanations concerning, for example, the origins of the virus, how much of a risk it presented and how effective were different interventions at combating its spread, the overall effect might be quite neutral as one frame cancelled out the effects of another. It is also possible that two frames might work together and magnify their individual effects.

One particular frame can have especially powerful effects, not just on understanding but also on attitudes and behaviour. This is the "blame frame". With events that spiral out of control or cause a great deal of damage, there will be an almost inevitable interest in why they occurred and more especially why. When addressing the "why?" question, explanations usually end up identifying what or who is to blame. The search for a source to blame is concerned with establishing who might take responsibility for what happened. There are occasions when events happen simply by accident or unintentionally and then no obvious source of blame can be found in terms of a specific actor (Iyengar, 1994; Lagnado & Channon, 2008). This outcome can sit uncomfortably with some people who seek someone to blame anyway in order to achieve some kind of explanatory closure in understanding a damaging event (Iyengar, 1994). When events are interpreted as planned or intentional, then a source of blame is critical to subsequent understanding and explanation of its occurrence. With harmful events, there is usually an intention to learn lessons from it, usually to minimise the possibility of its repetition Ames & Fiske, 2015; Rogers et al., 2019).

The blame frame can trigger behavioural intentions. If an actor is identified as being to blame for a damaging incident or event and when the belief develops that they acted with intent and perhaps will little concern for the harm that might be caused, strong negative feelings can develop about that actor among those affected by their actions. These feelings can then in turn motivate an intention or a wish for retribution (Shariff et al., 2014; Levin et al., 2016). Sometimes blame frames will identify a number of contributory factors to an outcome and on other occasions the blame may settle more acutely on one particular cause or actor. The more acute in this way the attribution of blame, the more those affected will seek some kind of reparation or retribution (Javeline, 2003).

Hence, if a specific individual kills a victim in a road accident and is found guilty of dangerous driving, the blame is attached very specifically to one source and there will be an expectation on the part of others, not least those directly affected by this event, that that perpetrator should be punished. If an incident that causes harm to one or more individuals is attributed to a range of causes, then "society" might be held to blame or the government which has the power to make policy changes to make society safer. A road accident that kills an innocent bystander as a vehicle drove off road to avoid a running down a cyclist who was seen only at the last minute at a notorious black-spot for these kinds of accidents could be attributed to the driver, to the cyclist or to the road conditions. There would still be calls for action, but the lessons learned in each case would be different and this would mean that subsequent behaviour changes in each case would be different and would involve different individuals or groups of people. The assignment of responsibility for what happened would vary in its application (Major, 2011; Kim, 2015).

The differential attribution of blame frames and then the variance in subsequent outcomes have characterised explanations for pandemics. In respect of the first SARS epidemic in China in 2003, which fortunately did no spread worldwide like the second SARS coronavirus in 2020, was identified as a zoonotic virus that jumped from an animal species into humans. On that occasion, the origin of this human version of the virus was identified as Guandong. As with the 2020 virus, the first SARS outbreak was explained by some in terms of the cultural practices in China relating to the presence of specific wild animal species in the human food chain there and the unsanitary conditions in which these animals were kept in the markets where they could be bought (Eichelberg, 2007). This frame gained traction round the world and particularly in the United States where Americans who subscribed to this explanation felt desire for retribution against China.

Similar narratives surfaced in 2020. The desired retribution for some people in the West was that the China should be held responsible and made to pay damages foe the economic harm wrought by the pandemic on other countries beyond China. China should therefore be pressured to pay up. Coupled with this blame frame and the need for financial reparations was a further sub-debate which went beyond determining that the virus originated in China, but then considered how this came about. Was it an accident waiting to happen in food markets or was it an outcome of scientific research that went wrong? The suggestion that the virus emerged as a result of deliberate actions in China placed a more acute form of blame in that direction.

An alternative frame emerged, that was reinforced by statements emanating from China, that the novel coronavirus that emerged for the first time in 2019 had not originated in China. Instead, it had been brought into China by foreigners. One version of this alternative blame frame proposed that this action had been deliberate and a less acute version suggested that it had been accidental. Depending upon which of these frames we might sign up to, the kinds of lessons learned and resolutions perceived to be more relevant and appropriate will also vary.

In terms of lessons learned from all of this for the psychological impact of the 2020 pandemic, a further behavioural outcome of blame games needs to be mentioned. Conspiracy theories often propose that specific events, such as pandemics (and the follow-on interventions used by governments), are motivated by hidden agendas that have usually got something to do with taking advantage of a situation in which people will accept removal of their usual freedoms of action to gain longer-term control over them. Signatories to these theories have then been found to be less willing to engage in prosocial behaviour to play their part in dealing with a crisis and its causes. This outcome was observed in the context of individuals' willingness to reduce their own carbon footprints as their contribution towards tackling the problems of climate change (Jolley & Douglas, 2014; van der Linden, 2015).

This similar suspension of personal altruism was also found to occur during the 2020 pandemic (Goldberg et al., 2020; Heffner et al., 2020; Jordan et al., 2020). Notwithstanding the many stories in the media about acts of kindness performed by people to help out others, for example, who could not leave their homes to shop for essentials because, as special "at-risk" cases, they were shielding at home, in more general terms willingness to help to protect others by staying home, maintaining social distancing and wearing face masks could be weakened for those signing up to specific blame frames (Pennycook et al., 2020).

One study investigated this phenomenon during the early phase of lockdown in April and May 2020 (Bolsen et al., 2020). The researchers assigned over 1,000 participants recruited online to four different conditions. In three conditions, the participants were presented with a headline and an accompanying brief news story which described different explanations of the origin of COVID-19. Those in the fourth condition received no news content. In one frame, the novel coronavirus was described as a naturally occurring zoonotic transmission event. In a second frame, it was described as laboratory made. In a third frame, both of the above two possibilities were considered. All participants were also required to read a statement explaining that there was no evidence that the coronavirus had been engineered as a biological weapon. After reading the story assigned to them, all respondents, including those in the control condition were required to answer a number of questions.

Among the questions presented were statements measuring the degree to which participants believed that the coronavirus originated in animals and jumped to humans versus originated in a laboratory; that the coronavirus originated in animals and jumped into humans; that the coronavirus originated in a laboratory; and that the coronavirus had been created by the Chinese government as part of a biological weapons programme. Responses to these items were found to be highly inter-correlated and this led the researchers to combine their scores into a single index. Two further questions asked participants whether they thought China should be financially responsible for the costs of the outbreak and whether other governments, states and organizations should be able to sue China to reveal more about the origin of the virus.

Finally, further items questioned participants concerning their views of whether the US government should increase spending on research into zoonotic viruses; and then about how necessary they felt it was for people to continue wearing face masks, frequently wash hands and maintain six-feet physical distance from others. Together these items comprised a prosocial behaviour index.

People who read the zoonotic virus frame about it jumping from animals to humans were more likely to believe this explanation subsequently. Similarly, exposure to the explanation that the virus originated in a Chinese laboratory led to a greater likelihood of acceptance of that frame. The competitive frame, which considered both of these explanations, produced no significant impact on participants subsequent beliefs about the origin of the novel coronavirus as one frame cancelled out the other. These beliefs did make a difference also to the willingness of participants to seek punitive reparations from China. Subscribers to the frame that the virus originated in a Chinese laboratory were the most likely to want to seek compensation from China for the economic damage caused by the pandemic in other countries. Belief in the frame that this is a zoonotic virus did not feel like this so strongly. Those who believed that this was a zoonotic virus were, however, stronger adherents to the view that there should be greater investment in research to understand these viruses better.

Finally, a number of frame-related predictors of prosocial behaviour intentions emerged from this study. Those who had been exposed to the conspiracy frame about the virus originating in a Chinese laboratory and those exposed to the frame that entertained by the zoonotic and laboratory explanations tended to be less likely to sign up to the necessity to persist with social distancing, face mask wearing and hand washing behaviours (Bolsen et al., 2020). The evidence was clear. When people are exposed to theories that profess some kind of conspiracy behind damaging events, they are less inclined to believe in the efficacy of prosocial behaviours designed to reduce their effects or minimise their repetition. Such behaviour might be seen as unsubstantiated by science and as unlikely to prove effective (Lewandowsky et al., 2013; Oliver & Wood, 2014). The concern about this type of reaction in the context of COVID-19 is that some accepting certain blame frames might discourage people from engaging in potentially life-saving behaviour (Jerit et al., 2020).

Key Lessons

News coverage can play a significant role in the control of public behaviour during times of national crisis. This effect had been observed to be both important and helpful in relation to outbreaks of new and infectious diseases. There can be a pattern to news coverage during emergencies such as pandemics. Coverage can wax and wane during a pandemic as a new disease grows in prevalence and its impact on specific communities becomes increasingly serious. This was true of the COVID-19 pandemic as it had been of earlier 21st century pandemics.

As the disease itself evolves and changes course, news coverage will follow these developments. The public's awareness can be maintained over time, but the emotions experienced by people change as new facts are learned about the disease and the risks it poses to specific communities or to groups within communities. News media coverage, both via mainstream broadcast and print media and via online platforms, is sensitive to real-world developments. Hence, as infection case numbers, hospitalisations and deaths of COVID-19 grew, media news reporting reported these changes. Insofar as this news when received directly through others might cause individuals to revise their estimates of their own risk of infection, high-profile media reporting could magnify these risk perceptions further.

The way the news framed stories around the pandemic could also shape public beliefs and attitudes about it and ultimately could influence how people behaved. Increased beliefs in stories about risks of infection and risks of death once infected could motivate more cautious behaviour and greater compliance with behavioural restrictions imposed by government, if these were thought to offer greater personal protection and provided that people trusted their government.

Evidence emerged from around the world that as the pandemic in 2020 spread, mass publics paid more attention to the mainstream news. Through this news exposure they learned more about the disease and also about steps being taken by their government and public health authorities to protect them. Although not everyone accepted all of the restrictions being imposed on their everyday behaviours at this time, especially among young people, even objectors admitted compliance with at least some of the protective measures that had been recommended by the authorities. People's anxieties about the disease became more prevalent and more pronounced over time and these emotional responses undoubtedly played a part in motivating compliance with behavioural restrictions and the adoption of personal protective measures.

The huge volume of information in circulation about the pandemic in the mainstream media and conveyed on different sites over the internet was not all homogeneous. Although, much of the messaging encouraged people – directly and indirectly – to comply with various restrictions to their behaviour, other messages had the opposite effect. False messaging that derived from mischief makers, rumour mongers and those who had justifiable reasons to be hesitant about trusting the authorities, could make people rethink their opinions and behaviour. It was discovered early on during the 2020–2021 coronavirus pandemic that clear government messaging could set the scene for public understanding and leave less room for unproven conspiracy theories to gain traction. Ambiguous government messaging or indecisiveness of the part of government, in contrast, could lead to people being left unsure what the believe and rendering them more susceptible to the influences of fake stories and conspiracies.

People also evaluate the news they receive. This is often done in terms of its perceived relevance for them. When confronted with news from local services and national services, some people might regard the former as having more relevance to them because it is far more likely than national news to address their specific concerns. Hence, if national news conveys messages from the national authorities that fail to resonate with local concerns, and yet local news does, local coverage could then have greater influence. The outcome then depends on whether the local and national are in harmony. If they are not, and the local does not support behavioural restrictions in the same way that the national coverage does, local public compliance in some communities might be rejected by many who live there. This was an issue that had had some influence on state-to-state variances in pandemic strategies, public behaviour and COVID-19 case levels across the United States.

The news can frame stories in different ways. This means they offer audiences different explanations for events. These frames can influence public understanding and opinion, and where relevant, these internal cognitive responses can also shape related public behaviour. One of the big debates about the novel coronavirus in the mainstream media, which also resonated with the online media echo chambers of microblogging and social networking sites, was about where the virus came from. Was it zoonotic – that is crossing over from an animal species into humans – or was it mad-made and escaped from a laboratory? Evidence was presented for both explanations, but this tended to be circumstantial rather than conclusive. One reason for this had been a reluctance on the part of the government and authorities in China to cooperate fully with independent inquiries into the genesis of the virus, despite a general belief that it originated on mainland China.

The cultivation of blame, which can take on different forms in different communities, can affect public beliefs and behaviour. In both terms, public responses in this context can manifest in the form of stereotypes and prejudices about causes and about the sources of these causes. This phenomenon often results in one community blaming another and where those being blamed represent a minority within a bigger community, the targets of blame can become targets of unsocial behaviour. Once again, false understanding that has not been helped by poor use of media to communicate clear, explanatory messaging about the causes of a pandemic, creates conditions for unhelpful public behaviour.

References

Ali, I. (2020) The COVID-19 pandemic: Making sense of rumor and fear. *Medical Anthropology*, 39(5): 376–379. doi:10.1080/01459740.2020.1745481

Ames, D. L., & Fiske, S. T. (2015) Perceived intent motivates people to magnify observed harms. *Proceedings of the National Academy of Sciences*, 112(12): 3599–3605. doi:10.1073/pnas.1501592112

Bolsen, T., Palm, R., & Kingsland, J. T. (2020) Framing the origins of COVID-19. *Science Communication*, 42(5): 562–585. doi:10.1177/1075547020953603

Bordia, P., & Difonzo, N. (2004) Problem solving in social interactions on the internet: Rumor as social cognition. *Social Psychology Quarterly*, 67(1): 33–49.

Boukes, M., Damstra, A., & Vliegenthart, R. (2019) Media effects across time and subject: How news coverage affects two out of four attributes of consumer choice. *Communication Research*, 48(3): 454–478.

Brooks, S. K., Webster, R. K., Smith, L. E., Woodland, L., Wessely, S., Greenberg, N., & Rubin, G. J. (2020) The psychological impact of quarantine and how to reduce it: Rapid review of the evidence. *The Lancet*, 395(10227): 912–920. doi:10.1016/S0140-6736(20)30460-8

Buck, R., & Ferrer, R. (2012) Emotion, warnings, and the ethics of risk communication. In S. Roeser, R. Hillerbrand, P. Sandin, & M. Peterson (Eds.) *Handbook of risk theory: Epistemology, decision theory, ethics and social implications of risk* (pp. 640–717). London, UK: Springer.

De Vreese, C. (2005) News framing: Theory and typology. *Information Design Journal*, 13(1): 51–62.

Dong, M., & Zheng, J. (2020) Letter to the editor: Headline stress disorder caused by Netnews during the outbreak of COVID-19. *Health Expectations*, 23(2): 259–260. doi:10.1111/hex.13055

Druckman, J. N. (2001) The implications of framing effect for citizen competence. *Political Behavior*, 23(3): 255–286.

Eichelberg, L. (2007) SARS and New York's Chinatown: The politics of risk and blame during an epidemic of fear. *Social Science & Medicine*, 65(6): 1284–1295. doi:10.1016/j.socscimed.2007.04.022

Entman, R. M. (1993) Framing: Toward a clarification of a fractured paradigm. *Journal of Communication*, 43(4): 51–58.

Freeston, M. H., Rhéaume, J., Letarte, H., Dugas, M. J., & Ladouceur, R. (1994) Why do people worry? *Personality and Individual Differences*, 17(6): 791–802. doi:10.1016/0191-8869(94)90048-5

Goldberg, M. H., Gustafson, A., Maibach, E., Ballew, M. T., Bergquist, P., Kotcher, J., Marlon, J. R., Rosenthal, S., & Leiserowitz, A. (2020) Mask-wearing increases after a government recommendation: A natural experiment in the U.S. during the COVID-19 pandemic. *PsyArXiv*. doi:10.31234/osf.io/uc8nz

Glik, D. C. (2007) Risk communication for public health emergencies. *Annual Review of Public Health*, 28, 33–54. doi: 10.1146/annurev.publhealth.28.021406.144123

Greenaway, K. H., & Cruwys, T. (2019) The source model of group threat: Responding to internal and external threats. *American Psychologist*, 74(2): 218–231. doi:10.1037/amp0000321

Heffner, J., Vives, M. L., & Feldman-Hall, O. (2020) Emotional responses to prosocial messages increase willingness to self-isolate during the COVID-19 pandemic. *PsyArXiv*. doi:10.31234/osf.io/qkxvb

Iyengar, S. (1994) *Is anyone responsible? How television frames political issues.* Chicago, IL: University of Chicago Press.

Jalali, R., & Mohammadi, M. (2020) Rumors and incorrect reports are more deadly than the new coronavirus (SARS-CoV-2). *Antimicrobial Resistance and Infection Control*, 9: 68. doi:10.1186/s13756-020-00738-1

Javeline, D. (2003) The role of blame in collective action: Evidence from Russia. *American Political Science Review*, 97(1): 107–121. doi:10.1017/S0003055403000558

Jerit, J., Paulsen, T., & Tucker, J. A. (2020) Confident and skeptical: What science misinformation patterns can teach us about the COVID-19 pandemic. *SSRN*. doi:10.2139/ssrn.3580430

Jiang, S. (2020) Information epidemic: The spreading of rumor about COVID-19 and the coping strategies. *Studies on Science Popularization* (in Chinese), 1: 70–78.

Jolley, D., & Douglas, K. M. (2014) The social consequences of conspiracism: Exposure to conspiracy theories decreases intentions to engage in politics and to reduce one's carbon footprint. *British Journal of Psychology*, 105(1): 35–56.

Jordan, J., Yoeli, E., & Rand, D. G. (2020) Don't get it or don't spread it? Comparing self-interested versus pro-socially framed COVID-19 prevention messaging. *PsyArXiv*. doi:10.31234/osf.io/yuq7x

Khosravi, M. (2020) Perceived risk of COVID-19 pandemic: The role of public worry and trust. *Electronic Journal of General Medicine*, 17(4): em203. doi:10.29333/ejgm/7856

Kim, S.-H. (2015) Who is responsible for a social problem? News framing and attribution of responsibility. *Journalism & Mass Communication Quarterly*, 92(3): 554–558. doi:10.1177/1077699015591956

Kim, E., Shepherd, M. E., & Clinton, J. D. (2020) The effects of big-city news on rural America during the COVID-19 pandemic. *Proceedings of the National Academy of Sciences of the United States of America*, 117(36): 22009–22014.

King, G., Schneer, B., & White, A. (2017) How the news media activate public expression and influence national agendas. *Science*, 358: 776–780.

Lagnado, D. A., & Channon, S. (2008) Judgments of cause and blame: The effects of intentionality and foreseeability. *Cognition*, 108(3): 754–770. doi:10.1016/j.cognition.2008.06.009

Levin, I., Sinclair, J., & Alvarez, R. (2016) Participation in the wake of adversity: Blame attribution and policy-oriented evaluations. *Political Behavior*, 38(1): 203–228. doi:10.1007/s11109-015-9316-6

Lewandowsky, S., Gignac, G. E., & Oberauer, K. (2013) The role of conspiracist ideation and worldviews in predicting rejection of science. *PLoS ONE*, 8(10): e75637. doi:10.1371/journal.pone.0075637. Erratum in: PLoS One. 2015; 10(8): e0134773

Liao, H.-P., & Wang, J.-L. (2021) The impact of epidemic information on the public's worries and attitude toward epidemic prevention measures during the COVID-18 outbreak. *Current Psychology*, 1–9. doi:10.1007/s121440021-01364-9. Retrieved from: https://link.springer.com/article/10.1007/s12144-021-01364-9

Liao, Q., Xiao, J., Cheung, J., Ng, W. Y., Lem, W. W. T., & Cowling, B. J. (2021) Community psychological and behavioural responses to coronavirus disease 2019 over one year of the pandemic in 2020 in Hong Kong. *Scientific Reports*, 11, 22480. doi:10.1038/s41598-021-00616-9

Major, L. H. (2011) The mediating role of emotions in the relationship between frames and attribution of responsibility for health problems. *Journalism & Mass Communication Quarterly*, 88(3): 502–522. doi:10.1177/107769901108800303

Meyerowitz, B. E., & Chaiken, S. (1987) The effects of message framing on breast self-examination, attitudes, intention and behavior. *Journal of Personality and Social Psychology*, 52(3): 500–510.

Olagoke, A. A., Olagoke, O. O., & Hughes, A. M. (2020) Exposure to coronavirus news on mainstream media: The role of risk perceptions and depression. *British Journal of Health Psychology*, 25: 1–10. doi:10.1111/bjhp.12427

Oliver, J. E., & Wood, T. J. (2014) Conspiracy theories and the paranoid style(s) of mass opinion. *American Journal of Political Science*, 58(4): 952–966. doi: 10.1111/ajps.12084

Oosterhoff, B., & Palmer, C. A. (2020) Psychological correlates of news monitoring, social distancing, disinfecting and hoarding behaviors among US adolescents during the COVID-19 pandemic. *JAMA Pediatrics*, 74(12): 1184–1190. doi:10.1001/jamapediatrics.2020.1876

Pennycook, G., McPhetres, J., Bago, B., & Rand, D. G. (2020) Predictors of attitudes and misperceptions about COVID-19 in Canada, the U.K., and the U.S.A. *PsyArXiv*. doi:10.31234/osf.io/zhjkp

Quattrone, G. A., & Tversky, A. (1988) Contrasting rational and psychological analyses of political choice. *American Political Science Review*, 82(3): 719–736.

Rogers, R., Alicke, M. D., Taylor, S. G., Rose, D., Davis, T. L., & Bloom, D. (2019) Causal deviance and the ascription of intent and blame. *Philosophical Psychology*, 32(3): 402–427. doi:10.1080/09515089.2018.1564025

Rosnow, R. L. (1980) Psychology of rumor reconsidered. *Psychological Bulletin*, 87(3): 578–591. doi:10.1037/0033-2909.87.3.578

Scheufele, D. A. (1999) Framing as a theory of media effects. *Journal of Communication*, 49(1): 103–122.

Shariff, A. F., Greene, J. D., Karremans, J. C., Luguri, J. B., Clark, C. J., Schooler, J. W., Baumeister, R., & Vohs, K. D. (2014) Free will and punishment: A mechanistic view of human nature reduces retribution. *Psychological Science*, 25(8): 1563–1570. doi:10.1177/0956797614534693

Tasnim, S., Hossain, M. M., & Mazumder, H. (2020) Impact of rumors or misinformation on coronavirus disease (COVID-19) in social media. *Journal of Preventive Medicine and Public Health*, 53(3): 171–174. doi:10.31235/osf.io/uf3zn

Tversky, A., & Kahneman, D. (1981) The framing of decisions and the psychology of choice. *Science*, 211(4481): 453–458.

van der Linden, S. (2015) The conspiracy-effect: Exposure to conspiracy theories (about global warming) decreases pro-social behavior and science acceptance. *Personality and Individual Differences*, 87: 171–173. doi:10.1016/j.paid.2015.07.045

Vaughan, E., & Tinker, T. (2009) Effective health risk communication about pandemic influenza for vulnerable populations. *American Journal of Public Health*, 99(SUPPL. 2): 324–332. doi:10.2105/AJPH.2009.162537

Wakefield, M. A., Loken, B., & Hornik, R. C. (2010) Use of mass media campaigns to change health behaviour. *The Lancet*, 376(9748): 1261–1271. doi:10.1016/S0140-6736(10)60809-4

Xiao, Y., Tang, S., & Wu, J. (2015) Media impact switching surface during an infectious disease outbreak. *Science Reports*, 5: 7838. doi:10.1038/srep07838

Xie, T., Yang, Z., Yang, S., Wu, N., & Li, L. (2014) Correlation between reported human infection with avian influenza A H7N9 virus and cyber user awareness: What can we learn from digital epidemiology? *International Journal of Infectious Diseases*, 22: 1–3. doi:10.1016/j.ijid.2013.11.013

Yamashita. (2012) A review of psychosocial assessments for disaster mental health studies. *Psychological Trauma Theory Research Practice and Policy*, 4(6): 560–567. doi:10.1037/a0025952

Yan, Q., Tang, S., Gabriele, S., & Wu, J. (2016) Media coverage and hospital notifications: Correlation analysis and optimal media impact duration to manage a pandemic. *Journal of Theoretical Biology*, 390: 1–13.

Yu, F., Yan, L., Wang, N., Yang, S., Wang, L., Tang, Y., Gao, G., Wang, S., Ma, C., Xie, R., Wang, F., Tan, C., Zhu, L., Guo, Y., & Zhang, F. (2020) Quantitative detection and viral load analysis of SARS-CoV-2 in infected patients. *Clinical Infectious Diseases*, 71(15): 793–798. doi:10.1093/cid/ciaa345

Chapter 10

Social Media, Behavioural Compliance and Other Outcomes

A great deal of varied information about the pandemic circulated on social media platforms. While some messaging was informed by or derived from official pandemic advice sources, much of the COVID content on these sites did not. What impact therefore did these sites have on public understanding of the pandemic and willingness to comply with behavioural advice from government and other authorities and from experts?

In trying to understand the effectiveness of public health measures in combatting the COVID-19 pandemic, it is important to direct attention to the multiple networking opportunities that exist over the Internet. These include the most popular micro-blogging services (e.g., Twitter) and social networks (e.g., Facebook, Instagram, YouTube and others). For many people, these sites served as important information sources. They frequently offered a broader range of insights, explanations and opinions about the pandemic than were found in the mainstream news media. The problem was that it was not always transparent who many of these online sources were or whether the information they provided was reliable (Atlani-Duault et al., 2020).

In spite of the general reliability of most mainstream news providers and the high public trust they commanded, when information from these "more reliable" sources migrated onto the Internet, it could be re-packaged and repurposed to a point where its original meaning and accuracy were compromised (Cuan-Baltazar et al., 2020).

Social media were sites of much fake news, false stories, rumours and other misleading information about the pandemic could undermine public confidence in official advice and encourage people to act inappropriate or ill-advisedly in relation to the pandemic. The authorities were often caught napping by the appearance of fake news and rumour which could circulate widely and rapidly online. One solution was the creation of interactive messaging that could counter the rumours and more especially identify when and where they occurred to enable people to spot them for themselves. These needed to be fast-acting and address the untruths of fake stories head-on and reference sources of advice that the public would (Depoux et al., 2020).

DOI: 10.4324/9781003274629-10

Social Media Use and Pandemic Behaviour

Research from China surveyed Chinese internet users to investigate links between their overall social media use and their use of specific categories of social media sites (public sites, professional sites and social sites) and what they knew and understood about COVID-19 and their compliance with preventive behaviours. The researchers surveyed people who were established Internet users. On average, these respondents used social media for two to three hours a day. In general, many respondents displayed a good knowledge of COVID-19. There was some evidence that heavier users of social media were more inclined to adopt preventive behaviours and also that this link was further mediated by being more generally knowledgeable about health issues, while knowing more about the disease weakened this relationship. Overall social media use was a good predictor of propensity to follow preventive behaviours, while use of other specific social media, run by major social media brands or on behalf of professional bodies were also linked significantly (but less strongly) to adoption of these behaviours. Official social media run government and other public bodies were less influential (Li, & Liu, 2020).

Compliance: Social Media Use and Self-Isolation Intention

People were required to isolate themselves at home when they became symptmatic and when requested by their health authorities to do so after being exposed to possible infection. Research found that exposure to social media chatter about COVID-19 and the importance of different interventions deployed to combat spread of the disease was related to the strength of motivation to self-isolate. Exposure to information about COVID-19, and especially on social media platforms, was related to public perceptions of the severity of COVID-19 and of their own ability to take control of the situation through taking cerytain actions, such as isolating socially. Exposure to online information about the virus was also linked to greater anxiety of the health risks posed by it – a symptom labelled as cyberchondria. As exposure to advisory information, ad hoc chatter and then accompanying anxieties grew, so too did the propensity to socially isolate (Farooq et al., 2020).

Social Media, Conspiracy Theories and Spin-Off Effects

Fake news circulates widely on social networking sites (Talwar et al., 2019). These sites provided a home for the rapid and widespread dissemination of false information about COVID-19 (Shaw et al., 2020). The origins of fake pandemic news is often traced back variously to rogue individuals, activist groups and movements and nation states. (Huang & Carley, 2020). There is also evidence that the online circulation of some conspiracy theories about COVID-19, such as one linking it to 5G mobile transmission signals, tended to be take the form of clusters of rumour spreaders, with many other Internet users ignoring or challenging them (Ahmed et al., 2020).

In seeking solutions to the fake news and conspiracy theory problem, some writers called for more involvement of medical and science experts in positioning robust evidence-based science on social networking sites that put the record straight in terms of the veracity of some of the more outlandish theories (Erku et al., 2021; O'Connor & Murphy, 2020; Orso et al., 2020).

There were other factors at play. Academic publication timeframes were reduced and pre-peer reviewed research released into the public domain to accelerate the development of interventions that were designed to protect people. News media had a strong appetite for research data and would report new findings at face value even before they had been properly checked for accuracy. This meant that unverified findings could gain currency online and spawn misleading narratives about the novel coronavirus and COVID-19 (King, 2020). Despite attempts by some legal systems to outlaw fake news about COVID-19, once misleading information was out there, its effects could linger even after misleading messages had been removed (Alvarez-Risco et al., 2020; Kadam & Atre, 2020).

As false news gained traction on micro-blogging and social networking sites, it could undermine the impact of official guidance about the pandemic. People struggled to distinguish between official and scientifically verified information and false and misleading narratives. There were signs that public confusion followed on and could weaken compliance with government advice and restrictions (Ahmad & Murad, 2020; Naseem & Bhatti, 2020).

Conspiracy Theories and Public Compliance with Authorities

As we have seen, there are many people who believe conspiracy theories about major national and international crises and disasters, whether naturally occurring or man-made. The attraction of these theories, despite the falsehoods on which they tend to be based, is that they can offer some certainty where there is little or none (Fritsche et al., 2017; van Prooijen & Douglas, 2018). Pre-pandemic research had already shown that during such crises people seek explanations and they often seek to assign blame. This can lead to disparate explanations being offered to account for a crisis being generated by different stakeholders or decision-makers seeking to defend their own position. At the same time, people seek out these explanations to find meaning where there is only uncertainty (Bale, 2007; van Prooijen, 2018).

The search for explanation is driven by the psychological discomfort caused by uncertainty which can also trigger significant levels of public anxiety. In searching for explanations for crises, people must also weigh up the credibility and trustworthiness of different sources (van Prooijen & Douglas, 2018). People want to understand the nature of a crisis, where it poses and clear and present danger to themselves. They need to know how to alleviate personal risk, rid themselves of fear and find workable solutions.

In the COVID-19 pandemic, most people turned first to their national governments and public health services for assurance and protection. For those who already lacked trust in the authorities, they turned instead to conspiracy theories or alternative scientific explanations from those being given by their government. In states of crisis, for the most extreme sceptics, even mainstream science is often rejected (van der Linden, 2015; Douglas et al., 2017). The alternative science adopted by sceptics is usually not driven by the proven veracity of their theories over the evidence offered by the authorities but simply by a generic distrust of government and of experts believed to be aligned with government. Sceptics might also rely upon highly selective scientific findings which mainstream science and scientists regard as outliers. The lack of association with (and rejection by) the mainstream often authenticates these outliers for sceptics (Bogart et al., 2010; Jolley & Douglas, 2014; Lamberty & Imhoff, 2018; Georgiou et al., 2020).

When people reject official advice and guidance and the science upon which they are based, their willingness to comply with government-imposed restrictions on their behaviour will be weakened. Although, generally regarded as unhelpful, conspiracy theories offer alternative views of the world that raise questions about the official viewpoints which then need to refuted. In doing so, the accuracy and veracity of official theories can then be tested and strengthened. These challenges also force governments and related authorities to be transparent in their own decision-making (Swami & Coles, 2010). There have been instances where conspiracy theories, despite lacking robust empirical support, sparked debates and the testing and re-testing of mainstream theories that accelerated the development of research and practice to the benefit of the public (Ford et al., 2013; Ojikutu et al., 2021). Another problematic outcome of conspiracy theories is that they can discourage people's prosocial tendencies during times of crisis and encourage a blame game that can magnify divisions of opinion and trigger inter-group conflict (Abalakina-Paap et al., 1999; Bilewicz & Sędek, 2015; Jolley et al., 2019).

Research in Poland found that a perceived lack of personal control during the pandemic prdicted an increased likelihood of being persuaded by conspiracy theories. Signing up to general cospiracy beliefs enabled individuals to acquire a stronger sense of community control, of which they could become a part. Such individuals did not tend to be more likely to subscribe to a different conspiracy theory about the pandemic being a government plot. Adherents to a general conspiracy orientation were also more likely to exhibit xenophobic beliefs and to be suspicious of other group than their own. Holding conspiracy theories about government was linked more specifically to distrust in government and in the context of the pandemic people who held on to these beliefs were less compliant in terms of handwashing and social distancing recommendations of government and health authorities (Oleksy et al., 2021).

The research comprised two studies. In the first part, data were collected via computer-assisted interviewing online. This research was conducted between 13th and 15th March 2020 with over 1,000 people aged 18 to 70 years. At ths time, Poland had just implemented its first set of major restrictions which included closures of schools, many shops and restaurants and advised observance of social distancing recommmendations. The second study comprised another online survey of Polish adults across the same age range a little later between 19th and 24th March 2020. The day following the end of this data collection period, the Polish government had announced the introduction of further restrictions.

The researchers collected data about how much control respondents felt they had oer their lives, how well protected people in Poland are against the virus, their views about some conspiracy theories of a general nature and more especially about the government, their support for xenophobic policies concerning additional controls over certain ethnic groups in the country, and their willingness to give emotional support to people experiencing dificulties under lockdown.

The first study revealed that adherence to compiracy theory about the government was predicted by experiencing a lack of personal control and also sensing that people across the country felt that their lives were spiralling out of control. People were less likely to endorse government-linked conspiracy theory when they felt more protective towards others. More general cyncism about COVID-19 was related to stronger xenophobic beliefs.

In the second study, both general and government-specific conspiracy theories were assocated with a lack of personal control and peprceiving a wider lack of collective control. Conspiracy theory adherence was also linked, once again, to xenophobia. Conspiracy beliefs were not mitigated by holding more protective attitudes towards other people.

Our central interest in this book is with the issue of behavioural compliance by the public in relation to government advice, recommendations and restrictions. This Polish study revealed that the more the respondents here believed in a government-driven conspiracy underlying COVID-19, the less frequently they reported following hygience rules such as hadwashing and the less they observed social distancing rules. Hence, if people believe that their government does not have their best interests at heart, they are less inclined to comply with any restrictions it imposes upon their behaviour and lives (Oleksy et al., 2021).

Conspiracy Mindsets and Pandemic Response

An accompanying psychological dynamic that might underpin a willingness to embrace conspiracy theories is the cognitive confusion and associated anxiety generated by complex topics for which simplified and personally comprehensible explanations are sought (Richey, 2017). Hence, having what some theorists have called a "conspiracy mentality", that is a tendency to believe any conspiracy theories rather than the statements of untrusted outgroups (i.e., authorities), seems to be underpinned by adherence to right-wing authoritarianism and social dominance orientation (Van der Linden et al., 2020; Dyrendal et al., 2021). There has also been a further and ongoing debate about whether it is misleading to treat conspiracy theory adherence as a general belief orientation (much like a personality characteristics) or whether those who adopt conspiracy theories differentiate between the ones they have chosen to accept and others they reject (Wood & Gray, 2019). In other words, it a discriminatory cognitive judgment that is situation specific rather than a general psychological orientation. There is evidence for both points view. There is no space here for further detailed examination of this important theoretical and empirical debate.

In the context of conspiracies and the COVID-19 pandemic, what we can say is that there was evidence that an enthusiasm for some conspiracy theories clearly seemed to play into the mindset that might be expected of those with more authoritarian and social dominance orientations. A theory that the novel coronavirus was developed as a bioweapon would be expected to appeal to those suspicious of governments and pan-government organisations and hierarchies from which their own social group weas excluded. Adopting this explanation would also appeal to people who believed that their own government should adopt a more robust foreign policy in dealing with perceived sources of this biological threat. Similar principles have been believed to apply to explanations of adoption of other conspiracies. One example might be the view that 5G technology represented a threat within the context of COVID-19. Bogus evidence might be presented that could be hard for many to accept, but for conspiracy theorists this may be less relevant that the identified sources of the perceived cause. In this case, 5G was a new technology that received strong government backing.

The government is generally distrusted by conspiracy theorists characterised by attributes such as right-wing authoritarianism and social dominance orientation. Through association therefore if 5G is regarded as a government "conspiracy" any theories connecting it to COVID-19, no matter how tenuous, will be accepted because it is psychologically consistent with the idea that government cannot be trusted and therefore why should this new technology be trusted (Sturm & Albrecht, 2020). Research has shown that the belief that the coronavirus was a complete hoax was associated with right-wing authoritarianism and social dominance orientation (Imhoff & Lamberty, 2020).

In a direct test among people in the UK, evidence emerged that individuals with right-wing authoritarianism and social dominance orientations were more likely to believe that the virus was created in a research laboratory in Wuhan, China and that it was caused by 5G technology. These same individuals also exhibited significant less trust in scientists which seemed in turn to strengthen their conspiracy theory beliefs about COVID-19. Such people said they also relied more on family members and friends as sources of information along with tabloid newspapers, but not other mainstream media. Social media played into the mix as well as an information source they turned to (Hartman et al., 2020).

Social Media Use and Positive Health Impact

The impact of social media sites on negative health outcomes has been well documented. Evidence has also emerged that public health objectives can be positively benefited via social media platforms with the appropriate messaging. Given the serious consequences of COVID-19 socially and economically for so many countries, being able to put these ubiquitous platforms to good use could represent a significant contribution to recovery for the pandemic. One illustration of how this could work was provided by a study conducted in Jordan (Al-Dmour et al., 2020).

More than 2,500 social media users were surveyed online about their social media habits and their health-related behaviour during the COVID-19 pandemic. Respondents were questioned about their public health awareness and what could or did learn from social media. The research indicated that social media platforms could be used positively to influence people's awareness of behaviour changes needed to tackle the pandemic and protect themselves and others against this new disease.

Key Lessons

One of the significant developments of the 2020–2021 coronavirus pandemic was the extensive role played by the Internet and the many different websites that conveyed pandemic-related content. This content originated from mainstream news suppliers, non-mainstream news operators, public health and government sources, independent scientific experts and specialist think-tanks and consultancies, charities and citizens. Some sources were peddlers of inaccurate and misleading information about COVID-19, sometimes labelled as fake news or as conspiracy theories. Other sources were treated as reasonable conscientious or scientific objectors to mainstream thought about this new disease.

The "chatter" about COVID-19 on the Internet often mirrored the news agendas of the major news media. There was also a considerable volume of information in circulation that offered alternative agendas and perspectives. Understanding the impact of these different agendas was important, not just as an academic exercise, but also for policy-makers trying to control a major health crisis without much established medical knowledge or known treatments. It was important for nation-states' populations to understand as much as possible about the new disease and also about the interventions their governments had taken to control its transmission. This understanding was crucial if people were also going to work in partnership with their governments to bring this rampant disease under control.

Social media emerged as information sources upon which many people relied. Among young people, in particular, for many social media were more important as news sources than were the major mass media. Social media sources were used more often and were trusted more. When social media provided information that was resonant with that of the mainstream news providers and largely comprised notices and advice from government, their use was linked to greater public compliance with restrictions placed on their behaviour. When social media sources offered a different perspective and different interpretations and explanations from the news mainstream, the outcome was different. Compliance with the will of authorities was less often embraced with enthusiasm or even at all.

Online debates, often fronted by established online performers or "influencers", who might not be known to many members of the public, but enjoy considerable patronage from regular social media users, could prove to be powerful forces in discouraging people from taking up any advice or guidance offered by government or even by scientists (Wiley, 2021). Alternative policies grounded in alternative science were typical in this parallel virtual reality.

These alternative pandemic narratives achieved considerable currency among people who felt they lacked personal control in an uncertain crisis situation in which their government and associated health authorities had failed to provide sufficient clarity about the disease and the efficacy of the many interventions that had been activated against it. Alternative viewpoints or behaviour frames would be readily adopted among people for whom there was a lack of trust in the competence of authorities. Even though these "conspiracies" frequently lacked solid evidence bases, the certainty that characterised the tone of delivery of their proponents had great appeal to minorities for whom their government had offered little reassurance. In some settings, the divisions in national populations could cut deep and signatories to alternative to mainstream science frames might be matched numerically by those rejecting these frames. This pattern was clearly apparent in Trump's America (and beyond) where Democrat and Republican supporters held considerably different opinions of and understanding about COVID-19. These differences then became manifest in their different behavioural responses to the pandemic.

More reassuringly, evidence did emerge that even social media sites could be used to get across positive health messages to the masses. Their ability to approach individuals on a mass scale with personalised messages or messages that at least seemed to be targeted specifically at them, often rendered them more powerful than mainstream news coverage. The cue here for governments and authorities is to recognise the diversification of communication channels through which people can now be reached and to understand better the relative impact of these different channels and the sections of national populations to which they each hold the most powerful appeal. Through this understanding, clear and authoritative communication strategies can be devised that diminish the opportunities for alternative explanatory frames of a pandemic to emerge and gain traction with the public.

References

Ahmad, A. R., & Murad, H. R. (2020) The impact of social media on panic during the COVID-19 pandemic in Iraqi kurdistan: Online questionnaire study. *Journal of Medical Internet Resesearch*, 22(5). doi:10.2196/19556

Ahmed, W., Vidal-Alaball, J., Downing, J., & López Seguí, F. (2020) COVID-19 and the 5G conspiracy theory: Social network analysis of twitter data. *Journal of Medical Internet Resesearch*, 22(5). doi:10.2196/19458

Abalakina-Paap, M., Stephan, W. G., Craig, T., & Gregory, W. L. (1999) Beliefs in conspiracies. *Political Psychology*, 20(3): 637–647.

Al-Dmour, H., Masa'deh, R., Salman, A., Abuhashesh, M., & Al-Dmour, R. (2020) Influence of social media platforms on public health protection against COVID-19 pandemic via the mediating effects of public health awareness and behavioural changes: Integrated model. *Journal of Medicine and Internet Research*, 22(8): e1996. doi:10.2196/19996

Atlani-Duault, L., Ward, J. K., Roy, M., Morlin, C., & Wilson, A. (2020) Tracking online heriosation and blame in epidemics. *Lancet Public Health*, e137–e138. doi:10.1016/S2468-2667(20)30033-5

Alvarez-Risco, A., Mejia, C. R., Delgado-Zegarra, J., Del-Aguila-Arcentales, S., Arce-Esquivel, A. A., Valladares-Garrido, M. J., Rosas Del Portal, M., Villegas, L. F., Curioso, W. H., Sekar, M. C., & Yáñez, J. A. (2020) The Peru approach against the COVID-19 infodemic: Insights and strategies. *American Journal of Tropical Medicine and Hygiene*, 103(2): 583–586. doi:10.4269/ajtmh.20-0536. Advance online publication.

Bale, J. M. (2007) Political paranoia vs. political realism: On distinguishing between bogus conspiracy theories and genuine conspiratorial politics. *Patterns of Prejudice*, 41(1): 45–60. doi:10.1080/00313220601118751

Bilewicz, M., & Sędek, G. (2015) Conspiracy stereotypes. Their sociopsychological antecedents and consequences. In M. Bilewicz, A. Cichocka, & W. Soral (Eds.) *The psychology of conspiracy*. London, UK: Routledge.

Bogart, L. M., Wagner G., Galvan F. H., & Banks D. (2010) Conspiracy beliefs about HIV are related to antiretroviral treatment nonadherence among African American men with HIV. *Journal of Acquired Immune Deficiency Syndromes*, 53(5): 648–655.

Cuan-Baltazar, J. Y., Muñoz-Perez, M. J., Robledo-Vega, C., Pérez-Zepeda, M. F., & Soto-Vega, E. (2020) Misinformation of COVID-19 on the internet: Infodemiology study. *JMIR Public Health Surveillance*, 6(2): e18444. doi:10.21 96/18444

Depoux, A., Martin, S., Karafillakis, E., Preet, R., Wilder-Smoth, A., & Larson, H. (2020) The pandemic of social media panic travels faster than the COVID-19 outbreak. *Journal of Travel Medicine*, 27(3): taaa031. doi:10.1093/jtm/taaa031

Douglas, K. M., Sutton, R. M., & Cichocka, A. (2017) The psychology of conspiracy theories. *Current Directions in Psychological Science*, 26(6): 538–542. doi:10.1177/0963721417718261

Dyrendal, A., Kennair, L. E. O., & Bendixen, M. (2021) Predictors of belief in conspiracy theory: The role of individual differences in schizotypal traits, paranormal beliefs, social dominance orientation, right wing authoritarianism and conspiracy mentality. *Personality and Individual Differences*, 173: 110645. doi: 10.1016/j.paid.2021.110645

Erku, D. A., Belachew, S. A., Abrha, S., Sinnollareddy, M., Thomas, J., Steadman, K. J., & Tesfaye, W. H. (2021) When fear and misinformation go viral: Pharmacists' role in deterring medication misinformation during the 'infodemic' surrounding COVID-19. *Research in social & administrative pharmacy: RSAP*, 17(1): 1954–1963. doi:10.1016/j.sapharm.2020.04.032

Farooq, A., Laato, S., & Islam, A. K. M. N. (2020) Impact of online information on self-isolation intention during the COVID-19 pandemic: Cross-sectional study. *Journal of Medical Internet Research*, 22(5): e19128. doi:10.2196/19128

Ford, C., Wallace, S., Newman, P., Lee, S.-J., & Cunningham, W. (2013) Belief in AIDS-related conspiracy theories and mistrust in the government: Relationship with HIV testing among at-risk older adults. *The Gerontologist*, 53(6): 1–12. doi:10.1093/geront/gns192

Fritsche I., Moya M., Bukowski M., Jugert P., de Lemus S., Decker O., Valor-Segura, I., & Navarro-Carrillo G. (2017) The great recession and group-based control: Converting personal helplessness into social class in-group trust and collective action. *Journal of Social Issues*, 73(1): 117–137. doi:10.1111/josi.12207.1/j.1751-2409.2011.01027.x

Georgiou N., Delfabbro P., & Balzan R. (2020) COVID-19-related conspiracy beliefs and their relationship with perceived stress and pre-existing conspiracy beliefs. *Personality and Individual Differences*, 166: 110201. doi:10.1016/j.paid.2020.110201

Hartman, T. K., Marshall, M., Stocks, T. V. A., McKay, R., Bennett, K., Butter, S., Gibson-Miller, J., Hyland, P., Levita, L., Martinez, A. P., Mason, L., McBride, O., Murphy, J., Shevlin, M., Vallières, F., & Bentall, R. P. (2020) Different conspiracy theories have different psychological and social determinants: Comparison of three theories about the origins of the COVID-19 virus in a representative sample of the UK population. *Frontiers in Political Science*. doi: 10.3389/fpos.2021.642510

Huang B., & Carley K. M. (2020) Disinformation and misinformation on Twitter during the novel coronavirus outbreak. Retrieved from: https://arxiv.org/abs/2006.04278

Imhoff, R., & Lamberty, P. (2020) A bioweapon or a hoax? The link between distinct conspiracy beliefs about the coronavirus disease (COVID-19) outbreak and pandemic Behavior. *Social Psychological and Personality Science*, 11(8): 1110–1118. doi:10.1177/1948550620934692

Jolley D., & Douglas K. M. (2014) The effects of anti-vaccine conspiracy theories on vaccination intentions. *PLoS One*, 9(2): e89177. doi:10.1371/journal.pone.0089177

Jolley D., Meleady R., & Douglas K. M. (2019) Exposure to intergroup conspiracy theories promotes prejudice which spreads across groups. *British Journal of Psychology*, 111(6): 1–19. doi:10.1111/bjop.12385

Kadam A. B., & Atre S. R. (2020) Negative impact of social media panic during the COVID-19 outbreak in India. *Journal of Travel Medicine*, 27(3). doi:10.1093/jtm/taaa057.taaa057

King A. (2020) Fast news or fake news? The advantages and the pitfalls of rapid publication through pre-print servers during a pandemic. *EMBO Reports*, 21(6). doi:10.15252/embr.202050817

Lamberty P., & Imhoff R. (2018) Powerful pharma and its marginalized alternatives? *Social Psychology*, 49: 255–270.

Li, X., & Liu, Q. (2020) Social media use, eHealth literacy, disease knowledge, and preventive behaviors in the COVID-19 pandemic: Cross-sectional study on Chinese netizens. *Journal of Medicine and Internet Research*, 22(10): e19684. doi:10.2196/19684

Naseem S. B., & Bhatti R. (2020) The Covid-19 "infodemic": A new front for information professionals. *Health Information and. Libraries Journal*, 37(3): 233–239. doi:10.1111/hir.12311

O'Connor C., & Murphy M. (2020) Going viral: Doctors must tackle fake news in the covid-19 pandemic. *BMJ (Clinical Research. Edition.)*, 369. doi:10.1136/bmj.m1587.m1587

Ojikutu, B. O., Stephenson, K. E., Mayer, K. H., & Emmons, K. M. (2021) Building trust in COVID-19 vaccines and beyond through authentic community investment. *American Journal of Public Health*, 111(3): 366–368. doi:10.2105/AJPH.2020.306087

Oleksy, T., Wnuk, A., Maison, D., & Lys, A. (2021) Content matters. Different predictors and social consequences of general and government-related conspiracy theories on COVID-19. *Personality and Individual Differences*, 168: 110289. doi:10.1016/j.paid.2020.110289

Orso D., Federici N., Copetti R., Vetrugno L., & Bove T. (2020) Infodemic and the spread of fake news in the COVID-19-era [published online ahead of print, 2020 23rd April]. *European Journal of Emergency Medicine*, 27(5): 327–328. doi:10.1097/MEJ.0000000000000713

Richey, S. (2017) A birther and a truther: The influence of the authoritarian personality on conspiracy beliefs. *Political Policy*, 45(3): 465–485. doi:10.1111/polp.12206

Shaw R., Kim Y., & Hua J. (2020) Governance, technology and citizen behavior in pandemic: Lessons from COVID-19 in East Asia. *Progress in Disaster Science*, 6:100090. doi:10.1016/j.pdisas.2020.100090

Sturm, T., & Albrecht, T. (2020) Constituent COVID-19 Apocalypses: Contagious Conspiracism, 5G, and Viral Vaccinations. *Anthropological Medicine*, 28(1): 122–139. doi:10.1080/13648470.2020.1833684122-139

Swami V., & Coles R. (2010) The truth is out there: Belief in conspiracy theories. *The Psychologist*, 23(7): 560–563.

Talwar S., Dhir A., Kaur P., Zafar N., & Alrasheedy M. (2019) Why do people share fake news? Associations between the dark side of social media use and fake news sharing behavior. *Journal of Retailing and Consumer Service*, 51: 72–82. doi:10.1016/j.jretconser.2019.05.026

Van Bavel, J. J., Baicker, K., Boggio, P. S., Capraro, V., Cichocka, A., Cikara, M., Crockett, M. J., Crum, A. J., Douglas, K. M., Druckman, J. N., Drury, J., Dube, O., Ellemers, N., Finkel, E. J., Fowler, J. H., Gelfand, M., Han, S., Haslam, S. A., Jetten, J., Kitayama, S., Mobbs, D., Napper, L. E., Packer, D. J., Pennycook, G., Peters, E., Petty, R. E., Rand, D. G., Reicher, S. D., Schnall, S., Shariff, A., Skitka, L. J., Smith, S. S., Sunstein, C. R., Tabri, N., Tucker, J. A., Linden, S. V., Lange, P. V., Weeden, K. A., Wohl, M. J. A., Zaki, J., Zion, S. R., & Willer, R. (2020) Using social and behavioural science to support COVID-19 pandemic response. *Nature and Human Behaviour*, 4(5): 460–471. doi:10.1038/s41562-020-0884-z

van der Linden S. (2015) The conspiracy-effect: Exposure to conspiracy theories (about global warming) decreases pro-social behavior and science acceptance. *Personality and Individual Differences*. 87: 171–173. doi:10.1016/j.paid.2015.07.045

Van der Linden, S., Panagopoulos, C., Azevedo, F., & Jost, J. T. (2020) The paranoid style in American politics revisited: An ideological asymmetry in conspiratorial thinking. *Political Psychology*, 42: 23–51. doi:10.1111/pops.12681

van Prooijen J. W. (2018) Empowerment as a tool to reduce belief in conspiracy theories. In J. E. Uscinski (Ed.) *Conspiracy theories and the people who believe them*. Oxford, UK: Oxford University Press.

van Prooijen J. W., & Douglas K. M. (2018) Belief in conspiracy theories: Basic principles of an emerging research domain. *European Journal of Social Psychology*. 48(7): 1–12. doi:10.1002/ejsp.2530

Wood, M. J., & Gray, D. (2019) Right-wing authoritarianism as a predictor of pro-establishment versus anti-establishment conspiracy theories. *Personality and Individual Differences*, 138: 163–166. doi:10.1016/j.paid.2018.09.036

Wiley, S. (2021, 4th February) Influencer marketing's surprising rise of the 'everyperson'. Forbes.

Chapter 11

Pandemic, Media and Ageism

According to the World Health Organization (WHO) ageism is one of the most significant health issues challenging the modern world. It is generally expected that as people grow older, their health will eventually start to deteriorate. This can mean that their declining state of health results in the elderly placing a disproportionate strain on public health services. Negative stereotypes about older people have surfaced in different parts of the world which label them as having a generally poorer state of health and well-being than younger people, as being more dependent on the help and support of others, and therefore inferring that they are, in different ways, a drain and a strain on society. Research evidence over many decades has shown that these stereotypes are further reinforced by representations of old people and ageing in the media.

Further research has shown that negative stereotypes about old age place older people at a disadvantage in all kinds of situations. They are confronted with prejudice about their capabilities. They might be patronised when they exhibit abilities young people have seen as beyond them. They might not be taken seriously by policy-makers. Most significantly of all in a health context, they may fail to receive the same treatment as younger people, even though they might benefit from it just as much. Sometimes there is a sense that the elderly are perceived as less worthy of care.

Writing about COVID-19 in the United States and comparing it with other parts of the world, Aronson (2020) asked whether the fact that older people were more likely to become seriously ill and die from this new virus affect the way different countries responded to the pandemic. As a doctor, the author claimed to have witnessed first-hand the way in which ageism not only figured in thinking about how to treat different patients, but could actively affect how patients were treated. She claimed that while some hospitals in the United States had created protocols for how to treat child and young adult COVID-19 patients, no such protocols were apparently in place for the elderly. Yet, both the virus and drugs that might have been used to treat COVID-19 patients did not behave the same in young and old patients.

Aronson lamented that medical schools spend considerable time teaching students about the principles of paediatrics and adult-related conditions,

DOI: 10.4324/9781003274629-11

but relatively little time on geriatrics. Some American health authorities did not even both to count deaths from specific conditions for elderly patients. Until 2018, the California Department of Public Health counted deaths from influenza only for children and adults aged under-65. These culturally endemic ageist biases in judgements about older people were, if anything, magnified during the COVID-19 pandemic. Some young people joked on-line about COVID-19 as the "boomer remover".

Such prejudice is an altogether unhealthy state of affairs. It may once have been the case that that the chronological shape of the population might be triangular, with large numbers of very young, slightly fewer in their middle ages and far fewer in old age as people died relatively early. In the 21st century, this geometrical analogy no longer makes a good fit for most con-temporary developed societies (Soto-Perez-de-Celis, 2020). Greater longevity beyond retirement means that more developed nations have age top-heavy populations. It is far more normative to be older and retired and also fit and healthy and mentally and physically active. This older age category, especially at the younger end – often referred to as "third agers" or the "young old" – are not a burden on society. Quite the reverse, they have considerable assets and spending power. They continue to pay income taxes from pensions and investments and as big purchasers contribute more sales tax than most other age groups.

It is unfortunate then that a heavy focus in the media on death rates, especially among the "old, old" (over-80s) conveys the idea that this group and the more active 60- and 70-somethings are generically vulnerable when often they are not. The fact that age emerged as perhaps the most critical indigenous risk factor for COVID-19, with death rates being highest of all for people aged over-80. Decade by decade, over the age of 50, people became progressively more at risk of becoming seriously ill if they were infected by the novel coronavirus. The very old were often told to "shield" themselves which meant being placed under a kind of house arrest whereby they were advised not to leave their homes at all.

On concern about the legacy of the 2020 pandemic is that it might fur-ther strengthen ageist stereotypes, placing older people at a bigger dis-advantage than they already have been. Given that ageism is known to have serious consequences for people's general state of health, and persistent victims can experience a deterioration in their physical and mental health, any such consequences of the pandemic would create further long-term strain for public health services (WHO, 2021, 18th March).

Ageism and Health

The coronavirus pandemic has affected many people around the world but it has disproportionately affected specific sub-groups, most notably racial minorities those who live in poorer and more crowded household, and most of all the elderly. In general, the probability of dying from COVID-19 is quite low, but it was found to grow proportionately bigger with age. Despite the greater risk of serious symptoms among older people, they did not feature prominently in much policy-making around COVID-19 (Soto-Perez-de-Celis, 2020).

In some countries, such as the United Kingdom, during the early phase of the pandemic, older people in residential care facilities were not prioritized for protection. In the UK, hospitals released many elderly COVID-19 patients back into care homes prematurely as the demand for hospital beds from those infected grew exponentially (United Nations, 2020) For some commentators, this oversight was underpinned by an endemic ageism (Soto-Perez-de-Celis, 2020).

In reviewing a large body of evidence that has accumulated over time about ageism and its health consequences, one group of reviewers concluded that the health effects of ageism had probably been underestimated (Chang et al., 2020). In this analysis, over 13,000 publications were identified and over 600 papers covering more than 400 studies were reviewed. This body of research had been amassed across 45 countries from all parts of the world. Ageism therefore is not a problem exclusive to one or two cultures.

Breaking down the evidence, health outcomes of ageism were linked to 11 health domains. These comprised: exclusion of older people from health research; devaluing the lives of older people; lack of work opportunities; denial of access to specific healthcare treatments; reduced longevity; poorer quality of life and well-being; risky health behaviours; poor social relationships; physical illness; mental illness; and cognitive impairment. In all of these domains, there was evidence from around the world that ageism disadvantaged older people.

Older people were more likely than young people to be excluded from health research which meant that clinical and medical understanding of older persons was under-developed. In fictional vignettes, in which choices had to be made about who to save first in highly life-threatening situations, older people were more likely to be sacrificed than younger people.

More generally, discrimination against older people in health care settings meant that they were more exposed to situations in which their physical and mental health and cognitive functioning would suffer. Ageism might have an immediate impact on older people by making them feel worse about themselves or by placing them at greater risk. It could also bias medical professionals against offering certain kinds of healthcare and treatment to older people that would willingly have been given to younger people. In some extreme instances, it is riskier for an old person to get seriously ill than a young person, not simply because the older person may be less fit to survive the illness, but because medical professionals would not offer the same treatment in each case.

Another important set of findings to emerge from this extensive review was that ageism effects can combine with and be magnified by other factors such as a poorer education and being a member of a minority ethnic group. Ageism can adversely affect health through both psychological and physiological pathways. It can demoralise and older person leaving them anxiety, guilty or depressed and these psychological responses can, in turn, weaken their resolve when confronted with a serious personal health condition. Ageism can also result in direct physical harm when medical and health professionals fail to give enough attention to correct diagnosis or withhold certain types of care and treatment (Chang et al., 2020).

According to some experts in the field, the negative concepts of the elderly and old age were regularly rehearsed in the media during COVID-19 pandemic. Not only that, but the generation-linked differences in opinions about older people became more acute. Conventional stereotyping of old people tended to regard them as being as warm and friendly as younger generations but as less physically and mentally competent (Cuddy et al., 2002). Such perceptions can, in turn, result in wider beliefs that the "old" need more help and support (Fiske et al., 2002; North & Fiske, 2012, 2013).

Yet, in spite of these discouraging observations, elsewhere recognition has been given to the value the Internet, World Wide Web and social networking sites can bring into the lives of older people, not least as a health information source. Moreover, efforts have been made to create user-friendly and content relevant sites that the older generations can and will use. There is an overriding belief that older people, contrary to the negative press they sometimes receive from young generations about their online competencies, are perfectly capable of using these online services and reaping personal benefits from them (Trentham et al., 2015; Taipale et al., 2018).

Media and Ageism

It is widely recognized that how we approach old age is conditioned upon culture. Media is undoubtedly the largest cultural arena in which societal images and attitudes towards old age and older people are formed. The existing research usually discusses the process of underrepresentation and misrepresentation of old age and older people. However, media as an important part of everyday realities among older people are also about creation and active use of media and their content (Wilinska & Iverson, 2017). It is therefore pertinent to the study of ageism to not only understand how different types of online and offline media represent ageing and old age, but also how people of different ages access and use those media and what types of knowledge about media and old age dominate.

Before turning to the ageism in established mainstream media and in newer online media, it is worth pausing to consider briefly the history of "ageism" in the media. Although one of the less popular topics for academic research, evidence has accumulated over many years to show that the major media, across the range of their content genres, have bene guilty of ageist representations of older people.

Close examination of these representations can uncover dominant social and cultural narratives about people at the older end of the age spectrum and about the process of ageing. Analyses of portrayals of older people on television in the 1960s through 1980s showed that the elderly were largely missing from mainstream fictional drama and other entertainment shows, especially older women. When older characters were used, they tended not to be central to the story-telling. When they did appear, they were generally less competent and vigorous than younger people and more dependent upon the support of the young (Peterson, 1973; Aronoff, 1974; Northcott, 1975; Harris & Feinberg, 1977; Greenberg et al., 1979; Davis & Kubey, 1982).

One body of work conducted in the United States revealed on mainstream television drama that character portrayals were dominated by people aged between 28 and 55. The over-65s, who at the time comprised 16 per cent of the American population, made up only two per cent of the television drama population (Gerbner et al., 1980).

Media portrayals of old people can shape public attitudes and beliefs about older adults. This includes the shaping of older-people's self-perceptions and the ideas and impressions that younger people form about them. Often, these impressions are negative rather than positive (Ayalon et al., 2020; Fraser et al., 2020). Public perceptions of old people can vary from country to country. They tend to be more positive in Eastern cultures than in Western cultures (Levy & Langer, 1994; Yoon et al., 2000).

More recently, ageism has been identified in news coverage across different media. Qualitative analyses of three Swedish newspapers coverage of old people and ageing presented narrative portraying older people as a strain on society and as a threat in terms of their demands for healthcare and welfare spending. The gradual ageing of the population is therefore presented as a worrying development that will require political and societal adjustment in the context of finding solutions to the problems it presents. The increased demand for resource for the older generations could also create a divide with the younger generations who make much less demand on the system (Lundgren & Ljuslinder, 2011).

Analysis of newspaper coverage and corporate media content concerning 50 large-scale Dutch organisations between 2006 and 2013 showed that while older employees were portrayed as high in terms of warmth and trustworthiness, they were generally presented as lower in competence. Other stereotypes indicated the value of older employees in terms of mentoring, but also the costs they might incur because of the lower perceived abilities with technology and lower adaptability to change (Kroon et al., 2016b).

In an experimental study, participants were shown a newspaper article portraying older workers in a stereotypical manner (or not) such as high rather low in warmth and low rather than high in competence. Stereotyped descriptions evoked more negative perceptions about the employability of older workers (Kroon et al., 2016a). Further evidence emerged from The Netherlands that as the volume of more news coverage of older workers' age discrimination claims increased, so too did the volume with which such claims were made by this age group (Kroon et al., 2019).

Previous research had shown that as concerns grew about older workers' health status and propensity to make insurance claims, employers were less willing to employ them for fear that older workers' problematic heath status might affect their productivity and health costs (Conen et al., 2011). Positive media coverage about older workers in which they are shown to be reliable and experienced did not significantly affect age discrimination claims, one way or another. Indeed, positive media stereotypes seemed unable to counter the impact of negative media stereotypes (Krings et al., 2011; Kroon et al., 2015).

Pandemic, News Media and Ageism

According to some commentators, it was not only the novel coronavirus that spread extensively during the pandemic, but also misleading beliefs about the pandemic and most especially about specific categories of people. One of the primary targets of this phenomenon were older people. They attracted a lot of public attention, driven to a significant extent by voluminous media coverage, because they had greater risk of dying from COVID-19 than most other population sub-groups. This vulnerability encouraged discussion of how dependent they might become on the help and support of others. Such coverage in the media reinforced pre-existing stereotypes about increased weakness and dependency of elderly folk. Despite the heterogeneity of people aged 60+ in terms of the socio-economic circumstances and health status, there was often a blanket homogeneous impression created that "they were all the same" (Previtali et al., 2020).

From early in the pandemic, COVID-19 was presented as a problem primarily for older adults. Young adults could catch the virus, but it did not generally make them very ill (Zhou et al., 2020). Ageism was witnessed for many years before 2020 and was characterised by positive and negative stereotypes (Ayalon & Tesch-Romer, 2018). During the COVID-19 pandemic, however, more emphasis was placed on the vulnerabilities of older people and this resulted in negative stereotypes about this age group being more widely aired than positive ones (Ayalon, 2020). The plight of the elderly has been seen in reports of how those less well-off have struggled to find the resources to procure extra protection in the form of face masks and sanitisers (Eckersley, 2020).

There was also a predominant view, that eventually became formal advice, that those aged 70+ was so vulnerable they should hide away completely in their homes and not venture out for anything (Sparrow, 2020). Social distancing was recommended to everyone, but especially to those of an older age. In part, the justification for this advice was that many of the older people had their pensions and would not suffer financially from staying home unlike younger people who still needed to work to pay their bills. The outcome of these age-related beliefs was to create an old versus young divide (Ayalon, 2020).

Analysis of mainstream Chinese media between January and May 2020 examined the way the media constructed narratives about older people in the context of reporting on COVID-19 (Zhang & Liu, 2021). There was evidence that old people were represented as passive recipients of the virus who then sought help from family, public institutions and government bodies. Older people were collectively described as a group that were at greater risk during the pandemic. This conclusion was based on medical evidence which had indicated that they were proportionately more likely to become seriously ill and die from tis new disease. Such coverage also reinforced a generational divided between young and old, with young people coming to regard older people as a threat to public health because of their vulnerability. The researchers called upon the media to be sensitive to these narratives and the public perceptions they can encourage and to strive not to promote or cultivate them.

In a Spanish study, researchers analysed over 500 newspaper headlines linked to the COVID-19 pandemic that were also related to older people. Formal analysis of the language used in these headlines revealed that most (71%) represented older adults in an unfavourable way. Older people were associated with deaths, deficiencies in residential care and were presented as being especially vulnerable. It was concluded that typical frontline news reporting reinforced ageist stereotypes of old age and older people (Bravo-Segal & Viller, 2020).

Pandemic, Social Media and Ageism

The mainstream media have been identified over several decades regular reinforcers of ageist stereotypes. Old people have frequently been depicted in media drama as dependent on the young, unable to cope and in need of social and familial support. They have been shown as physically past their peak, with fading mental faculties. These stereotypes continued during the pandemic and extended to social media (United Nations, 2020).

Negative stereotypes about older people in relation to their use of online social media can impact their perceptions of their own competence in this sphere. Research conducted in Canada, indicated that older people who had internalised negative stereotypes about their own generations information technology literacy seemed to believe what they were being told and downgraded their personal online competencies (Lagacé et al., 2015). Interviews with young people in Italy, when asked about their parents' information technology abilities, also indicated that the young do not hold their elders in high regard when it comes to the latter's online competencies (Piccioni et al., 2020).

Social media became important information sources during the pandemic used by governments, news media, medical professionals and members of the public. They often provided catalysts to the spread of new research and diagnostic evidence at a time of international emergency. They were also sites responsible for spreading much misinformation about COVID-19. They were permeated by conspiracy theories about the virus, vaccines and treatments. The presence of hate speech about older people and COVID-19 was an example of potentially harmful ageism. To establish more systematically how serious this negative language had become, researchers conducted large-scale analyses of the content of social media sites.

Social media were found to contain frequent negative comments about COVID-19 and older people. Some of the messages posted almost amounted to hate speech. Jokes abounded about the virus targeting the elderly. This speech was perhaps most succinctly exemplified by references to COVID-19 as a "Boomer Remover". This comment made reference to Baby Boomers or people born between 1946 and 1964 and aged between 56 and 74 years at the time of the 2020 pandemic. On Twitter, this derogatory reference was further emphasised by attaching a hashtag to it.

An analysis of tweets about COVID-19 posted in the ten days after a pandemic had been declared found that one in four played down the seriousness of the virus (Jimenez-Sotomayor et al., 2020). The same methodology was applied by a different group of researchers to analyse a large sample of tweets posted between January and April 2020, during the early phase of the COVID-19 pandemic. Tweets were found to be laden with opinions about the pandemic but there were fewer (12% judged to be ageist. Furthermore, the sentiments expressed in tweets started with a degree of age-related negativity soon after the pandemic had been declared, but then decreased in prevalence over time (Xiang et al., 2020).

Another analysis of over 18,000 tweets from which a sub-set was found that were identified through the use of key words such as "elderly", "older" and "Boomer" together with "COVID-19" or "coronavirus" found around one in three (32%) offered personal opinions, three in ten (30%) were informative and one in seven (14%) contained jokes or ridicule. Although by no means all tweets were offensive to older people, a significant minority were critical, off-hand or made fun of them in the context of the pandemic. These findings only start to develop meaning when compared with more general topic analysis of tweets during the pandemic. One such analysis of tweets between January and May 2020, drawn from a master sample of nearly 14 million English-language Twitter posts found that the most prevalent types of tweets made reference to the impact of the pandemic on the economy, the spread of the disease and growth in cases, treatment and recovery issues, the impact on the healthcare sector and the government's response (Chandrasekaran et al., 2020).

Further evidence emerged of cultural differences in the presence of ageism in online comments and posts. Around one-tenth of tweet content was found to contain ageist comments in a Spanish study. In contrast, an analysis of comparable behaviour in China, on its equivalent to Twitter, known as Weibo, where comments were more respectful of older people and their contributions to society (Xi et al., 2020).

Historically, Chinese people have been found to have positive impressions of old people. They are highly regarded for the contribution they have made in the past but also venerated for the wisdom they carry forward into old age (Vauclair et al., 2017). Another factor at play, which differentiates China from the western world is that more online activity is generated by organisations rather than individuals and they are acutely sensitive to their own public image. Criticism of old people is unlikely to be culturally well-received and so it is better to be seen to be positive rather than negative towards them (Oscar et al., 2017).

Confirming the cultural discrepancies in respect for old age, in the United States, the great majority of older adults (80%+) said that they felt they had been discriminated against. Yet, in other countries, such as Mexico (18%) and Spain (4%), this perception was much less widely held by older people (Palmore, 2004; INEGI, 2017; Ministerio De Sanidad, Servicios Sociales E, 2020). These variances might have more than on explanation. They could be attributed to cultural values linked to ageing and the elderly or it might be linked to the age profile of a country.

Another potentially important and relevant observation is that there is a generation-linked digital divide in use of micro-blogging and social networking sites (Pew Research Center, 2019). In the United States, for instance, the use of these sites was found to be far more prevalent among adolescents and young adults than mong the over-65s. Older adults do use these sites, but do so less often and generate far less content on them than do younger people (Campos-Castillo & Laestadius, 2020). Hence, any age-related prejudicial or stereotyped messages in this environment were more likely to be witnessed by the young than the old.

Lessons Learned

In summing up, the media consumption patterns of younger and older generations have diversified. While both used mainstream media more than usual during the pandemic, the young paid more attention to alternative sources of information found online than did the old and middle-aged. In the online sphere, more space was given to alternative frames of explanation of the pandemic and of the efficacy of different interventions implemented by governments to control virus transmission.

The use of media coverage in different ways might also have played a part in generational differences in personal risk interpretation. From early in the pandemic, there was an established view that older people were at greater risk of dying from this new disease than were younger people. This finding gave some succour to younger people who were able to co-opt such evidence in constructing their own anti-compliance rationales in relation to behavioural restrictions that did not play well with them. This did not mean wholescale rejection of behavioural restrictions by the young, but it did encourage those more disposed to display psychological reactance to loss of freedom to act upon their negative feelings about the authorities and their COVID-19 interventions.

Different patterns of use of information sources, offline and online, can provide interesting insights into the types of messages about ageing to which different generations might be exposed. A further important part of this understanding, however, derives from assessments of the nature of messaging about older people in these different settings. As some of the evidence presented in this chapter indicated, there was plenty of online messaging that was characterised by disparaging remarks about older people and elderly specifically within the context of the COVID-19 pandemic. Although some evidence was referenced that ageism had typified mainstream media outputs over decades, the recent phenomenon of social media had provided another echo chamber for such commentary and in some instances had magnified and intensified it.

References

Aronoff, C. (1974) Old age in prime-time. *Journal of Communication*, 24: 86–87.

Aronson, L. (2020, 28th March) Ageism is making the pandemic worse. *The Atlantic*. Retrieved from: https://www.theatlantic.com/culture/archive/2020/03/americas-ageism-crisis-is-helping-the-coronavirus/608905/

Ayalon, L. (2020) There is nothing new under the sun: Ageism and intergenerational tension in the age of the COVID-19 outbreak. *International Psychogeriatrics*, 32(10): 1221–1224.

Ayalon, L., Chasteen, A., Diehl, M., Levy, B., Neupert, S. D., Rothermund, K., Tesch-Römer, C., & Wahl, H. W. (2020) Aging in times of the COVID-19 pandemic: Avoiding ageism and fostering intergenerational solidarity. *The Journals of Gerontology, Series B: Psychological Sciences and Social Sciences.* doi:10.1093/geronb/gbaa051

Ayalon, L., & Tesch-Romer, C. (Eds.) (2018) *Contemporary perspectives on ageism*. Berlin, Germany: Springer Open.

Bravo-Segal, S., & Viller, F. (2020) Older people representation on the media during COVID-19 pandemic: A reinforcement of ageism? *Revista Espanola de Geriatria y Gerontologia*, 55(5): 266–271.

Campos-Castillo, C., & Laestadius, L. I. (2020) Racial and ethnic digital divides in posting COVID-19 content on social media among US adults: Secondary survey analysis. *Journal of Medical Internet Research*, e20472. doi:10.2196/20472

Chandrasekaran, R., Mehta, V., Valkunde, T., & Moustakas, E. (2020) Topics, trends, and sentiments of tweets about the COVID-19 pandemic: Temporal infoveillance study. *Journal of Medical Internet Research*, 22(10): e22624. doi: 10.2196/22624

Chang, E.-S., Kannoth, S., Levy, S., Wang, S.-Y., Lee, J. E., & Levy, B. R. (2020) Global reach of ageism on older persons' health: A systematic review. *PLoS One*, 15(1): e02220857. doi:10.1371/journal.pone.0220857

Conen, W. S., Henkens, K., & Schippers, J. J. (2011) Are employers changing their behavior toward older workers? An analysis of employers' surveys 2000–2009. *Journal of Aging and Social Policy*, 23(2): 141–158.

Cuddy, A. J. C., Fiske, S. T., & Glick, P. (2002) Warmth and competence as universal dimensions of social perception: The stereotype content model and the BIAS map. *Advances in Experimental Social Psychology*, 40(07): 61–149. doi: 10.1016/S0065-2601(07)00002-0

Davis, R. H., & Kubey, R. W. (1982) Growing old on television and with television. In D. Pearl, L. Bouthilet, & J. Lazar (Eds.) *Television and behaviour: Ten years of scientific progress and implications for the eighties*. Rockville, MD: National Institute of Mental Health.

Eckersley, P. (2020) Elderly Chinese woman is confronted by police on a bus after refusing to wear face mask during coronavirus outbreaks. *Daily Mail*. https://www.dailymail.co.uk/news/article-7944045/Chinese-woman-confronted-police-refusing-wear-face-mask-coronavirus-outbreaks.html

Fiske, S. T., Cuddy, A. J. C., Glick, P., & Xu, J. (2002) A model of (often mixed) stereotype content: Competence and warmth respectively follow from perceived status and competition. *Journal of Personality & Social Psychology*, 82(6): 878–902. doi:10.4324/9781315187280

Fraser, S., Lagacé, M., Bongué, B., Ndeye, N., Guyot, J., Bechard, L., Garcia, L., Taler, V., CCNA Social Inclusion and Stigma Working Group, Adam, S., Beaulieu, M., Bergeron, C. D., Boudjemadi, V., Desmette, D., Donizzetti, A. R., Éthier, S., Garon, S., Gillis, M., Levasseur, M., Lortie-Lussier, M., & Tougas, F. (2020) Ageism and COVID-19: What does our society's response say about us? *Age and Ageing*, 49(5):692–695. doi:10.1093/ageing/afaa097

Gerbner, G., Gross, L., Signorielli, N., & Morgan, M. (1980) Ageing with television: Images on television drama and conceptions of social reality. *Journal of Communication*, 30: 37–47.

Greenberg, B. S., Korzenny, F., & Atkin, C. (1979) The portrayal of the ageing trends on commercial television. *Research on Ageing*, 1: 319–334.

Harris, A., & Feinberg, J. (1977) Television and ageing: Is what you see what you get? *Gerontologist*, 17: 464–468.

INEGI. (2017) Encuesta nacional sobre discriminación (ENADIS). Retrieved from: https://www.inegi.org.mx/programas/enadis/2017/

Jimenez-Sotomayor, M. R., Gomez-Moreno, C., & Soto-Perez-de-Celis, E. (2020) Coronavirus, ageism, ad twitter: An evaluation of tweets about older adults and COVID-19. *Journal of the American Gerontological Association*, 68(8): 1661–1665.

Krings, F., Sczesny, S., & Kluge, A. (2011) Stereotypical inferences as mediators of age discrimination: The role of competence and warmth. *British Journal of Management*, 22(2): 187–201.

Kroon, A. C., Van Selm, M., Ter Hoeven, C., & Vluengenthart, R. (2015) Age at work explaining variation in frames of older employees in corporate and news media. *Journalism Studies*. doi:10.1080/1461670X.2015.1111162

Kroon, A. C., van Selm, M., Ter Hoeven, C. L., & Vliengenthart, R. (2016a) Poles apart: The processing and consequences of mixed media stereotypes of older persons. *Journal of Communication*, 66(5): 811–833.

Kroon, A. C., van Selm, M., Ter Hoeven, C. L., & Vliengenthart, R. (2016b) Reliable and unproductive? Stereotypes of older employees in corporat and news media. *Ageing and Society*. doi:10.1017/S01446X16000982

Kroon, A. C., Trilling, D., van Selm, M., & Vliegenthart, R. (2019) Biased media? How news content influences age discrimination claims. *European Journal of Ageing*, 16: 109–119.

Lagacé, M., Charmarkeh, H., Laplante, J., & Tanguay, A. (2015) How ageism contributes to the second-level digital divide: The case of Canadian seniors. *Journal of Technologies and Human Usability*, 11: 1–13. doi:10.18848/2381-922 7/CGP/v11i04/56439

Levy, B., & Langer, E. (1994) Aging free from negative stereotypes: Successful memory in China and among the American deaf. *Journal of Personality and Social Psychology*, 66(6): 989–997. doi:10.1037//0022-3514.66.6.989

Lundgren, A. S., & Ljuslinder, K. (2011) "The baby boom is over and the ageing shock awaits": Populist media imagery in news-press representations of population ageing. *International Journal of Ageing and Later Life*, 6(2). doi:10.3384/ijal.1652-8670.116233

Ministerio De Sanidad, Servicios Sociales E (2020) Igualdad. Estudio diagnóstico de fuentes secundarias sobre la discriminación en España. Retrieved from: https://sid.usal.es/idocs/F8/FDO27095/estudio_discrim_espana.pdf

North, M. S., & Fiske, S. T. (2012) An inconvenienced youth? Ageism and its potential intergenerational roots. *Psychological Bulletin*, 138(5): 982–997. doi:1 0.1037/a0027843

North, M. S., & Fiske, S. T. (2013) A prescriptive intergenerational-tension ageism scale: Succession, identity, and consumption (SIC). *Psychological Assessment*, 25(3): 706–713. doi:10.1037/a0032367

Northcott, H. C. (1975) Too young, too old – age in the world of television. *Gerontologist*, 15: 184–186.

Oscar, N., Fox, P. A., Croucher, R., Wernick, R., Keune, J., & Hooker, K. (2017) Machine learning, sentiment analysis, and tweets: An examination of Alzheimer's disease stigma on Twitter. *The Journals of Gerontology, Series B: Psychological Sciences and Social Sciences*, 72(5): 742–751. doi:10.1093/geronb/gbx014

Palmore, E. B. (2004) Ageism in Canada and the United States. *Journal of Cross-Cultural Gerontology*, 19: 41–46.

Peterson, M. (1973) The visibility and image of old people on television. *Journalism Quarterly*, 50: 569–573.

Pew Research Center. (2019) Social media fact sheet. Retrieved from: https://www.pewinternet.org/fact-sheet/social-media/

Piccioni, T., Scarcelli, C. M., & Stella, R. (2020) Inexperienced, addicted, at risk. How young people describe their parents' use of digital media. *Italian Journal of Sociology of Education*, 12: 270–292.

Previtali, F., Allen, L. D., & Varlamova, M. (2020) Not only virus spread: The diffusion of ageism during the outbreak of COVID-19. *Journal of Ageing and Social Policy*, 32(4-5): 506–514.

Soto-Perez-de-Celis, E. (2020) Social media, ageism, and older adults during the COVID-19 pandemic. *The Lancet: EClinicalMedicine*, 29: 100634. doi:10.1016/j.eclinm.2020.1000634

Sparrow, A. (2020) Coronavirus: UK over-70s to be asked to stay home "within weeks", Hancock says. *The Guardian*. Retrieved from: https://www.theguardian.com/world/2020/mar/15/coronavirus-uk-over-70s-to-be-asked-to-self-isolate-within-weeks-hancock-says

Taipale, S., Petrovcic, A., & Dolnicar, V. (2018) Intergenerational solidarity and ICT usage: Empirical insights from Finnish and Slovenian families. In Taipale, S., Wilska, T. A., & Gilleard, C. (Eds) *Digital technologies and generational identity: ICT usage across the life course* (pp. 69–86). London: Routledge.

Trentham, B., Sokoloff, S., Tsang, A., & Neysmith, S. (2015) Social media and senior citizen advocacy: An inclusive tool to resist ageism? *Politics, Groups, and Identities*, 3: 558–571. doi:10.1080/21565503.2015.1050411

United Nations. (2020, May) Policy brief: The impact of COVID-19 on older persons. Retrieved from: https://www.un.org/development/desa/ageing/wp-content/uploads/sites/24/2020/05/COVID-Older-persons.pdf

United Nations. (2020, May) Policy brief: The impact of COVID-19 on older persons. Retrieved from: https://www.un.org/development/desa/ageing/wp-content/uploads/sites/24/2020/05/COVID-Older-persons.pdf

Vauclair, C. M., Hanke, K., Huang, L. L., & Abrams, D. (2017) Are Asian cultures really less ageist than Western ones? It depends on the questions asked. *International Journal of Psychology*, 52(2): 136–144. doi:10.1002/ijop.12292

WHO. (2021, 18th March) Ageism is a global challenge: UN. Retrieved from: https://who.int/news/item/18-03-21-ageism-is-a-global-challenge-un

Wilinska, M., & Iverson, S. M. (2017, July) Media and ageism. *Innovation in Aging*, 1(suppl_1): 71. doi:10.1093/geroni/igx004.293

Xi, W., Xu, W., Zhang, X., & Ayalon, L. (2020) A thematic analysis of Weibo topics (Chinese Twitter Hashtags) regarding older adults during the COVID-19 outbreak. *Journals of Gerontology, B: Psychological Sciences and Social Science*, 6(7): e306–e312. doi:10.1093/geronb/gbaa148

Xiang, X., Lu, X., Halavanau, A., Xue, J., Sun, Y., Lai, P. H. L., & Wu, Z. (2020) Modern senicide in the face of a pandemic: An examination of public discourse and sentiment about older adults and COVID-19 using machine learning. *Journals of Gerontology B Psychological Science and Social Science*, 76(4): e190–e200. doi:10.1093/geronb/gbaa128

Yoon, C., Hasher, L., Feinberg, F., Rahhal, T. A., & Winocur, G. (2000) Cross-cultural differences in memory: The role of culture-based stereotypes about aging. *Psychology and Aging*, 15(4): 694–704. doi:10.1037//0882-7974.15.4.694

Zhang, J., & Liu, X. (2021) Media representation of older people's vulnerability during the COVID-19 pandemic in China. *European Journal of Ageing*, 18(2): 1–10. doi:10.1007/s10433-021-00613-x

Zhou, F., Yu, T., Du, R., Fan, G., Liu, Y., Liu, Z., Xiang, J., Wang, Y., Song, B., Gu, X., Guan, L., Wei, Y., Li, H., Wu, X., Xu, J., Tu, S., Zhang, Y., Chen, H., & Cao, B. (2020). Clinical course and risk factors for mortality of adult inpatients with COVID-19 in Wuhan, China: A retrospective cohort study. *The Lancet*, 395(10229): 1054–1062. doi:10.1016/s0140-6736(20)30566-3

Chapter 12

The Pandemic, the Media and Mental Health

In 2020, the world experienced the onset of a pandemic on a scale not seen for 100 years since the 1918–1919 influenza outbreak. In the absence of medical therapies and vaccines known to provide protection against this highly infectious virus, public health authorities had to rely on what were broadly labelled as "non-pharmaceutical interventions" (NPIs). Upon discovering that this new virus was mostly airborne, these NPIs took the form of interventions designed to reduce physical contact between people. Only in this way, could the primary mechanism for spread of the virus be controlled.

Reducing physical contact between people meant closing down spaces, public and private, where people normally interacted. These spaces included schools, shops, many workplaces, cultural, entertainment, hospitality and leisure venues, especially ones where large numbers of people might crowd together. In effect, most parts of entire societies and their economies were closed down. The closure of a society, however, had great cost. People lost their jobs as businesses large and small suspended all their activities and lost income. Restrictions on meetings between people from different households, even when they were family members, also wrought a psychological cost. Uncertainty about the future triggered widespread anxiety. Ignorance about the new disease and media focus on deaths from it, raised public risk estimates about it and generated fear for their own safety and that of their family. Restrictions on meetings between people meant that individuals could not turn to their families or friends for social and psychological comfort and support in such traumatic times. Such social isolation caused varying degrees of emotional distress. In the most extreme cases, among some social groups, some people were driven to suicide. In Japan, during 2020, there was a year-on-year rise of 83% in suicide deaths among women (*The Japan Times*, 2020).

Mental health breakdowns occur when individuals struggle to cope with the normal, everyday stresses of life. While some level of stress is not usually harmful and can even be beneficial in providing the motivation to learn new coping mechanisms when confronted with difficult problems. During times

DOI: 10.4324/9781003274629-12

of crisis, especially when they affect an entire community or population, stress can reach exceptional levels.

A national emergency such as a pandemic, spreading uncontrollably, and for which there are no effective medications, can prove particularly worrying because everybody faces the same threat and no one has a solution. Such a situations can create a psychological climate of no hope. When this happens, some vulnerable individuals may begin to conjure destructive thoughts that lead to problematic behaviour that sometimes might be targeted against others and sometimes is directed inwards towards themselves. Anxiety becomes more prevalent. If this mental state persists, it can evolve into more chronic and debilitating depression and from there to more damaging behaviour (Budhwani & Sun, 2020; Rovetta & Bhagavathula, 2020; Su et al., 2020; Wen et al., 2020; Zheng et al., 2020).

During the 2020 COVID-19 pandemic, many people became fearful of the disease and others were stressed by the interventions implemented by governments and public health authorities to combat it. People worried about catching the virus. They also worried about not being allowed to see family members and their friends, even when they got ill (Mertens et al., 2020; Rossi et al., 2020; Tull et al., 2020) The diversion of resources of health systems to dealing with COVID-19 meant that many other health conditions were side-lined, including some that were life-threatening (Brown et al., 2020; Fiorillo & Gorwood, 2020; Rajkumar, 2020). Hence, as well as the threat to public health represented by COVID-19, and the many deaths that arose from it, the interventions designed to protect public also harmed it through various types of collateral damage.

Another factor believed to have contributed to the mental distress caused by the pandemic was the continuous news coverage given to COVID-19 and evolving government intervention policies (Vasquez, 2020; Tangcharoensathien et al., 2020; Zheng et al., 2020). News agendas across all the major broadcast and print news media were dominated by the pandemic from March through to the end of 2020. Initial advice from governments and health authorities recommended light-touch interventions such as hand-washing and avoidance of face touching. Later, when it became clear that the virus was mostly airborne, people were told to keep their distance from each other. The dramatic way in which national governments suddenly shut down virtually their entire societies and required people to put themselves into voluntary house arrest was unprecedented. Many people were surprised and many in a state of shock once the gravity of this pandemic was no longer perceived as "somebody else's problem" (Reihani et al., 2020).

The negative aspects of the pandemic were given much early news prominence. In the United Kingdom, daily briefings from government ministers and their senior public health and scientific advisers reminded everyone of the serious cases and how much at risk they were of dying or of surviving, but then experiencing longer-term debilitating health conditions. This type of media coverage was found to produce mental stress ranging from mild to severe (Olagoke et al., 2020).

Media, COVID-19 and Mental Health

The frequently extreme measures implemented by governments to control public interpersonal contact persisted for many months and in some countries were re-imposed after periods of relaxation numerous times. These extreme circumstances lowered the mood states of most people and for a significant number they caused serious mental health issues. The worsening status of mental health for national populations had concerns about COVID-19 as their root cause, but there was evidence also that information flowing through the mass media and online social media also played their part in driving these reactions (Pimenta et al., 2020).

People around the world were reliant on the mass media for up-to-date and comprehensive information about the pandemic. Despite the constructive role many news media adopted in working with governments and public health authorities to keep people informed and reassured during an unprecedented crisis, evidence also emerged that repeated exposure to news about COVID-19 did increase public anxiety and stress (Garfin et al., 2020).

Research confirmed that media coverage played a part in determining public risk perceptions and emotional reactions during the pandemic. One study found statistically significant associations between people's reported frequencies of exposure to COVID-related news and these psychological reactions. A public health questionnaire was used to measure symptoms of anxiety and depression and other questions were designed to measure perceived risk from the coronavirus and also the frequency with which they got information about COVID-19 from various broadcast and print news sources. News exposure was found to be related to reporting of depressive symptoms after controlling for demographic factors. This relationship was also strengthened by greater perceived vulnerability to COVID-19 (Olagoke et al., 2020).

A large survey in Russia, conducted between 6th and 15th April 2020, investigated whether consuming COVID-related news was associated with the onset of state anxiety. The findings indicated that time spent following this kind of news was linked to increased anxiety. The relationship was progressive. The more COVID-19 news respondents read about, the greater their anxiety became. Many of the sample held high-confidence in the COVID-19 information they received, but they exhibited low overall trust in government and the authorities and generally had a poor opinion of their country's state of readiness to handle the pandemic (Nekliudov et al., 2020).

The news media were known to be able to shape public perceptions on the issues it covers. The news does not simply convey factual information, which does not always fully get through to people (Gunter, 2015). It can also create and impart impressions about people, places, institutions, events and issues that might or might not have a factual basis (Gunter, 1997). When this happens during times of crisis, when people are often more acutely tuned in to the news, its power potentially to shape public opinion grows (Leo & Lacasse, 2008; Meadows et al., 2011; Seabrook et al., 2016).

Knowing that the news media can exert these influences, it is imperative during a major crisis such as the COVID-19 pandemic that they present information that is accurate, balanced, relevant and timely information, that offers a measured interpretation of pandemic events and a clear explanation and analysis of the interventions announced and imposed on national or regional populations and communities by governments and their public health authorities (Cowper, 2020; Keles et al., 2020).

People needed to understand what was happening and, in particular, to be willing to comply with restrictions on their behaviours because they knew why these measures were being taken. They needed to be motivated to comply and this response would probably be achieved through rational argument, understanding of personal risks and through subtle emotional threats. In part, the restrictions were imposed to protect the vulnerable and also to protect the capacity of health services to cope. In addition, messages about the pandemic needed to explain the personal risks to all individuals. These risk perceptions would drive emotional reactions and these anxieties would, in turn, motivate behavioural intentions to comply with pandemic restrictions (Bish & Michie, 2010; Park et al., 2019). Apart from these important behavioural outcomes, however, persistent anxiety can eventually cause a range of other mental health complications. Mainstream news media were not the only sources of information and influence in people's lives during the COVID-19 pandemic. Many people turned also to the Internet and their microblogging and social media sites for alternative sources of insight.

Social Media, COVID-19 and Mental Health

There was evidence from pre-pandemic research that regular users of social media sites already exhibited a degree of anxiety proneness. These online settings were places where users could be exposed to many different kinds of problematic content giving rise to misinformation, enhanced risk perceptions and fear responses, sometimes leading to more chronic and persistent anxiety symptoms (Coyne et al., 2019; de Bérail et al., 2019). Sometimes, the adverse psychological responses were triggered by remarks directed at the user (Ruggieri et al., 2020). Vulnerable people prone to swallow unsubstantiated rumours can end up experiencing unncesaary anxiety that can in some cases cause even more serious mental health problems (Roy et al., 2020).

In the context of the 2020 pandemic, further evidence emerged that anxiety responses could also occur in response to exposure to news online (Moghanibashi-Mansourieh, 2020). One possible psychological dynamic at play here was that in thinking about COVID-19 more often, people also become more worried about it (Huang & Zhao, 2020). There was further evidence that people were spending more time online during the pandemic, often seeking out information it or simply being exposed by virtue of spending more time in that environment (Hutchinson, 2020). The more time they spent in that setting, the more likely they were to become anxious as a result (Hawes et al., 2020).

Wong, Liu Leung and colleagues (2020) found that greater exposure to COVID-19 information on social media among people living in Hong Kong was associated with higher levels of anxiety. This anxiety also gave rise to lower trust in COVID-19 information, but also greater behavioural compliance. Hence, older people in Hong Kong who engaged with greater amounts of COVID information on social media sites also exhibited higher levels of anxiety. While anxiety may have motivated people to comply mor with behavioural restrictions, there was no direct behavioural influence of level of exposure to COVID-19 information on social media sites (Wong et al., 2021).

Media, Pandemic and Self-Harm

Among the most extreme mental health risks associated with the pandemic were projections that suicide rates could increase. With many people experiencing anxiety about infection, social isolation and loneliness and uncertainties about their future studies or empployment, the scene was set for a wave of more severe mental health synptoms, most espeiclaly depression. These in turn might lead some especially vulnerable people to consider taking more extreme measures to end the considerable psychological discomfort they were experiencing. History has indicated that pandemics can create the conditions in which self-harm behaviour rises. There was evidence of this from the United States during the 1918–1919 Spanish influenza pandemic and from Hong Kong during the 2003 severe acute respiratory syndrome (SARS) outbreak of 2003 Wasserman, 1992; Cheung et al., 2008).

People with pre-existing mental health problems tend to be the most at risk. If restrictions deployed by public heallth authorities to slow the spread of a highly infectious new virus meant that the usual support networks were closed down or significantly reduced in capacity, then many of those with severe psychiatric disorders would have experienced difficulties coping with everyday life. On the basis of pre-pandemic evidence, measures deployed during the 2020 pandemic such as social isolation and physical distancing coupled with widespread fear about the new virus itself created a cocktail of interventions that meant that those with dispositions towards chronic anxiety and depression were likely to experience difficulties coping with societal lockdowns (Stuckler et al., 2009; Gunnell et al, 2020). Carried to an even further extreme, social isolation and feeling trapped and lonely, even at home, could then have contributed to an increased suicide risk (O'Connor & Kirtley, 2018). Not just that but constant coverage of the pandemic and its negative effects on people's lives could have triggered suicidal tendencies in people reflecting upon suicidal thoughts (Niederkrotenthaler et al., 2020).

Suicide rates increased during the Great Depression of the 1930s, but it was principally stories in the media of the day about political leaders taking their lives, rather than suicides among other groups that were significantly associated with public suicides (Stack, 1992). Further research revealed that media stories about suicides were most likely to exhibit a statistical assoiciaiton with suicides only during times of crisis or difficulty, such as periods went the rates of unemployment were high (Stack, 1993).

In the context of the 2020 pandemic, the health concern rested on the possibility that anxiety-triggering experiences such as uncertainties about infection risks and lockdown side-effects (eoconmic and psychological) could generate widespread depression that might then lead more susceptible individual to entertain suicidal thoughts (Sher, 2020). In the United Kingdom, higher than normal rates of anxiety, stress and depression were recorded in a large population cohort during the first month of the first lockdown in April 2020, especially among younger adults, females and those with pre-existing mental health issues (Jia et al., 2020). Other relevant evidence emerged from the 2020 novel coronavirus pandemic that exposure to media coverage was linked to public fear responses (Garfin et al., 2020).

Early evidence of increased propensities of self-abuse, self-harm and having suicidal thoughts emerged from a large British panel study that collected data weekly and then monthly from respondents across the country from March 2020 to the end of the year. Relevant questions about self-harm and suicidal tendencies were included routinely in this survey. One early report examined evidence collected across the first month of the first UK lockdown in the spring 2020. This study was not able to show whether suicide risk had risen during the pandemic, but the distribution of such risk mirrored pre-pandemic evidence, with higher levels being recorded amog younger people, women, those experiencing economic problems, the unemployed, those with disabilities and chronic physical illnesses and mental disorders. The research also found that people diagnosed with COVID-19 displayed high rates of abuse and self-harm thoughts. Although the researchers could not rule out that those infected could also have been at greater risk because of the nature of their work and lifestyle factors that might also explain their mental health condition (Iob et al., 2020). No evidence was presented in this study about possible media effects.

Despite evidence that some people had entertained self-harm tendencies that could have evolved into suicidal thoughts, initial soundings taken around the world in high income countries reported no increases in suicide rates (Faust et al., 2020; Qin & Mehlum ,2020; Ueda et al., 2020). Findings from lower-income countries were less clear cut with some indicative evidence from police data in one case showing that suicide rates had risen during the pandemic (Pokhrel et al., 2020). Yet, this finding was not replicated in other developing countries (Calderon-Anyosa & Kaufman, 2020).

An interesting study from India tracked suicides during the country's lockdown, between 21st March and 3rd May 2020, that were reported in online news publications. These reports were compared with ones identified during the same period in 2019. In all, 339 cases of suicides and attempted suicides were detected in 2020 and 220 in 2019. This represented a 68% year-on-year increase. This cannot be taken as an unequivocal measure of suicide rates because reporting choices could have been influenced by journalists' decisions about the newsworthiness of specific stories. Suicide stories were analysed in detail to identify characteristics of cases, including their demography and reasons for self-harm.

The researchers found that in 2020, as compared with 2019, suicide cases tended to be older, male, married and unemployed. It was speculated that the stresses lockdown restrictions on male heads of household, many of whom lost their jobs, could have contributed to this behaviour. Since there was no substantive evidence that journalists had generally changed their reporting practices, the greater presence of these stories in news media could serve as a proxy measure for actual suicide rates. Further evidence that COVID-19 was linked to suicides and attempts derived from the finding that in 157 cases out of 339 reference had bene made to fear of COVID, concern about the impact of lockdown or about being quarantined (Pathare et al., 2020).

Media Practices to Counter Adverse Mental Health Effect

The application of extensive and profound behaviour controls and re-strictions required people on a mass scale to suspend their regular, everyday lives. This locking down of societies was one of the principal interventions used to bring highly infectious and rapidly spreading diseases under control. Even though pandemics can bring considerable pain and suffering to po-pulations, extensive closures of societies can be equally damaging, eco-nomically, socially and psychologically. For individual members of the population, these kinds of restrictions can prove difficult to cope with. If they persist over time, the psychological repercussions can be severe.

As evidence gathered around the COVID-19 pandemic showed, public fear and anxiety were widespread. Being socially isolated generated feelings of loneliness. Uncertainty about when the pandemic would be over meant that finding effective psychological coping mechanisms was problematic. People were reliant on the mainstream news media for much of their information from official sources. In the 21st century, however, the Internet had made available a multitude of other information sources. While much of this information originated with government and public health organisations and was published by established news operations, there was also much content that derived from sources of uncertain identity and agenda and information of poorly established provenance. Not all the information flowing via unofficial sources therefore could be trusted and this, in turn, caused futher psychological impact by frightening people or encouraging them to behave in ways not being encouraged by the authorities.

There were also unfortunate consequences stemming from the sheer quantity of information being generated. Many people were overwhelmed by information overload. Others might be confused by different messages from different sources. Others might simply misunderstand the information even from the most established and professional of news providers, as journalists and editors tried to fit vast amounts of information about ofen complex issues into limited news space.

Even among the trusted news operators, there was an agenda at play other than objective news reporting. They were competing for audiences and readers and therefore needed to create news that stood out from the crowded news marketplace. News needed to be interesting and this often meant that it needed to be entertaining. When entertainment becomes a part of the news agenda, it can mean that story-telling styles adapt by introducing features designed to play to people's emotions as well as their intellects. This approach can result in reports that focus on dramatic developments and these tend more often than not to feature "bad" news rather than "good" news. Even good news stories – for example, featuring the personal stories of patients recovering from serious illness with COVID-19 – reminds people of the most adverse consequences of this disease. In absolute statistical terms such cases are relatively rare (or certainly of low probability), but the special attention they receive in the news can make they appear more prevalent than they really are. This reporting can cause greater public anxiety as personal risks ecome exaggerated.

The mainstream media must also monitor their own audiences and the extent to which they are exposed to different types of information and also ensure there were no unforeseen consequences of the reports and briefings they covered. When newsmakers get the packaging right, mainstream media briefings can have a positive impact (Christensen & Lægreid, 2020; Colfer, 2020; Kabiraj & Lestan, 2020; Li et al., 2020; Liu et al., 2020; Trevisan et al., 2020).

Despite the concerns already mentioned about the spreading of misinformation over the Internet, the major technology firms such as Facebook,

Google and Twitter could also play important roles in ensuring that accurate and useful information about the pandemic was circulated widely. These companies were capable of writing algorithms that could find and prioritise information verified by science and scientists through the usual peer reviewing processes and ensure that narratives explaining and justifying government pandemic polices were effectively presented (Chen et al., 2020). The overall aim here must be to reduce public anxiety stemming from uncertainty than in turn derives from ambiguity in terms of the facts about the pandemic, the SAR-CoV-2 virus and the COVID-19 disease that flows from it.

As the pandemic progress. there were calls also for further support for the public in deciphering the massive quantities of news and information in circulation about COVID-19 and the pandemic (Chen et al., 2020). Citizens needed to be able to identify for themselves which pandemic narratives and information sources they could and should believe. This objective could be achieved through educational programmes and also content classification and verification systems (Hale et al., 2020; Liu et al., 2020; Okan et al., 2020; Trevisan et al., 2020; Zhang et al., 2020). All these safeguarding interventions would be targeted at enhancing the overall quality of pandemic news by putting the most reliable and trusted information in the foreground and counteracting misleading messages that only caused confusion or motivated people to make the wrong behavioural choices, putting themselves and others at harm.

While the large technology companies, might legitimately be called upon to play their part in controlling the circulation of obviously misleading or false information, the mainstream news media could support this process by reporting on any spreading false messages and conspiracy theories associated with the pandemic and presenting evidence to dispel the effects of these messages (Mheidly & Fares, 2020; Pennycook et al., 2020; Roth & Pickles, 2020).

If these steps are taken, progress could be made in improving the quality of pandemic-related information in circulation. Tackling the damaging effects of misinformation, conspiracy theories and fake news is a goal worth investing in. The pandemic has been a global crisis and it is wrought damage on economies and societies all over the world. Perhaps equally significant have been the psychological consequences of the pandemic and governments' and public health authorities' interventions.

Significant medical and scientific research progress has been made during the pandemic and it is important that everyone understands what this means. The complexities of the science however are often best explained not by scientist themselves but by professional communicators. This is where journalists and other media professionals can come into play. New information needs to be understood by the public so that they take constructive steps as a result. Misunderstandings can produce distorted risk perceptions and fears that motivate the wrong behavioural responses

(Bhagavathula et al., 2020; Olum et al., 2020; Spoorthy et al., 2020; Taghrir et al., 2020). The last chapter will take these considerations further by examining the positive steps that media and communications system can play in supporting national and international-level actions that are taken to protect the world's populations from highly infectious new diseases.

Selective Use of Media to Alleviate Mental Health Problems

The impact of COVID-19 on mental health stemmed mostly from the interventions deployed by governments and public health authorities to combat the disease. These measures were initially the only ones available because vaccines and tried-and-tested drug treatments had not been developed in advance. It was the physical and social distancing measures, above all, that affected many people. Restrictions on going out and meeting with other people triggered feelings of loneliness. Coupled with the anxiety arising from the uncertainties surrounding the new coronavirus, isolation from usual networks of social support meant that large numbers of people felt chronically down and for some depression set in.

The restrictions imposed by lockdowns meant that people had to find alternative methods of keeping in touch with each other and occupying their time. Having no outdoor entertainment available, being encouraged to work from home, losing their jobs and having nowhere to go, meant that people sought distractions and these included spending more time in front of screens consuming mediated information and entertainment and interacting with others remotely. Research evidence emerged that those experiencing the most stress during pandemic lockdowns turned to the media to fill time, provide distraction and life their mood.

One online study, with participants from Canada and the east coast of the United States, conducted between 20th March and 20th April 2020, during the early phase of the pandemic, found that those experiencing the most COVID-19-related stress reported greater use of Facebook, mainstream television, YouTube and streaming services such as Netflix (Pahayahay, & Khalili-Mahani, 2020). Those individuals who reported being in a generally poor state of mental health (saying it was "not good") turned to streaming services such as Netflix twice as much as others. Women turned to social media twice as much as did men during this time, while younger people, aged under-35, turned to computer games three times as much as did older people. People's use and appraisal of media during the pandemic was not unconditional and was not invariably reported in positive terms. Evidence emerged that many people did turn to the mainstream media and social media as coping mechanisms but evaluated their usefulness in a positive way if the experiences they had were supportive and helped them to cope with the uncertainties of the pandemic through provision of factual and positive information.

Drawing together the evidence, it was clear in the first part of this chapter, that the pandemic did give rise to conditions that promoted increased mental health issues across populations around the world. The fears of the disease and concerns about how their lives had been disrupted by it translated for many into more chronic conditions such as anxiety, stress and depression. The media – offline and online – played their part in this process as purveyors of pandemic news and interpretation that fuelled peoples' mindsets and emotional responses. It is inevitable that the media will report bad news. There was so much bad news around at the start of the pandemic. It would have been irresponsible of major broadcasters not to present the facts to the public even when they might generate adverse reactions as side effects. Reassurance can be taken from evidence that the media can also offer the public hope and help with psychological coping. This more positive power of the broadcast, print and online media can be harnessed by governments and health authorities to help their populations understand what is happening an take some degree of personal psychological control in uncertain times.

References

Bhagavathula, A. S., Aldhaleei, W. A., Rahmani, J., Mahabadi, M. A., & Bandari, D. K. (2020) Knowledge and perceptions of COVID-19 among health care workers: Cross-sectional study. *JMIR Public Health Surveillance*, 6(2): e19160.

Bish, A., & Michie, S. (2010) Demographic and attitudinal determinants of protective behaviours during a pandemic: A review. *British Journal of Health Psychology*, 15(Pt 4): 797–824. doi:10.1348/135910710X485826

Brown, E., Gray, R., Lo Monao, S., O'Donoghue, B., Nelson, B., Thompson, A., Francey, S., & McGorry, P. (2020) The potential impact of COVID-19 on psychosis: A rapid review of contemporary epidemic and pandemic research. *Schizophrenia Research*, 222: 79–87. doi:10.1016/j.schres.2020.05.005

Budhwani, H., & Sun, R. (2020) Creating COVID-19 stigma by referencing the novel coronavirus as the "Chinese virus" on twitter: Quantitative analysis of social media data. *Journal of Medicine and Internet Research*, 22(5): e19301.

Calderon-Anyosa, R., & Kaufman, J. (2020) Impact of COVID-19 lockdown policy on homicide, suicide, and motor vehicle deaths in Peru. *medRxiv [Preprint.]* doi: 10.1101/2020.07.11.20150193

Chen, Q., Min, C., Zhang, W., Wang, G., Ma, X., & Evans, R. (2020) Unpacking the black box: How to promote citizen engagement through government social media during the COVID-19 crisis. *Computers in Human Behavior*, 110: 106380. doi:10.1016/j.chb.2020.106380

Cheung, Y. T., Chau, P. H., & Yip, P. S. (2008) A revisit on older adults suicides and severe acute respiratory syndrome (SARS) epidemic in Hong Kong. *International Journal of Geriatric Psychiatry*, 23, 1231–1238.

Christensen, T., & Lægreid, P. (2020) Balancing governance capacity and legitimacy: How the Norwegian government handled the COVID-19 crisis as a high performer. *Public Administration Review*, 80(5): 774–779. doi:10.1111/puar.13241

Colfer, B. (2020) Herd-immunity across intangible borders: Public policy responses to COVID-19 in Ireland and the UK. *European Policy Analysis*, 6(2): 203–225. doi:10.1002/epa2.1096

Cowper, A. (2020) COVID-19: Are we getting the communications right? *The BMJ*, 368: m919. doi:10.1136/bmj.m919

Coyne, S., Stockdale, L., & Summers, K. (2019) Problematic cell phone use, depression, anxiety, and self-regulation: Evidence from a three-year longitudinal study from adolescence to emerging adulthood. *Computers and Human Behaviour*, 96: 78–84. doi:10.1016/j.chb.2019.02.014

de Bérail, P., Guillon, M., & Bungener, C. (2019) The relations between YouTube addiction, social anxiety and parasocial relationships with YouTubers: A moderated-mediation model based on a cognitive-behavioral framework. *Computers and Human Behaviour*, 99: 190–204. doi:10.1016/j.chb.2019.05.007

Faust, J., Shah, S., Du, C., Li, S., Lin, Z., & Krumholz, H. (2020) Suicide deaths during the stay-at-home advisory in Massachusetts. *medRxiv [Preprint.]* doi: 10.1101/2020.10.20.20215343

Fiorillo, A., & Gorwood, P. (2020) The consequences of the COVID-19 pandemic on mental health and implications for clinical practice. *European Psychiatry*, 63(1): e32.

Garfin, D. R., Silver, R. C., & Holman, E. A. (2020) The novel coronavirus (COVID-2019) outbreak: Amplification of public health consequences by media exposure. *Health Psychology*, 39(5): 355–357.

Gunnell, D., Appleby, L., Arensman, E., Hawton, K., John, A., Kapur, N., Khan, M., O'Connor, R. C., & Pirkis, J. The COVID-19 suicide prevention research collaboration. (2020). Suicide risk and prevention during the COVID-19 pandemic. *The Pnacent Psychiatry*, 7(6): 468–471.

Gunter, B. (1997) *Measuring bias on television*. Luton, UK: University of Luton Press.

Gunter, B. (2015) *The cognitive impact of television news: Production attributes and information reception*. Basingstoke, UK: Palgrave Macmillan.

Hale, T., Angrist, N., Boby, T., Cameron-Blake, E., Hallas, L., Kira, B., Majumdar, S., Petherick, A., Phillps, S., Taflow, H., & Webster, S. (2020) Variation in government responses to COVID-19. *Blavatnik School of Government Working Paper*; BSG-WP-2020/032, p.31. Retrieved from: https://www.bsg.ox.ac.uk/sites/default/files/2020-12/BSG-WP-2020-032-v10.pdf

Hawes, T., Zimmer-Gembeck, M., & Campbell, S. (2020) Unique associations of social media use and online appearance preoccupation with depression, anxiety, and appearance rejection sensitivity. *Body Image*, 33: 66–76. doi:10.1016/j.bodyim.2020.02.010

Hutchinson, A. (2020) People are spending 20% more time in apps during the COVID-19 lockdowns. Retrieved from: https://www.socialmediatoday.com/news/people-are-spending-20-more-time-in-apps-during-the-covid-19-lockdowns-re/575403/ [Report]

Huang, Y., & Zhao N. (2020) Generalized anxiety disorder, depressive symptoms and sleep quality during COVID-19 outbreak in China: A web-based cross-sectional survey. *Psychiatric Research*, 288: 112954. doi:10.1016/j.psychres.2020.112954

Iob, E., Steptoe, A., & Fancourt, D. (2020) Abuse, self-harm and suicidal ideation in the UK during the COVIF-19 pandemic. *British Journal of Psychiatry*, 217(4): 543–546.

Jia, R., Ayling, K., Chalder, T., Massey, A., Broadbent, E., Coupland, C., & Vedhara, K. (2020) Mental health in the UK during the COVID-19 pandemic: Cross-sectional analyses from a community cohort study. *BMJ Open*, 10(9). doi:10.1136/bmjopen-2020-040620

Kabiraj, S., & Lestan, F. (2020) COVID-19 outbreak in Finland: Case study on the management of pandemics. In G. Babu, & M. Qamaruddin (Eds.) *International case studies in the management of disasters* (pp. 213–229). Bingley, UK: Emerald Publishing Limited.

Keles, B., McCrae, N., & Grealish, A. (2020) A systematic review: The influence of social media on depression, anxiety and psychological distress in adolescents. *International Journal of Adolescence and Youth*, 25(1): 79–93. doi:10.1080/02673843.2019.1590851

Leo, J., & Lacasse, J. R. (2008) The media and the chemical imbalance theory of depression. *Society*, 45: 35–45. doi:10.1007/s12115-007-9047-3

Li, Y., Chandra, Y., & Kapucu, N. (2020) Crisis coordination and the role of social media in response to COVID-19 in Wuhan, China. *American Review of Public Administration*, 50(6–7): 698–705. doi:10.1177/0275074020942105

Liu, W., Yue, X.-G., & Tchounwou, P. B. (2020) Response to the COVID-19 epidemic: The Chinese experience and implications for other countries. *International Journal of Environmental Research and Public Health*, 17(7): 2304. doi:10.3390/ijerph17072304

Meadows, M. E., & Foxwell-Norton, K. (2011) Community broadcasting and mental health: The role of local radio and television in enhancing emotional and social well-being. The *Radio Journal: International Studies in Broadcast and Audio Media*, 9: 89–106.

Mertens, G., Gerritsen, L., Duijndam, S., Salemink, E., & Engelhard, I. M. (2020) Fear of the coronavirus (COVID-19): Predictors in an online study conducted in March 2020. *Journal of Anxiety Disorders*,74: 102258. doi:10.1016/j.janxdis.2020.102258

Mheidly, N., & Fares, J. (2020) Leveraging media and health communication strategies to overcome the COVID-19 infodemic. *Journal of Public Health Policy*, 41(4): 410–420. doi:10.1057/s41271-020-00247-w

Moghanibashi-Mansourieh, A. (2020) Assessing the anxiety level of Iranian general population during COVID-19 outbreak. *Asian Journal of Psychiatry*, 51: 102076. doi:10.1016/j.ajp.2020.102076

Nekliudov, N. A., Blyus, O., Cheung, K. Y., Petrou, L., Genuneit, J., Sushentsev, N., Levadnaya, A., Comberian, P., Warner, J. O., Tudor-Eilliams, G., Teufel, M., Greenhawt, M., DunnGalvin, A., & Munblit, D. (2020) Excessive media consumption about COVID-19 is associated with increased state anxiety: Outcomes of a large online survey in Russia. *Journal of Medical Internet Research*, 22(9): e20955. doi:10.2196/20955

Niederkrotenthaler, T., Braun, M., Pirkis, J., Till, B., Stack, S., Sinyor, M., Tran, U. S., Voracek, M., Cheng, Q., Arendt, Florian., Scherr, S., Yip, P. S. F., & Spittal, M. J. (2020) Association between suicide reporting in the media and suicide: systematic review and meta-analysis. *BMJ*, 365: m575. doi:10.1136/bmj.m575.

O'Connor, R. C., & Kirtley, O. J. (2018) The integrated motivational-volitional model of suicidal behaviour. *Philosophical Transactions of the Royal Society London B: Biological Sciences*, 373(1754): 20170268. doi:10.1098/rstb.2017. 0268

Okan, O., Bollweg, T. M., Berens, E. M., Hurrelmann, K., Bauer, U., & Schaeffer, D. (2020) Coronavirus-related health literacy: A cross-sectional study in adults during the COVID-19 infodemic in Germany. *International Journal of Environmental Research and Public Health*, 17(15): 5503. doi:10.3390/ijerph17155503

Olagoke, A. A., Olagoke, O. O., & Hughes, A. M. (2020) Exposure to coronavirus news on mainstream media: The role of risk perceptions and depression. *British Journal of Health Psychology*, 25(4): 865–874.

Olum, R., Chekwech, G., Wekha, G., & Nassozi, D. R. (2020) Coronavirus disease-2019: Knowledge, attitude, and practices of health care workers at Makerere University teaching hospitals, Uganda. *Frontiers of Public Health*, 8: 181. doi:10.3389/fpubh.2020.00181

Pahayahay, P., & Khalili-Mahani, N. (2020) What media helps, what media hurts: A mixed methods survey study of coping with COVID-19 using the media repertoire framework and the appraisal theory of stress. *Journal of Medical Internet Research*, 22(8): e20186. doi:10.2196/20186

Park, S., Boatwright, B., & Avery, E. J. (2019) Information channel preference in health crisis: Exploring the roles of perceived risk, preparedness, knowledge and intent to follow directives. *Public Relations Review*, 45(5). Retrieved from: https://www.sciencedirect.com/science/article/abs/pii/S0363811118306192

Pathare, S., Vijayakumar, L., Fernandes, T. N., Shastri, M., Kapoor, A., Pandit, D., Lohumi, I., Ray, S., Kulkarni, A., & Korde, P. (2020) Analysis of news media reports of suicides and attempted suicides during the COVID-19 lockdown in India. *International Journal of Mental Health Systems*, 14, Article No. 88. doi:10.1186/s13033-020-00422-2

Pennycook, G., McPhetres, J., Zhang, Y., Lu, J. G., & Rand, D. G. (2020) Fighting COVID-19 misinformation on social media: Experimental evidence for a scalable accuracy-nudge intervention. *Psychological Science*, 31(7): 770–780. doi:10.1177/0956797620939054

Pimenta, I. D. S. F., Nayana de Sousa Mata, A., Braga, L. P., Silva de Medeiros, C. B., Morais de Azevedo, P., Bezerra, I. N. M., Hugo de Oliveira Segundo, V., de Franca Nunus, A. C., Santos, G. M., Grosseman, S., Nicolas, I. M., & Piuvesam, G. (2020) Media and scientific communication about the COVID-19 pandemic and the repercussions on the population's mental health: A protocol for the systematic review and meta-analysis. *Medicine (Baltimore)*, 99(5): e23298. doi:10.1097/MD000000000023298

Pokhrel, S., Sedhai, Y. R., & Atreya, A. (2020) An increase in suicides amidst the coronavirus disease 2019 pandemic in Nepal. *Medical Science and Law*. 25802420966501. doi:10.1177/0025802420966501 pmid:33036544

Qin, P., & Mehlum, L. (2020) National observation of death by suicide in the first 3 months under COVID-19 pandemic. *Acta Psychiatrica Scandinavia*, pmid:33111325

Rajkumar, R. P. (2020) COVID-19 and mental health: A review of the existing literature. *Asian Journal of Psychiatry*, 52: 102066.

Reihani, H., Ghassemi, M., Mazer-Amirshahi, M., Aljohani, B., & Pourmand, A. (2020) Non-evidenced based treatment: An unintended cause of morbidity and mortality related to COVID-19. *The American Journal of Emergency Medicine*, 39: 221–222. doi:10.1016/j.ajem.2020.05.001

Rossi R., Socci, V., Talevi, D., Mensi, S., Niolu, C., Pacitti, F., Di Marco, A., Rossi, A., Siracusano, A., & Di Lorenzo, G. (2020) COVID-19 pandemic and lockdown measures impact on mental health among the general population in Italy. *Frontiers of Psychiatry*, 11: 790. doi:10.3389/fpsyt.2020.00790

Roth, Y., & Pickles N. (2020) Updating our approach to misleading information: Twitter, Inc. Retrieved from: https://blog.twitter.com/en_us/topics/product/2020/updating-our-approach-to-misleading-information

Rovetta, A., & Bhagavathula, A. S. (2020) Global infodemiology of COVID-19: Analysis of Google web searches and instagram hashtags. *Journal of Medical Internet Research*, 22(8): e20673. doi:10.2196/20673

Roy, D., Tripathy, S., Kar, S., Sharma, N., Verma, S., & Kaushal, V. (2020) Study of knowledge, attitude, anxiety & perceived mental healthcare need in Indian population during COVID-19 pandemic. *Asian Journal of Psychoolgy*, 51: 102083. doi:10.1016/j.ajp.2020.102083

Ruggieri, S., Santoro, G., Pace, U., Passanisi, A., & Schimmenti, A. (2020) Problematic Facebook use and anxiety concerning use of social media in mothers and their offspring: An actor–partner interdependence model. *Addictive Behaviour Reports*, 11: 2100256. doi:10.1016/j.abrep.2020.100256

Seabrook, E. M., Kern, M. L., & Rickard, N. S. (2016) Social networking sites, depression, and anxiety: A systematic review. *JMIR Mental Health*, 3(4): e50. doi:10.2196/mental.5842

Sher, L. (2020) The impact of the COVID-19 pandemic on suicide rates. *QJM: An International Journal of Medicine*, 113(10): 707–712.

Spoorthy, M. S., Pratapa, S. K., & Mahant, S. (2020) Mental health problems faced by healthcare workers due to the COVID-19 pandemic-A review. *Asian Journal of Psychiatry*, 51: 102119. doi:10.1016/j.ajp.2020.102119

Stack, S. (1992) The effect of the media on suicide: The Great Depression. *Suicide and Life Threatening Behavior*, 22(2): 255–267.

Stack, S. (1993) The media and suicide: A nonadditive model, 1968-1980. *Suicide and Life Thtreatening Behavior*, 23(1): 63–66.

Stuckler, D., Basu, S., Suhrcke, M., Coutts, A., & McKee, M. (2009) The pulbic health effect of ecoonmic crises and alternative policy responses in Europe: An empirical analysis. *The Lancet*, 374: 315–323.

Su, Z., McDonnell, D., Wen. J., Kozak, M., Abbas, J., Segalo, S., Li, X., Ahmad, J., Cheshmehzangi, A., Cai, Y., Yang, L., & Xiang, Y.-T. (2021) Mental health consequences of COVID-19 media coverage: the need for effective crisis communication practices. *Global Health*, 17(1): 4. doi:10.1186/s12992-020-00654-4

Su, Z., Wen, J., Abbas, J., McDonnell, D., Cheshmehzangi, A., Li, X., Ahmad, J., Šegalo, S., Maestro, D., & Cai, Y. (2020) A race for a better understanding of COVID-19 vaccine non-adopters. *Brain, Behaviour & Immunity – Health Journal*, 9: 100159. doi:10.1016/j.bbih.2020.100159

Taghrir, M. H., Borazjani, R., Shiraly, R. (2020) COVID-19 and Iranian medical students; A survey on their related-knowledge, preventive behaviors and risk perception. *Archives of Iranian Medicine*, 23(4): 249–254.

Tangcharoensathien, V., Calleja, N., Nguyen, T., Purnat, T., D'Agostino, M., Garcia-Saiso, S., Landry, M., Rashidian, A., Hamilton, C., AbdAllah, A., Ghiga, I., Hill, A., Hougendobler, D., van Andel, J., Nunn, M., Brooks, I., Sacco, P. L., De Domenico, M., Mai, P., Gruzd, A., Alaphilippe, A., & Briand S. (2020) Framework for managing the COVID-19 infodemic: Methods and results of an online, crowdsourced WHO technical consultation. *Journal of Medical Internet Research*, 22(6): e19659.

Tasnim, S., Hossain, M. M., & Mazumder, H. (2020) Impact of rumors and misinformation on COVID-19 in social media. *Journal of Preventive Medicine and Public Health*. 53(3): 171–174.

The Japan Times. (2020) Japan suicides rise as economic impact of coronavirus hits home. [cited 2020 December 1st]; Available from: https://www.japantimes.co.jp/news/2020/11/11/national/japan-suicide-rise-coronavirus/

Trevisan, M., Le, L. C., & Le, A. V. (2020) The COVID-19 pandemic: A view from Vietnam. *American Journal of Public Health*, 110(8): 1152–1153.

Tull, M. T., Edmonds, K. A., Scamaldo, K. M., Richmond, J. R., Rose, J. P., & Gratz K. L. (2020) Psychological outcomes associated with stay-at-home orders and the perceived impact of COVID-19 on daily life. *Psychiatry Research*, 289: 113098. doi:10.1016/j.psychres.2020.113098

Ueda, M., Nordström, R., & Matsubayashi, T. (2020) Suicide and mental health during the COVID-19 pandemic in Japan. *medRxiv [Preprint.]* doi:10.1101/2020.10.06.20207530

Vazquez, M. (2020) Calling COVID-19 the "Wuhan Virus" or "China Virus" is inaccurate and xenophobic. Yale School of Medicine. Retrieved from: https://medicine.yale.edu/news-article/calling-covid-19-the-wuhan-virus-or-china-virus-is-inaccurate-and-xenophobic/

Wasserman, I. M. (1992) The impact of epidemic, war, prohibition and media on uicide: United States, 1910-1920. *Suicide and Life Threatening Behaviour*, 22: 240–254.

Wen, W., Su, W., Tang, H., Le, W., Zhang, X., Zheng, Y., Liu, X., Xie, L., Li, J., Ye, J., Dong, L., Cui, X., Miao, Y., Wang, D., Dong, J., Xiao, C., Chen, W., & Wang, H. (2020) Immune cell profiling of COVID-19 patients in the recovery stage by single-cell sequencing. *Cell Discovery*, 6: 31. doi:10.1038/s41421-020-0168-9. Erratum in: *Cell Discovery*, 20:6:41.

Wong, F. H. C., Liu, T., Leung, D. K. Y., Zhang, A. Y., Au, W. S. H., Kwok, W. W., Shum, A. K. Y., Wong, G. H. Y., & Lum, T. Y.-S. (2021) Consuming information related to COVID-19 on social media among older adults and its association with anxiety, social trust in information, and COVID-safe behaviors: Cross-sectional telephone survey. *Journal of Medical Internet Research*, 23(2): e26570. doi:10.2196/26570

Zhang, L., Li, H., & Chen, K. (2020) Effective risk communication for public health emergency: Reflection on the COVID-19 (2019-nCoV) outbreak in Wuhan, China. *Healthcare (Basel, Switzerland)*, 8(1): 64. doi:10.3390/healthcare8010064

Zhang, L., Zhang, D., Fang, J., Wan, Y., Tao, F., & Sun, Y. (2020) Assessment of mental health of Chinese primary school students before and after school closing and opening during the COVID-19 pandemic. *JAMA Network Open*, 3: e2021482. doi:10.1001/jamanetworkopen.2020.21482 pmid:32915233

Zheng, Y., Goh, E., & Wen, J. (2020) The effects of misleading reports about COVID-19 on Chinese tourists' mental health: A perspective article. *Anatolia*, 31(2). doi:10.1080/13032917.2020.174720

Chapter 13

Importance of the Media during a Pandemic

As the pandemic spread rapidly across the world in early 2020, it became clear that a global crisis was fast emerging that would need urgent protective action from national governments. In large part, the "protection" would need to derive initially from restrictions on the way people behaved. Many spaces in which people would normally interact, without a second thought, were compulsorily closed. People were told to stay home and not go into the workplace if they did not have to. Schools, shops, entertainment, leisure and hospitality venues were closed, as were many other physical spaces and people were told to keep their distance from each other. In needing to reach entire populations instantly with these messages, the mass media came into play as the primary communications platforms through governments could put out their notices.

Previous pandemics, such as SARS (2003), H1N1 (2009) and MERS (2012) had illustrated the important role that mass media could play in this context. While dealing with a new virus, about which relatively little was known, presented a fresh challenge, there was some relevant hindsight from earlier pandemics to draw upon in terms of public health communications strategies that could be effective.

The media quickly picked up on coronavirus, especially, as the first cases were recorded in their own country. News agendas became saturated by stories about the virus and the speed with which it was spreading. As is customary with mainstream news broadcasts and publications, "bad" news tended to command more attention, space and airtime than good news. During the early stages of the pandemic, there was plenty of bad news as the virus spread, seemingly out of control, and hospitalisation and death rates soared. Complete societal lockdowns were dramatically implemented as governments and their health systems suddenly found themselves confronted with the real likelihood that hospitals would be full and thousands of patients would die because of shortage of care.

The media played a major role in monitoring how the disease was spreading around the world, and how different national governments had chosen to tackle it. Comparisons also emerged through news reports and

DOI: 10.4324/9781003274629-13

analyses about the relative levels of performance of different countries through international comparisons based on specific metrics such as infection numbers, numbers admitted to hospital, numbers in intensive care and, most especially, numbers of deaths (expressed in absolute terms and as proportions of the population. Some media coverage clearly scared people. There was much uncertainty during the early stages of the pandemic. Even the authorities did not always seem to know what was going on or how to cope with it. When a crisis gets to the point where government asks people to stay home and not to mix with anyone outside their household, it is clearly serious.

Under these circumstances many people were motivated to comply with these extreme requests out of a sense of personal risk and accompanying fear. Starved of normal social contact, and with many facing the threat of job losses or significant income reductions, there was a psychological price for many. These reactions, however, depended on the information people received about what was going on. Information sources varied from other people through to mainstream and online media platforms.

The complexity of the impact of the mass media and the diversity of applications they could serve in a major health crisis of this kind means that much more needs to be understood about the role the media can play as a source of information, education, persuasion and behavioural control and psychological support (Anwar et al., 2020).

Media, Government Action and Public Protection

Governments around the world had to act promptly and decisively as the COVID-19 pandemic reached their shores. Measures were needed to stop the spread of the new virus. Once it became clear that it was airborne, this meant that people needed to be discouraged and even prevented from engaging in most forms of normal social interaction. This was the only way to protect mass publics from being infected in the absence of tried and tested vaccines.

To reach people quickly, governments had access to the established mass media and also to the Internet. Within the Internet, social networking sites were identified as having the potential to reach many people with messages they might be more likely to absorb even than news media reports. Of course, not everyone used these sites, but their penetration in many populations at the start of the second decade of the 21st century was deep enough to render them potentially useful and effective communications channels. Early evidence emerged that this channel could be effective, when used alongside news media, in China, both to advise people what steps to take to protect themselves as well as to inform the public about the actions being taken by their government and related authorities (Chen et al., 2020).

One key factor in mediated influences is trust in sources. Governments were principal sources of advice and guidance to their populations during the pandemic. Social identity theorists argued that identifying with a source because they are a member of a trusted group is critical when persuading people to adopt new behaviour patterns. If groups or their leaders are not trusted, however, their ability to command public respect and behavioural compliance will be significantly diminished. In contrast, shifting individuals' attitudes or beliefs as precursors to changing their behaviour can be accelerated if a group has a respected and trusted leader (Steffens et al., 2014).

This type of influence can be significant at a nation-state level when the leader of the government commands public respect and trust. It was claimed that in New Zealand, Prime Minister Jacinda Ardern commanded sufficient public respect that the population collectively and quickly supported her tough lockdown measures against the pandemic (Vignoles et al., 2021). There was evidence from pre-pandemic research to show that when politicians invoked collective support and responsibility during times of crisis or major public decision-making, they could move populations to change (Steffens & Haslam, 2013; Haslam, 2020). The identification of the public with a political leader was built upon investing sufficient trust in her or him (Haslam et al., 2020). When the people believe that their leader genuinely does have their best interest at heart, they are more likely to comply with their requests for wholescale change in public behaviour (Bennhold & Eddy, 2020).

When leaders are not perceived as being "one of us" and are positioned instead in a different "outgroup", their ability to move their people with them is diminished (Haslam, 2020). This can be a volatile scenario, however, with the way political leaders respond to events being capable of shifting public attitudes and beliefs about their leader from being positive to negative within one dramatic incident. In the United Kingdom, the behaviour of the Prime Minister's most senior adviser, Dominic Cummings, in breaking pandemic restrictions and then being unapologetic about it, severely damaged trust in the government and most especially in the Prime Minister (Fletcher et al., 2020). It also weakened the government credibility and authority in relation to commanding continued public compliance with severe behaviour restrictions (Mahese, 2020).

Public tolerance towards rule-breakers was found to be low whether those breaches were perpetrated by members of another group or their own group (Van Assche et al., 2020). In the United Kingdom, for instance, the public widely and quickly accepted draconian restrictions to their everyday behaviours with relatively little fuss (Drury et al., 2020). There was widespread compliance with guidance from the start (Duffy, 2020). Even though some exaggeration of compliance might have been expected, initial signs were that most people really meant it when they said they had followed pandemic-related guidance (Daoust et al., 2020).

The only serious non-compliers were people who could not adhere to all the restrictions if this meant they could no longer afford to earn enough money to keep their families safe and fed (Atchison et al., 2020).

Social groups can bring benefits to individuals during times of crisis through their social support (Haslam, 2020; Jetten et al., 2021). The UK government frequently made reference to the need for collective action during the first national lockdown of the country that started in March 2020. This appeal played on an established group phenomenon of social resilience in which members of a group confront a threat together (Drury et al., 2016, 2019; Neville et al., 2020).

On recognising the significance of group processes in their influence on people's behaviour, it is essential that governments and authorities that seek to control public behaviour n times of emergency ensure that principal reference groups identify with government goals. People will be less likely to comply with government advice if groups they belong take a different view Livingstone et al. (2011).

The Public: Better Informed and Better Prepared

Juan-Bin Li from the Education University of Hong Kong found that people who felt better informed about the virus were more acutely aware of its severity and risks, and were more inclined to adopt precautionary behaviour, which generally meant cutting back on their usual social activities (Li et al., 2020). These steps were taken by most people and especially by the better educated and by women.

The precise reasons for being behaviourally cautious were not the same for everyone. Those who felt more vulnerable because they were older or had chronic health conditions withdrew behaviourally because they were scared and felt they needed to protect themselves by staying away from other people. Those who were fitter and healthier, adopted more controlled behaviour patterns because they believed it gave them more control in an uncertain situation. Behavioural caution was not simply people said they observed, it was actually shown to occur based on a scale of frequency of engaging in specific activities. The findings from this study showed some consistency with other investigations (e.g., Blanchard-Fields et al., 1997; Harvey et al., 2010). Having more knowledge about the new coronavirus and increased risk perceptions associated with it led people to take more precautions to protect themselves and others (Brug et al., 2004; Dorfan & Woody, 2011; Vartti et al., 2009). As we will see, as we sum up key evidence, studies from different parts of the world confirmed that keeping the public informed with accurate advice and comprehensible explanation is key to procuring and sustaining people's cooperation and compliance with restrictions on their everyday behaviours.

News Media, Public Awareness and Behavioural Compliance

The news media, especially when combined with the online world, can be effective at promoting COVID compliance among the public. Messages about matters such as personal hygiene and physical distancing can remind the public of the need to be mindful of these interventions in their own lives, describe how to adopt them and encourage a positive attitude towards these behaviours.

Research from The Netherlands found that some compliance behaviours were apparently more frequently adopted than others when people were asked about them. Many people in The Netherlands indicated that they following advice on coughing and sneezing into their elbow, but hand washing, face touching and physical distancing measures were less often adopted. Researchers were interested in what steps could be taken via the media to improve upon this behaviour (Yousof et al., 2020).

An article was placed in a major national newspaper and an accompanying video was made by a social media influencer to remind people about these COVID compliance behaviours. The newspaper article was reported online two million times and the video was watched more than 80,000 times. Information was presented in infographic form in the article.

The findings showed that when people were surveyed after these messages had been published, exposure to the video and infographics and exposure just to the infographics predicted increased likelihood of reported hand washing. Exposure to COVID compliance messages in these two formats also produced more reported hand washing compared with a matched group of people who had not seen any of this health massaging. Compared to those who had not seen the video or news coverage, those witnessing both forms of messaging and the infographic alone were more likely to observe physical distancing, but only if a respondent had experienced COVID-19 symptoms, and there was further evidence that message exposure also improved face touching behaviour (Yousof et al., 2020).

The Internet, Public Awareness and Behavioural Compliance

The Internet was an important platform for mass publics around the world to access repositories of information about the pandemic. It provided a communications infrastructure for mainstream news operators to reach their regular audiences and others who did not normally tune into their traditional offline world outputs. The Internet was also used by specialists and experts such as scientists and research groups. In this context it expedited the distribution and sharing or new scientific discoveries. Then there were the social community websites, some almost as big as the entire

Internet, and often colloquially grouped together under the heading of "social media". Most especially, these sites included the popular micro-blogging sites (e.g., Twitter) and social networking sites (e.g., Facebook, Instagram, YouTube). These widely used sites provided pandemic information from a diverse array of sources that was constantly being refreshed and updated. Not all the sources behind this information were readily identifiable and the accuracy, objectivity and trustworthiness of the content they disseminated could not always be proven. This meant that, for social media information to be effective for individual users, the users themselves needed to have some understanding of the online world in order to be able to distinguish between information they could rely on and that they could not.

Despite these concerns, the Internet has emerged as a highly effective mechanism for disseminating important information to the public at times of major health crisis. With the emergence in China of a new avian influenza A H7N9 virus in the spring of 2013, local authorities utilised the Internet, communications about the disease spread rapidly with days via blogging sites. The interactive nature of these sites facilitated a great deal of public chatter that included well-informed comment and inquiries from people who knew very little about what was going on, combined in turn with fake news and unsubstantiate conspiracies. By monitoring this chatter, it was possible for public health authorities to detect public concerns from early on and also to identify where false or misleading messaging was in circulation. It was then possible to engage with this world to put the record straight about what was happening and how people could take steps to protect themselves and their families (Gu et al., 2014).

The various sites subsumed under the heading of "social media" were recognised as having a similar information and public awareness potential during the COVID-19 pandemic. Equally, it was noted that false information could be as widespread as true information and it was important to have the right tools in place to sort one type of content from another and to counter or neutralise the impact of misinformation (Gonzalez-Padilla & Tortolero-Blanco, 2020).

Social Media Behaviour and Public Well-Being

Keeping people safe and well can be divided into two broad camps. During a pandemic, there is a need for people to know how to safeguard themselves and those close to them from a new and highly infectious disease. In practical terms, this means ensuring that people follow expert advice and comply with it, even when it means, as during the 2020 COVID-19 pandemic, indefinite suspension of everyday life. The second aspect is dealing with the collateral damage caused by the extreme interventions implemented to tackle spread of the disease. These included an exaggerated sense of personal risk, anxiety about this and other longer-lasting mental and physical health side effects.

On the direct effects of pandemic interventions, evidence emerged from China that use of social media was associated with showing more awareness and knowledge of the disease and having a better sense of how to find useful health information online. Better COVID knowledge and eHealth awareness were, in turn, significant related to greater adopt of preventive behaviours such as personal hygiene measures (e.g., hand-washing), face mask wearing and social distancing (Li & Liu, 2020).

Further research conducted in Hong Kong corroborated the findings from the China mainland that eHealth Literacy was directly linked to people's propensities to observe preventive behaviours such as earing face masks, washing hands regularly and social distancing (Guo et al., 2020).

The above findings were confirmed in research conducted in the United States. An adult sample drawn online from across the country completed a series of questions about COVID knowledge and prevention compliance behaviour and completed a test designed to assess their general health literacy. More than a quarter of the people surveyed (29%) were found to possess poor COVID knowledge, there was enough variance in knowledge across the sample to show that those with better genera health literacy also had better COVID knowledge and that better COVID knowledge was related to an increased tendency to comply with recommended COVID prevention behaviours (An et al., 2020).

Social media communities were found able to offer some alleviation of these effects. They could provide reassuring information not just from official sources with identifiable expertise and authenticity but also from family members and friends (Brooks et al., 2020). These sites enabled people to maintain social contact during times when they were prohibited from physically meeting with people from other households. Advice could be distributed rapidly across these sites from public health authorities and could be updated multiple times a day. These sites could also be used by experts and professionals in medical and science fields actively working to develop protective drugs and treatments to accelerate pace of research and development and public protection protocols (Allen et al., 2013; Chan et al., 2020).

The importance of ensuring people understand what is happening during a health crisis such as the 2020 pandemic is critical for the public to know how to protect themselves. Evidence from previous disasters revealed that false information can be extremely damaging by undermining official advice and instruction not least because misinformation can spread more rapidly than a pandemic, giving rise to a parallel "infodemic" of unhelpful conspiracies and false claims concerning the nature of a crisis and the motives of governments and authorities (Depoux et al., 2020; Hua & Shaw, 2020).

Social Media Use to Reach Specific Communities

The public, even within the same country, do not comprise a single homogeneous mass of people. Instead, they can be differentiated by age, gender, socio-economic status, family structure, religion, ethnicity and cultural group and a range of other factors. These factors are important not just as descriptors that reveal the diversity intrinsic in many communities, but also social and psychological agents that can dynamically influence the way people behave.

In the context of the pandemic, evidence emerged population-wide statistics concerning such metrics as infection rates, hospitalisation rates and death rates attributable to COVID-19 and behaviours such as adoption of preventive measures such as wearing face coverings, hand washing and, most importantly, social distancing disguised considerable degrees of variance between different population sub-groups. This volume does not deal with these differences in depth, but it is useful to note here that the major distinguishing factors in terms of these metrics included age, ethnicity and a number of chronic health factors. Other factors made some difference, these three variables made a big difference to personal risk posed by COVID-19.

Evidence emerged also, as already seen, that knowledge and understanding about COVID-19 and about the reasons for deployment of specific behavioural restrictions and other interventions were closely linked to the propensity of people to follow expert and official advice concerning self-protective measures. Researchers in the social sciences developed tests to measure people's health literacy. This was both generic and tied specifically to COVID-19. These tests were developed for use with health professionals and with members of the public (Do et al., 2020). The more people knew, the more they were also compliant with behaviour restrictions imposed upon them. Yet, there were still variances between population sub-groups in health literacy levels. There was evidence from China that older people displayed poorer health literacy than younger people, but that people who were better educated and had higher income were more knowledgeable (Guo et al., 2020; Shiferaw et al., 2020).

Given that there was considerable ignorance in some sectors of populations about COVID-19 and how to tackle it, and a reluctance to comply with behavioural restrictions anyway even when there was awareness of the risk posed by this new disease, there were calls for more to be done to ensure that as many people as possible did understand how serious the situation was and also that they could help themselves as well as the authorities to bring the spreading of new coronavirus under control. In this context, some researchers turned their attention to the use of the Internet and more specifically of social media sites to engage with people in ways that might convince them to find out more and to accept and act upon official COVID advice.

Boosting Pandemic Knowledge and Understanding: Role of Different Media

One finding that has emerged consistently from research into the media and the 2020 pandemic is that if people have more useful information, that enhances their knowledge and understanding of the new disease itself and of the protective steps being taken by national governments and public health authorities, they are then better equipped to help themselves and to help wider society in bringing a crisis situation to an end.

The "news" in the mainstream mass media (i.e., television, radio, newspapers) can play a part in this process. The Internet is another important environment in which positive influence can be exerted. Both offline mass media and the information flowing across the online world can also undermine attempts to persuade the public to support government-imposed interventions, principally by complying with them. Media news editors and reporters can draw excessive attention to the most dramatic pandemic developments and then cultivate an exaggerated sense of personal risk and fear that might motivate some constructive behaviours (such as staying home), but also causes people to behave less constrictively (e.g., panic buying). The Internet, mainly through the most popular social media, can convey much useful information that help people to understand more and take positive and constructive action, but it is also the biggest purveyor of false and misleading information about the pandemic that causes people to eschew compliance with behaviour restrictions. Yet, both media domains can adopt or encourage practices that will have a more positive outcome in general.

With the Internet, research has explored the efficacy of specific message applications designed to provide the public with balanced and relevant advice and support that will render people better equipped psychologically to cope with a pandemic emergency. An analysis of YouTube videos about the novel coronavirus, covering the 1st and 2nd February 2020, found that they had already attracted millions of views even though the virus was mostly linked to China and few cases had been recorded elsewhere (Khatri et al., 2020). The study examined made in English-language and Mandarin. Trained reviewers used a formal analysis system to classify the videos as "useful", "misleading" or "news" using a specific, pre-determined set of criteria.

The videos analysed in this way had attracted over 21 million views. Although, English-language videos were categorised as "useful" more often than Mandarin videos, overall, these videos were classed as helpful in the information they contained more often than misleading or as offering relatively neutral news. The researchers concluded that YouTube could be an effective platform for getting health information over the people and that more health agencies, poorly represented in this research sample, might consider using the site in this way.

TikTok has been one social media site that has been used as a platform for promoting constructive support advice associated with COVID-19. One of these applications concerned whether video on the subject could encourage people to wear face masks as a barrier to slow the spread of the virus. Researchers identified 100 videos, with the hashtag #WearAMask, that had already attracted a lot of attention on TikTok together with 32 videos that had been posted on this site by the World Health Organization. They studied the attention these videos received and any online evidence that they had struck a chord with viewers (Basch et al., 2021).

Any videos posted on TikTok that had the hashtag #WearAMask were found to have bene viewed nearly 500 million times. Videos posted by the WHO had attracted almost 57 million views. Although there were three times as many #WearAMask videos as WHO videos, the former had attracted ten times as many views and so were relatively more popular. The #WearAMask videos were found to contain more humour than the WHO videos. Over one in four of the #WearAMask videos also included dance. The dance videos alone accumulated 130 million views.

Further research was conducted by the same research group into the potential information utility of TikTok during the pandemic. The researchers analysed 100 videos posted under the hashtag #Coronavirus and a further 17 videos posted by the World Health Organization. Together these videos were viewed nearly 1.2 billion times. In classifying the contents of the videos, one in seven (15%) was characterised by dealing with public anxiety and these alone attracted over 190 views. One in ten dealt with quarantine-related matters and fewer than one in ten videos dealt with how the virus was spread, symptoms and prevention. WHO videos tended to deal more often with transmission and symptoms, but, even then, only a small minority of their posts dealt with these important matters (Basch et al., 2020).

TikTok users base consists predominantly of people aged 13 to 24 years. This age group tended to have low risk of symptomatic or serious infection, but even so, they could become infected and pass it on to others. TikTok was regarded as a potentially useful medium for reaching this age group and for getting through to them with crucial health information, if not for self-protection, then certainly of relevance to the protection of others at greater risk than themselves.

Evidence emerged from one investigation, conducted among people of Asia origin in the United States, that the use of social media, especially for posting private messages and browsing and commenting upon the messages of others, was associated with more experience of discrimination. Much of the social media activity with which participants in this study engaged offered supportive messages designed to contribute to subjective well-being of site users, especially from within that ethnic community. Enhanced subjective well-being was most likely to be promoted among those who actively engaged in relevant debates, but les so among those who simply browsed the posts of others (Yang et al., 2020).

Modelling Health Communications during a Pandemic

There was significant collateral damage caused by the pandemic and by some of the interventions implemented to tackle it. The closure of businesses and workplaces had devastating effects on the financial circumstances of many people and on the economies of nations. Even for those who did not suffer financially, social isolation and misinformation about the pandemic gave rise to a raft of other problems for their mental health as anxiety and depression levels rose along with increases in excess alcohol consumption, domestic violence and gambling (Davidson et al., 2020).

One of the key sources of bad influences were the ubiquitous social media sites which spread fake news stories and distorted and untrue information about the pandemic and the effectiveness of different interventions, especially vaccines. The public had already been frightened by mainstream news coverage of the pandemic. Their fears were then often exacerbated by the continuous flow of misinformation online. The largely uncontrolled circulation of inaccurate and warped "facts" about the pandemic was labelled as an "infodemic" – a wave of misleading stories and reports spreading from person to person as rapidly and damagingly as the virus itself. The online world had, however, created a whole new set of communications dynamics to those usually studied in relation to the role played by the conventional mass media (e.g., television, radio and newspapers) that needed a new theoretical approach in terms of modelling communications' impacts on people.

Micro-blogging and social networking sites are both widely used and regularly used by those who tune in. Many people who used these sites also reported that they did turn to them and rely on them for health information (Zhang et al., 2017; Sun et al., 2020). In China, for example, more than 500 WeChat accounts were identified during the pandemic that operated varyingly at province, municipal and county levels providing health education driven by the circumstances on the ground with COVID-19 in different parts of the country (Sun et al., 2020).

Despite being labelled as a source of toxic information about health issues, many people turned to social media sites for public health advice. One major review of reviews of evidence on social media and public health indicated that research findings did not provide overwhelming support for the hypothesis that social media sites convey information that benefits the public (Giustini et al., 2018). Yet, within the literature, evidence did emerge that specific health education benefits could be achieved through effective deployment of social media platforms. These sites are places where wide-ranging debates and discussions of important issues occur, such as on the efficacy of immunisation or vaccination as protection against diseases (Orr et al., 2016; Broniatowski et al., 2018).

Research has shown that while the mainstream mass media can serve as important health information vehicles, they often tend to present public health messages from official sources and hence provide a somewhat narrow perspective in health issues around which they is still considerable medical and scientific debate. Social media sites were found to offer commentaries from a more diverse range of sources based not just on science but also on individual experience. This more open discussion could be destructive but could equally be helpful in providing different and yet valid perspectives on controversial health treatment methods about which some sections of the public had concerns (Orr et al., 2016).

Attempts have been made to establish an overriding model for conceptual and analytical purposes to investigate the part that social media can play in public health. One such model was called SPHERE (Social media and Public Health Epidemic and REsponse). Within this model, social media were conceived to have potential influences that could cause a misinformation contagion, that could encourage risky behaviours, that could stop the spread of false information, that could enable people to monitor a disease outbreak in real time, that could then also spread health-promoting and protection guidance, and also encourage people proactively to seek to protect themselves or to seek treatment (Schillinger et al., 2020).

The model also incorporated features that identified and defined different attributes of health communications, examining the way they were framed, their sources and the latter's credibility, the timing and volume of messages, platform factors that could magnify or inhibit the impact of health messages, and apply rules, regulations and standards to check on the quality and integrity of information and advice being circulated. Further analysis would focus on the nature of the pathogen and disease ensuring people were familiar with how it is spread, the nature of its symptoms and steps they can take to protect themselves. There would be transparency checkers enabling people to reassure themselves about the standards operated by the platform and by the sources of key evidence. The authors of this model recommended the development of artificial intelligence systems to automate this body of analysis to facilitate its scaling up across the vast expanses of the World Wide Web and to deliver timely, accurate and dispassionate assessments of relevant and validated evidence.

Closing Comments

As this book draws to a close, it is worth reflecting that media systems played highly significant roles during the 2020–2021 novel coronavirus pandemic. Traditional news media were centrally important to national governments and their health authorities in reaching out to their publics to keep them appraised of the progress of the pandemic, to outline steps people could take to protect themselves, and at different times to frighten people and given them reassurance when different motives were needed to control public behaviour.

There were times when media professionals had a crucial role to play in simplifying complex scientific issues and the confused or mixed messages of governments. In liberal democracies the mainstream media also called governments and politicians to account over their handling of the pandemic. The media, however, could also distort and sensationalise pandemic-related stories for their own aesthetic and competitive purposes. The mainstream media were confronted with competition for ears and eyeballs from the multitude of new information sources supplied over the Internet. In this online environment, the authority and even the identity of sources of particular pandemic stories was not always clear. While the traditional mass media represented megaphones for governments, online information sources often represented unknown or mischievous interests bent on stirring up public uncertainty about the risks of the novel virus and of the latest drug treatments and vaccines designed to protect the public against it.

Understanding how different pandemic narratives were played out on different communications technology platforms and what impact they had on mass publics or different population subgroups became essential if official information and advisory campaigns were to have traction. The wrong information could lead anxious and confused people to fail to take appropriate protective measures or to engage in behaviours that would ultimately cause them harm. When the world starts to review that way governments and international authorities managed the pandemic, the role played by different information sources will need to be placed centre-stage.

The aim must be to enhance understanding of what happened and to be honest and truthful about mistakes that were made without heavy focus on assigning blame. Blame will only lead to defensiveness and in turn less than frank debates about who did what, why and with what impact? Any such reviews must gather as much relevant evidence as they can and critically assess the contributing science disciplines and their methodologies to ensure that any "truths" that emerge are comprehensively reinforced by relevant data with demonstrable validity and reliability.

References

Allen, H. G., Stanton, T. R., Di Pietro, F., & Moseley, G. L. (2013) Social media release increases dissemination of original articles in the clinical pain sciences. *PLoS One*, 8(7): e68914. doi:10.1371/journal.pone.0068914

An, L., Bacon, E., Hawley, S., Yang, P., Russell, D., Hufffman, S., & Resnicow, K. (2020) Relationship between coronavirus-related eHealth Literacy and COVID-19 knowledge, attitudes, and practices among US adults: Web-based survey study. *Journal of Medical Internet Research*, 23(3): e25042. doi:10.2196/25042

Anwar, A., Malik, M., Taees, V., & Anwar, A. (2020) Role of mass media and public health communications in the COVID-19 pandemic. *Cureus*, 12(9): e10453.

Atchison, C., Bowman, L., Vrinten, C., Redd, R., Pristera, P., Eaton, J. W., & Ward, H. (2020) *Perceptions and behavioural responses of the general public during the COVID-19 pandemic: A cross-sectional survey of UK adults*. Health Sciences. doi:10.1101/2020.04.01.20050039

Basch, C. H., Fera, J., Pierce, I., & Basch, C. E. (2021) Promoting mask use on TikTok: Descriptive, cross-sectional study. *JMIR Public Health Surveillance*, 7(2): e26392. doi:10.2196/26392

Basch, C. H., Hillyer, G. C., & Jaime, C. (2020) COVID-19 on TikTok: Harnessing an emerging social media platform to convey important public health messages. *International Journal of Adolescent Medicine and Health*. doi:101515/ijamh-2020-0111

Basch, C. H., Hillyer, G. C., Meleo-Erwin, Z. C., Jaime, C., Mohlman, J., & Basch, C. E. (2020) Preventive behaviors conveyed on YouTube to mitigate transmission of COVID-19: Cross-sectional study. *JMIR Public Health Surveillance*, 6(2): e18807. doi:10.2196/18807

Bennhold, & Eddy. (2020) Germany bans groups of more than 2 to stop coronavirus as Merkel self-isolates. *The New York Times*. Retrieved from: https://www.nytimes.com/2020/03/22/world/europe/germany-coronavirus-budget.html

Blanchard-Fields, F., Chen, Y., & Norris, L. (1997) Everyday problem-solving across the adult life span: Influence of domain specificity and cognitive appraisal. *Psychology and Ageing*, 12(4): 684–693.

Broniatowski, D. A., Jamison, A. M., Qi, S., AlKulaib, L., Chen, T., Benton, A., Quinn, S. C., & Dredze, M. (2018) Weaponized health communication: Twitter bots and Russian trolls amplify the vaccine debate. *American Journal of Public Health*, 108(10): 1378–1384. doi:10.2105/AJPH.2018.304567

Brooks, S. K., Webster, R. K., Smith, L. E., Woodland, l., Wessely, S., Greenberg, N., & Rubin, G.J. (2020) The psychological impact of quarantine and how to reduce it: Rapid review of the evidence. *The Lancet*, 395: 912–920.

Brug, J., Aro, A. R., Oenema, A., de Zwart, O., Richardus, J. H., & Bishop, G. D. (2004) SARS risk perception, knowledge, precautions, and information sources, the Netherlands. *Emerging Infectious Diseases*, 10: 1486–1489. doi:10.3201/eid1008.040283

Chan, A. K. M., Nickson, C. P., Rudolph, J. W., Lee, A., & Joynt, G. M. (2020) Social media for rapid knowledge dissemination: Early experience from the COVID-19 pandemic. *Anaesthesia*, 75(12): 1579–1582. doi:10.1111/anae.15057

Chen, Q., Min, C., Zhang, W., Wang, G., Ma, X., & Evans, R. (2020) Unpacking the black box: How to promote citizen engagement through government social media during the COVID-19 crisis. *Computing and Human Behavior*. 110: 106380. doi:10.1016/j.chb.2020.106380

Davidson, I., Pimenta, S. F., Nayan de Sousa Mata, A., Braga, L. P., Bandeira Silva de Medeiros, C., Morais de Azevedo, P., Bezerra, I. N. M., Higo de Oliveira Segundo, V., Clara de Franca Nunes Santos, G. M., Nocilas, I. M., & Piuvezam, G. (2020)

Media and scientific communication about the COVID-19 pandemic and the repercussions on the population's mental health: A protocol for a systematic review and meta-analysis. *Medicine (Baltimore)*, 99(50): e23298. doi:10.1097/MD.00000000000 23298

Depoux Martin, S., Karafillakis, B., Preet, R., Wilder-Smith, A., & Larson, H. (2020) The pandemic of social media panic travels faster than the COVID-19 outbreak. *Journal of Travel Medicine*, 27: taaa031. doi:10.1093/jtm/taaa031

Do, B. N., Tran, T. V., Phan, D. T., Nguyen, H. C., Nguyen, T. T. P., Nguyen, H. C., Ha, T. H., Dao, H. K., Trunh, M. V., Do, T. V., Nguyen, H. Q., Vo, T. T., Nguyen, N. P. T., Trao, C. Q., Tran, K. V., Duong, T. T., Pham, H. X., Nguyen, L. V., Nguyen, K. T., Chang, P. W. S., & Duong, T. V. (2020) Health literacy, eHealth literacy, adherence to infection prevention and control procedures, lifestyle changes, and suspected COVID-19 symptoms among health care workers during lockdown: Online survey. *Journal of Medical Internet Research*, 22(11): e22894. doi:10.2196/22894

Dorfan, N. M., & Woody, S. R. (2011) Danger appraisals as prospective predictors of disgust and avoidance of contaminants. *Journal of Social and Clinical Psychology*, 30: 105–132.

Daoust, J. F., Nadeau, R., Dassonneville, R., Lachapelle, E., Bélanger, É., Savoie, J., & van der Linden, C. (2020) How to survey citizens' compliance with COVID-19 public health measures? Evidence from three survey experiments. *Journal of Experimental Political Science*, 1–8. doi:10.1080/13548506.2017.1338736

Drury, J., Brown, R., González, R., & Miranda, D. (2016) Emergent social identity and observing social support predict social support provided by survivors in a disaster: Solidarity in the 2010 Chile earthquake. *European Journal of Social Psychology*, 46(2): 209–223. doi:/10.1002/ejsp.2146

Drury, J., Carter, H., Cocking, C., Ntontis, E., Tekin Guven, S., & Amlôt, R. (2019) Facilitating collective resilience in the public in emergencies: Twelve recommendations based on the social identity approach. *Frontiers in Public Health*, 7: 141. doi:10.3389/fpubh.2019.00141

Drury, H., Reicher, S., & Stott, C. (2020) COVID-19 in context: Why do people die in emergencies? It's probably not because of collective psychology. *British Journal of Social Psychology*, 59: 686–693. doi:10.1111/bjso.12393

Fletcher, R., Kalogeropoulos, A., & Nielsen, R. K. (2020) *Trust in UK government and news media COVID-19 information down, concerns over misinformation from government and politicians up. UK COVID-19 news and information project: Factsheet 4*. Reuters Institute and University of Oxford. Retrieved from: https://reutersinstitute.politics.ox.ac.uk/sites/default/files/2020-06/UK_COVID-19_ News_and_Information_Factsheet_4_FINAL.pdf

Giustini, D., Ali, S. M., Fraser, M., & Kamel Boulos, M. N. (2018). Effective uses of social media in public health and medicine: a systematic review of systematic reviews. *Journal of Public Health Informatics*, 10(2): e215. doi:10.5210/oj phi.v10i2.8270.

Gonzalez-Padilla, D. A., & Tortolero-Blanco, L. (2020) Social media influence in the COVID-19 pandemic. *International Brazilian Journal of Urology*, 46(1). doi:10.1590/s1677-5538.ibju.2020.s121

Gu, H., Chen, B., Zhu, H., Jiang, T., Wang, X., Chu, L., Jiang, Z., Zheng, D., & Jiang, J. (2014) Importance of internet surveillance in public health emergency control and prevention: Evidence from a digital epidemiologic study during avian influenza A H7N9 outbreaks. *Journal of Medical Internet Research*, 16(1): e20. doi:10.2196/jmir.2911

Guo, Z., Zhao, S. Z., Guo, N., Wu, Y., Wen, X., Wong, J. Y.-H., Lam, T. H., & Wang, M. P. (2020) Socioeconomic disparities in e-Health literacy and preventive behaviors during the COVID-19 pandemic in Hong Kong: Cross-sectional study. *Journal of Medical Internet Research*. doi:10.2196/24577

Harvey, A., Nathens, A. B., Bandiera, G., & LeBlanc, V. R. (2010) Threat and challenge: Cognitive appraisal and stress responses in simulated trauma resuscitations. *Medical Education*, 44: 587–594.

Haslam, S. A. (2020) Leadership. In J. Jetten, S. D. Reicher, A. A. Haslam, & T. Cruwys (Eds.) *Together apart: The Psychology of COVID-19* (pp. 25–30). Sage.

Haslam, S. A., Reicher, S. D., & Platow, M. J. (2020) *The new psychology of leadership: Identity, influence and power* (2nd Ed.). Hove, UK: Psychology Press.

Hua, J., & Shaw, R. (2020) "Infodemic" and emerging issues through a data lens: The case of China. *International Journal of Environmental Research and Public Health*, 17: 2309.

Jetten, J., Haslam, C., & Haslam, S. A. (2012) *The social cure: Identity, health and well-being*. Psychology Press Taylor & Francis Group.

Khatri, P., Singh, S. R., Belani, N. K., Yeong, Y. L., Lohan, R., Lim, Y. W., & Teo, W. Y. (2020) YouTube as source of information on 2019 novel coronavirus outbreak: A cross sectional study of English and Mandarin content. *Travel Medicine and Infectious Disease*, 35: 101636. doi:10.1016/j.tmaid.2020.101636

Li, J.-B., Wang, A., Dou, K., & Wang, L.-X. (2020) Chinese public's knowledge, perceived severity and perceived controllability of the COVID-19 and reactions, social participation and precautionary behaviour: A national survey. https://www.researchgate.net/publication/33950638

Li. X., & Liu, Q. (2020) Social media use, eHealth literacy, disease knowledge, and preventive behaviors in the COVID-19 pandemic: Cross-sectional study on Chinese netizens. Cross-sectional study on Chinese netizens. *Journal of Medical Internet Research*, 22(10): e19684. doi:10.2196/19684

Livingstone, A. G., Young, H., & Manstead, A. S. R. (2011) "We drink, therefore we are". *Group Processes & Intergroup Relations*, 14(5): 637–649. doi:10.1177/1368430210392399

Mahese, E. (2020) Covid-19: UK government's defence of senior aide has damaged public and NHS confidence, says experts. *British Medical Journal*, 369. doi:10.1136/bmj.m2109

Neville, F. G., Templeton, A., Smith, J. R., & Louis, W. R. (2021) Social norms, social identities and the COVID-19 pandemic: Theory and recommendations. *Social and Personality Psychology Compass*, 15(5): e12596. doi:10.1111/spc3.12596

Orr, D., Baram-Tsabari, A. M., & Landsman, K. (2016) Social media as a platform for health-related public debates and discussions: The polio vaccine on Facebook. *Israel Journal of Health Policy Research*, 5(1): 34. doi:10.1186/s13584-016-0093-4

Shiferaw, K. B., Tilahun, B. C., Endehabtu, B. F., Gullslett, M. K., & Mengiste, S. A. (2020) E-health literacy and associated factors among chronic patients in a low-income country: A cross-sectional survey. *BMC Medical Information and Decision Making*, 20(1): 181. doi:10.1186/s12911-020-01202-1

Schillinger, D., Chittamura, D., & Ramirez, A. S. (2020) from "infodemics" to health promotion: A novel framework for the role of social media in public health. *American Journal of Public Health*, 110: 1393–1396.

Steffens, N. K., & Haslam, S. A. (2013) Power through "us": Leaders' use of we-referencing language predicts election victory. *PLoS ONE*, 8(10): e77952. doi:10. 1371/journal.pone.0077952

Steffens, N. K., Haslam, S. A., Reicher, S. D., Platow, M. J., Fransen, K., Yang, J., Ryan, M. K., Jetten, J., Peters, K., & Boen, F. (2014) Leadership as social identity management: Introducing the Identity Leadership Inventory (ILI) to assess and validate a four-dimensional model. *The Leadership Quarterly*, 25: 1001–1024. doi:10.1016/j.leaqua.2014.05.002

Sun, M., Yang, L., Chen, W., Luo, H., Zheng, K., Zhang, Y., Lian, T., Yang, Y., & Ni, J. (2020). Current status of official WeChat accounts for public health education. *Journal of Public Health*, 43(3): 618–624. doi:10.1093/pubmed/fdz163.

Van Assche, J., Politi, E., van Dessel, P., & Phalet, K. (2020) To punish or to assist? Divergent reactions to ingroup and outgroup members disobeying social distancing. *British Journal of Social Psychology*, 59: 594–606. doi:10.1111/bjso.12395

Vartti, A. M., Oenema, A., Schreck, M., Uutela, A., de Zwart, O., Brug, J., & Aro, A. R. (2009) SARS knowledge, perceptions, and behaviors: A comparison between Finns and the Dutch during the SARS outbreak in 2003. *International Journal of Behavioral Medicine*, 16: 41–48.

Vignoles, V.L., Jaser, Z., Taylor, F., & Ntontis, E. (2021) Harnessing shared identities to mobilise resilient response to the COVID-19 pandemic. *Political Psychology*, 42(5): 817–826. doi:10.1111/pops.12726

Yang, C.-C., Tsar, J.-Y., & Pan, S. (2020) Discrimination and well-being among Asians/Asian Americans during COVID-19: The role of social media. *Cyberpsychology. Behaviour and Social Networking*, 23(12): 865–870.

Yousof, H., Corbin, J., Sweep, G., Hofstra, M., Sherder, E., van Gorp, E., Zwetsloot, P. P., Zhao, J., van Rossum, B., Jiang, T., Lindemans, J.-W., Narula, J., & Hofstra, L. (2020) Association of a public heath campaign about coronavirus disease 2019 promoted by news media and a social influencer with self-reported personal hygiene and physical distancing n the Netherlands. *JAMA Network Open*, 3(7): e2014323. doi:10.1001/jamamnetworkopen.2020.14323

Zhang, X., Wen, D., Liang, J., & Lei, J. (2017) How the public uses social media WeChat to obtain health information in China: A survey study. *BMC Medical Information and Decision Making*, 17(suppl 2): 66.

Index

A

acute stress from pandemic 4
advice sources, official pandemic 151
advisers, scientific 178
age groups 164, 168, 203
ageing 163, 166–67, 171
ageism 163–76
alternative information sources 37
amount of media coverage 52, 122
analyses of micro-blogging 44
anger 23, 39, 124, 126
anxiety 4, 7, 70, 76–77, 126–29, 138,
    152, 178–83, 186, 200, 204
    economic 52
    heightened 91, 137
    public 22, 127, 154, 179, 184, 203
anxiety levels 4, 7, 127, 181
anxiety symptoms 7
arguments 73–74, 109–10
audiences 9, 19–22, 26, 29, 62, 69–70,
    73–76, 122, 130, 184
authoritative information 28
avian influenza virus 129

B

behaviour, preventive 152, 200
behavioural compliance 7, 10, 106–7,
    135–150, 151–162, 181, 196, 198
behavioural restrictions 10–11, 36, 41,
    44, 61–62, 101, 105, 107–8, 112,
    132, 138, 145, 201
behavioural research 11
behavioural sciences 11, 91
belief in conspiracy theories 107
blame 71, 113, 132, 141–42, 153
blame frames 140–44
broadcast news airtime 2

broadcast news operators 26
broadcast news sources 56–57

C

chatter regarding COVID 36–48, 68,
    92–94, 106, 122, 140, 158, 199
China 1–3, 8, 18, 20–21, 40–41, 45, 59,
    91, 111, 126–28, 131, 135–39,
    141–44, 171, 199–202
Chinese government 8, 21, 45, 111, 143
circulation of misinformation 100
climate change 20, 24, 87, 142
confidence in public in news/journalism
    49–67
compliance, behavioral 135–150,
    151–162
comprehensive information 179
confusion 28, 55, 100, 102, 105, 185
conspiracy theories 60, 68, 73–74, 86,
    89, 100, 102–13, 142, 145,
    153–57, 185
coronavirus, novel 8, 10, 19, 21, 24, 41,
    43–45, 60, 62, 75–76, 90, 92,
    142–44, 153, 156
coronavirus fear 129–30
coronavirus outbreak 18, 58,
    76–77, 128
    novel 18, 125
coronavirus pandemic 4, 53, 76–77,
    145, 157, 164
    novel 182, 205
COVID-19 2–6, 8–10, 19–29, 36–45,
    53–55, 57–58, 71–74, 90–94,
    100–102, 104–8, 111–12, 126–30,
    137–40, 152–53, 155–58, 163–65,
    168–70, 178–79, 181–85, 201
    catching 132

classed 3
conspiracy theory beliefs 108
covered 57
crisis 45, 113
elderly 165
epidemic 139
fatigue 19
mortality rate 3
online chatter regarding 36–48
outbreak 49, 58, 69
public sentiments abut, 40 young
    adult patients 163
restrictions 140
sources of 1–2, 42, 56–57, 59, 62, 71,
    74, 86, 88, 105, 107, 128–31,
    157–58, 184–85
stories 5, 52

D
death rates 2, 4–5, 18–19, 22, 25, 49,
    53, 60, 68, 72, 164, 194, 201
Democrat supporters 27–28, 57–58
depression 88, 178–79, 182
disease risks 25
distribution, willful 42
distrust 102, 104, 112, 155

E
employers 52, 168
English-language news sources 23, 28
ethnicity 201
evidence
    diagnostic 170
    medical 169
    substantive 183
    validated 205
    widespread 112
explanations 19, 24, 73–74, 102–4,
    111, 113, 140–43, 151, 153–54,
    156, 158
exposure to COVID-19 information on
    social media 181
exposure to media coverage 102, 122,
    129, 182

F
fake news 11, 43, 88, 100, 106, 111,
    152, 185, 199–200, 205
    outlaw 153
    political 104
    exposure 100

fear 7–10, 21, 23, 27, 39, 70, 76–77,
    121–134, 136, 183, 185, 202, 204
framing 70, 73, 76–77, 123–24

G
gain frame 122–25
global pandemics 2, 7, 91
government advice 23, 112, 153,
    155, 197
government interventions 11, 23, 89,
    109, 113
lockdowns 2
pandemic polices, justifying 185
restrictions 73

H
hand washing 5, 198, 201
    regular 4
    behaviours 144
    influence 75
harboured misunderstandings 73
hashtags 170, 203
health anxiety 130
health authorities 37, 40, 43, 88, 91,
    93–94, 100, 107, 138–39, 152, 155
health behaviours 165
health campaigns 108
healthcare 165, 167
healthcare workers 87
health information 24, 37, 202–4
    public 36, 87
    online 200
health literacy
    better genera 200
    measure people's 201
    poorer 201
health literacy levels 201
health messages 205
health status 129, 168
historical evidence 5
hydroxychloroquine 29
hygiene rules 155

I
illness 3, 40, 101, 165, 184
    mental 165
    physical 165
    severe respiratory 2
images
    public 171
    societal 166

visual 70, 130
immunisation 205
impact of media on public
    understanding 68–85
implications
    commercial 9
    important 10
    long-term 4
income
    lost 177
    reductions 195
    lower 52
Independents 54
infection
    possible 152
    case numbers 144
    levels 92, 135
    numbers 195
    outbreaks 37
    prevention 136
    risks, mitigating 38
    transmission rates 75, 77
information
    quality 20, 42–43, 45, 88, 90, 128
    popular 60
    sources of 1–2, 42, 56–57, 59, 62, 71,
        74, 86, 88, 105, 107, 128–31,
        157–58, 184–85
information technology abilities 170
information to communities 1
information utility, potential 203
internet, perception of pandemic by
    public 86–99
isolation, social 88, 177, 181–82, 204

J
jobs 27, 53, 56, 62
journalism, public confidence in 49–67
journalists 6, 21, 43, 49, 53, 55–56,
    58–60, 94, 183–85
    believed 59
    trusted 56
judgments 24, 55, 125
    cognitive 156
justification, scientific 132

K
key policy messages 26
kits, first-aid 9
knowledge 11, 26, 41–42, 72, 75, 90,
    100, 137, 166, 197, 200–202
    actionable 74

actual 72
authoritative 37
medical 111, 158
pre-existing 69
public 18

L
lack of trust 104, 158
language
    emotive 126
    multiple 90
    negative 170
lessons 1, 138, 141–42
liberal democracies, open 6
lifestyle, healthy 101
lockdowns
    country's 183
    first 72, 182
    major 121
    repeated 2
    extension 125
    restrictions 62, 125, 130
    rules 122
loneliness 181, 184, 186
loners, isolated 71
longevity, reduced 165
loss frame 122–25
loss of income 52, 126

M
mainstream broadcast news bulletins
    59, 92
mainstream mass media 20, 202, 205
mainstream media 11, 17, 20–21, 45,
    49, 75–77, 88, 90, 101–2, 130, 132,
    180, 184–85
    operators 198
major news media 1, 5, 11, 26, 45, 69,
    89, 94, 131, 138, 158
mass media 4–6, 17–18, 24, 68, 105,
    179, 194–95, 204
    major 6, 69, 102, 105, 158
    offline 202
    traditional 2, 4
measured interpretation 180
media
    ageism 163–176
    behavioral compliance 151–162
    high-profile 145
    initial 21
    mainstream 43
    mental health 177–193

positive 168
regular 129
reputable news 23
traditional 51, 59, 87
traditional local new 61
unofficial 128
media content, corporate 167
media coverage 2, 4, 7, 17–35, 52–53,
    101–2, 109, 121–22, 125–26, 129,
    131, 179, 182
importance of, during pandemic
    194–210
initial 21
    mainstream 43
    positive 168
    relentless 19
media drama 169
media exposure 7, 122, 126, 128–29
media news coverage 26, 69, 125
media sources, social 61, 158
mental disorders 182
mental health 177–193
methodologies
    common 59
    linguistic analysis 29
    people meter 129
microblogging 45, 60, 180
    sites 105
minor sources for news 58
misinformation 23, 25, 37–38, 42, 57,
    60, 86–87, 100–102, 104, 106–8,
    110–11, 184–85, 199–200
    conspiracy theories 7, 60, 86
    contagion 205
    narratives 26
    online 204
misleading pandemic information
    100–120, 128, 153

N
new coronavirus 2–3, 8, 18, 37, 41, 86,
    88, 132, 139–40, 197, 201
news coverage 5, 7, 17–18, 24, 28–29,
    39–40, 55, 57–58, 70–72, 76–77,
    127, 135, 140, 144, 167–68
news entertainment value 9
news headlines 23, 53
news markets 29, 49, 63
news media 17–35, 39, 51–54, 56–63,
    68–77, 136, 178–80, 183, 195, 198
    anxiety from 127
    coverage 26, 49, 72, 144

effect on public understanding 68–85
    exposure to 127
    public confidence in 68–85
    reports 5, 195
news organizations 5, 43, 45, 53–54,
    62, 70
newspaper journalists 55–56
newspapers 18, 20, 22, 25–26, 29,
    49–51, 56–57, 127, 130, 202, 204
news sources 19, 37, 51, 55–57, 61,
    75–77, 158, 179
news stories 23–24, 29, 69–71, 104,
    111, 126, 130, 143
    fake 104, 109–11, 138, 204

O
objective news 184
objective statistical probabilities 71
observational study, quantitive 82, 117
official sources 89, 132, 184, 200, 205
offline outlets 85
older adults 160, 167–168, 171,
    174–175, 192
older youth 71
online behavior 37, 45, 100
online chatter, COVID-related 36–48
online, high-traffic news sites 18
online information sources 50
    emergent 17
online media exposure and public
    fear 128
online sources 61–62, 127, 151
opinion polls, public 72, 93, 121
orientation
    psychological
    right-wing authoritarianism 156–57
outcome of conspiracy theories 154
over use of emotion 30

P
pandemics
    major 10
    regional 11
pandemic
    control, initial 73
    developments 58, 92, 202
    fears of 130
    importance of media during 194–210
    lockdowns 7, 107, 186
    mental health 177–193
    narratives 185
    restrictions 27, 138

sources 51
statistics 40
physical contact 177
politicians 26–29, 49, 56–57, 61, 74,
    101, 104, 112, 138, 196
populations
    local 131
    national 158, 179
    sub-groups 87, 168, 201
preferred news 61, 63
pre-pandemic research 1, 75–76, 153,
    180, 196
protocols, public protection 200
psychological reactions 7, 58, 69–70,
    106, 137, 179
psychopathology 103
public
    effect of media on during
        pandemic 1–16
    misleading pandemic information to
        100–120
public compliance 52–53, 107, 122,
    153, 158, 196
public confidence
    in authorities 26, 100
    in news/journalism 49–67
public disquiet 4
public perception of pandemic 86–99
public trust
    in journalists 59
    in news media 59
public understanding, impact of news
    media on 68–85

Q
qualitive analysis 41, 97, 167
quality of COVID news 17–35
quarantine
    enhanced community 83
    massive 185
    restrictions 40
quarantining 40, 50

R
radio 20, 61, 127, 202, 204
reactions
    cognitive 140
    public 34, 39, 57, 72, 76–77, 93, 139
    xenophobic 8
reality 71, 79
    social 173
    virtual 158

reassurance, evidence-backed 28
recovery 38–39, 157
restrictions
    extreme 123
    draconian 122, 196
    limited 93
right-wing authoritarianism
    156–157, 162
risk perceptions 121–134
    exaggerated 22, 110
    increased 197
    personal 4
    warped 90
rumors, unsubstantiated 180

S
sceptics 154
sensationalism 25
sensitivity to news 127
sentiment analysis 23, 39, 41
shift, in perception point 61, 130
social cognition 146
social distancing 27, 40, 94, 111, 137,
    139, 144, 169, 200–201
    maintaining 143
    measures 186
    requirements 125
social identity theory 196
social media
    behavioral compliance 151–162
    chatter 152
    communities 200
social media sites 9–10, 44–45, 60–61,
    87–89, 91, 104, 108, 110–11, 127,
    131, 180–81, 201, 203–5
    major 108
    preferred 128
social media use 10, 108, 152,
    200–201, 203
strain
    disproportionate 163
    long-term 164
stress 88, 91, 177–79, 182, 186
suicide rates 77, 181–83
supply chains 9
symptoms
    advanced 88
    depressive 52, 179, 188

T
tacit knowledge capacity
tactics, fear-evoking 53

technology literacy 6, 170
technology platform 94
televised news 22, 29, 140
threats
    emotional 180
    perceived 7, 107
topic modeling analysis 96, 47
toxic information 204
tracked public trust in television 56
trust in scientists 157
tweets 38–41, 44, 93, 106, 170–71

U
understanding of news media by public
    68–85
unknowns 5, 24, 136
unreliable information sources 10
urban centers 139–140
user awareness, cyber 149

V
vaccination beliefs 43
variances 17, 25, 61, 93, 130, 141, 171,
    200–201
verified information 6, 153
vested interests, verified represented 45
videos 17, 20–21, 25, 75, 90, 127, 198,
    202–3
violence, domestic 204
visual imperatives 24

W
warning signals, early 41, 88
wave, initial 40
websites 1, 42, 86, 102, 129, 157
    low credibility 42
    microblog 37
    professional 129
    social community 198
WHO (World Health Organization) 3,
    8, 37, 163–64, 203
women 52, 177, 182, 186, 197
    older 167
words
    cataloguing 23
    key 45, 170
    semantically-related 126
worldviews, alternative 104, 112

X
xenophobic policies 155
xenophobic reactions 8

Y
younger generations 17, 36, 94, 166–67
YouGov polls 56
YouTube 1, 9, 86, 90, 92, 105, 108,
    151, 186, 199, 202

Z
zoonotic viruses 143

Printed in the United States
by Baker & Taylor Publisher Services

Printed in the United States
by Baker & Taylor Publisher Services